CARVED IN STONE
THE GREEK HERITAGE

Basil S. Dawrol

12/6/01

CARVED IN STONE
THE GREEK HERITAGE

BY
BASIL DOUROS

FIVE AND DOT CORPORATION
RANCHO MURIETA, CA

Body text set in 11 point Adobe Minion, heads set in Adobe Lithos.
Book and Cover Design by Pete Masterson, Æonix Publishing Group.
http://www.aeonix.com

CARVED IN STONE
THE GREEK HERITAGE
Copyright © 1998, 1999 by Basil Douros
Published by
Five And Dot Corporation
7026 Colina Lane
Rancho Murieta, CA 95683
e-mail: 5plusdot@calweb.com

Library of Congress Catalog Number 98-95025
ISBN 0-9670593-1-3

4th printing, January 15, 2001

Printed in U. S. A.

ACKNOWLEDGMENTS

This book could not have been written without the encouragement and assistance of many people. Richard Fenaroli was the first to urge me to enter a writers contest. Another friend, Anthony Maris read and helped edit it more than once. My son, William Douros sacrificed many hours of his precious time reviewing it and offering advice. Robert Jones, Ruth Younger, Naida West, and Jack Tavalario were always available with words of advice and encouragement.

These are only a few of the people to whom I will forever be grateful for their assistance, encouragement and guidance.

TABLE OF PHOTOS

CAST OF CHARACTERS

TABLE OF CONTENTS

PREFACE

Most characters in this book were real people. Others are composites of people who actually existed. A few—such as the smuggler in Argos—are entirely fictitious. Many situations are portrayed exactly as they were told to me and as precisely as I could imagine them from the telling.

I have reported actual events that took place, but added circumstances and details in some situations. I recreated conversations since tape recorders did not exist at that time, and because memories—the listeners' and the teller's—are faulty at best. I've also inserted some characters into incidents that actually occurred, even though they were not directly involved.

The novel is best described as a fictional, historical tribute to a breed of people that do not and could not exist in this era. Today's world would be too small to contain them.

These people were my ancestors.

FAMILY RELATIONSHIPS

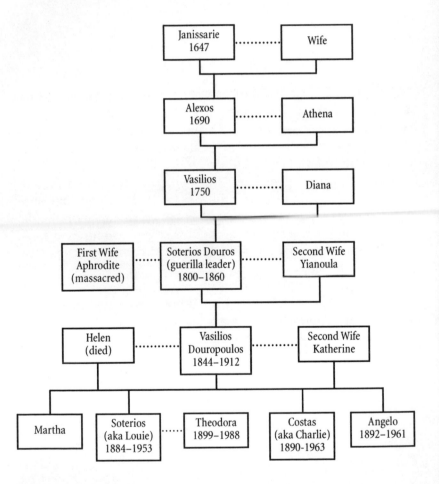

Diagram showing family relationships of characters in the text.

╝╝╝╝╝╝╝╝╝╝╝╝╝╝╝╝╝╝╝╝╝╝╝╝╝╝╝╝╝╝╝

INTRODUCTION

I n B.C. 133, the rulers of the Roman Empire assigned the conquered lands of the Hellenes to the noble family of Gracchus to govern, collect taxes, and eventually send new conscripts to replenish their dwindling armies. The people living in those lands were identified as belonging to the Gracchus clan. They would one day be known to the world as Greeks.

In A.D. 1399 the Greeks were thrown into confusion when the Turkish troops of the Ottoman Empire conquered the country, burning the holy churches of the Orthodox faith and slaughtering the priests. The Turks governed the land, harshly persecuting the Christian Greeks, collecting taxes, and inducting the young males for their armies. They ruled the land for 400 years, until the Greeks finally revolted and gained their independence in 1827/1832.

In more modern times, from 1870 to 1920, the Greeks fought a series of seemingly never-ending battles with Albania, Bulgaria, and Turkey. During this time Greece expanded to its present boundaries. It was coincidental that the conscription of young men to fill these armies came at the same time as the great emigration of young Greek males to America took place.

In 1900 the land was exhausted, having spent too many years baking under the hot sun and absorbing the blood of the thousands and thousands who had claimed the land as theirs. The people were exhausted. The nation had been conquered so many times by so many different bloodlines and cultures that the inhabitants no longer knew their heritage.

The young, bewildered and frustrated, left the homeland searching for dignity and a better life in other lands. The old asked the Christ to watch over their children and kissed them for the last time.

One who bent to receive a final kiss from his father was a young Greek called Soterios.

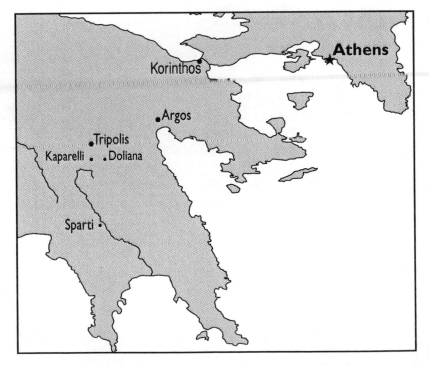

A portion of Greece, showing cities mentioned in the text.

1820

The wind violently shook the small mud and stone house. The small-est girl, probably four years old, cried loudly for her mother, more out of fear than from the cold. Around midnight the north winds had begun to drive more snow and ice down the steep, rocky slopes onto the villagers' homes.

"Shh, little golden one, Mother is outside checking on the goats," the older sister whispered. "You know she would make the cold wind go away if she could. She will be back soon. And tomorrow, maybe father will return from his mission."

The voice of her sister calmed the youngster, whose brown eyes quickly dried as she tried again to sleep. In a corner two young boys intermit-tently snored and wakened, as the wind increased and loose slate shingles skated across the roof to the ground. The old woman, bundled in a blan-ket in another corner, flashed her eyes at her grandchildren who shiv-ered in separate bedding. She cursed the Turks, the wind, the many mountainside winters she'd survived, the goats that froze last night, and her only living daughter's husband, who was gone once again to wage battle. She despised her son-in-law for leaving his wife and family to defend themselves against the winter storm. But she hated the Turks even more for giving her son-in-law reason to go.

"Keep the little one quiet," the old grandmother hissed to the eldest sister. "If her father comes home and hears her crying, he will beat her. If the Turks hear her crying, they will eat her ... after they have eaten you."

"Oh Grandmother, I have her quieted. She misses her father and she needs someone to tell her we are safe. I have done that. Besides nothing or no one outside could hear even the loudest screams in the house. The wind roars like the river after the snow melt. You should try to sleep too. Or put on your boots and go help Mother."

The eldest sister knew, from watching her mother, how to use a little logic to quiet her grandmother.

"Yes, I'll sleep," replied the old woman. "Your brother is stronger than I am, and together, he and your mother will find a way to keep the goats warm."

The eldest sister could see her grandmother close her eyes in the flick-ering lantern, but the wind was too loud to hear the old woman curse.

Soterios aka Louie

PART 1

SOTERIOS

CHAPTER 1

THE ORIGIN

Wait! *Before you go you must know where you came from so you will know who you can be."*

1906

Soterios watched as his father Vasilios stirred the fire so that the cool mountain wind could blow new life into the flames. Sparks snapped and popped from the dead branches of an olive tree. The warm autumn day, coming after many hot summer days, had kept the dead wood dry. For a split second, he wondered again if it was true that they resembled each other. Would he look like his father when he too was an old man of sixty-three? He felt a little shockwave as the earth moved from one of the frequent earthquakes. The trees that grew on both sides of the mountain separating the villages of Kaparelli and Doliana shook ever so slightly. Soterios had been born in Doliana but lived in Tripoli, where his father had moved after his first wife died.

ᒥᒧᒥᒧᒥᒧᒥᒧ_____

Soterios glanced at his father who continued to talk, and guiltily wondered whether the old man had noticed that his listener's mind had wandered once again. After all, Soterios reminded himself, his father had taken the time to spend an evening with him, talking and sleeping on the mountainside the night before he was to leave for America. He stretched his leg that had fallen asleep, hoping to relieve the painful cramps.

The movement caused his father to return mentally from the past. He had been reliving the memory of his own father, Soterios' grandfather, and another campfire in the mountains. For a moment Vasilios could not recall his father's name. It had been so long ago. Then he remembered. "Of course," he told Soterios, "my eldest son and my father would have the same name. That is how it has always been. What better way is there to remember the dead? What better way to give them the respect they earned? How else could you remind everyone from where the family had come?

"Son, you and your success are important to this family. We have saved money for the last three years so that one of us could go to America, make a good life, and eventually send for the rest. We have struggled on this old, dry mountainside for countless years. The mountain has grown weary of us. The soil has been used so many times that no one can prosper by farming here. There are more stones than dirt. No one comes to the bakery to buy more than one day's bread at one time. They can barely afford that much. That is why you must leave. But I can't let you leave dreaming of the life ahead of you until I am convinced you understand that the life you have now is the result of the ones who came before you."

Soterios winked at the fire, knowing that his father was going to lecture him again. He knew it would be a lesson he had heard before from his father or his uncles, but hopefully this time it would be with a new twist.

"Father, perhaps you should be the one to go to America. If one needs to know his origin before enjoying the adventures of a new life, then you are best suited."

Vasilios smiled at his son's attempt to lighten the mood, but said nothing. Because of the momentary silence, Soterios waved the smoke aside so he could see his father, whose smile had faded to a deep frown.

"Father! What are you thinking about? Are you all right?"

"Yes. Listen, I was thinking of names. Of your name, of my name, of our family name. That's what this evening is all about. I have told you before that most families have names that are meaningless. Every so often, though, a man might do something exceptional—something to make him stand out so that his deed becomes his name. Do you remember Nicholas Kouréas?"

"Yes, of course I do."

"Well," his father continued, "he was Nicholas Voultsionis until he went to Athens and became a barber. I never minded his old name, but others said he had to become 'Kouréas' so that all of his descendants, if he became a famous barber, would know what he had accomplished."

"Yes, Father, you have told me this before."

Vasilios' green eyes glared in response to his son's impatient tone. "Well, now it is time to tell you how our family got its name. The story is not a pretty one. There are some things I'm not proud of, but you need to hear it. You're old enough to know the truth and make your own decisions of what is right and what is wrong. Pay attention, because I want you to remember every detail. You must be able to tell anyone who cares enough about you to ask the origin of your family name. You are the oldest, and since you are going to America, everyone in this family is counting on you. Especially me, because I don't want our name to be forgotten. If you forget your ancestry, who will tell my grandsons who we were? Our ancestors suffered and struggled to live in such a way that their children would always be proud to carry their name. We are more than mules and animals who don't know or care where they come from. I have worked long hours in that cursed bakery so I can provide for you people. My lungs are so full of flour that sometimes you've seen me coughing nothing but flour dust."

The old man stretched his back to relieve the cramps from sitting on a flat, hard rock. He reached into his vest's watch pocket and pulled out a string of blue worry beads. He spun the beads in a circle around his ring finger, then squinted as he peered through the smoke at the clouds drifting in front of the half moon.

"I wanted to look at all this, and I wanted you to feel the land when I tell you the story," he said, gesturing to the scene below. Soterios got to his feet, walked to his father's side, and putting his hand on the old man's shoulder looked down into the little valley. The moonlight, partly obscured by moving clouds, was still bright enough to illuminate the rock walls checker-boarding the fields below. Treetops were silhouetted against the mysterious gray background that was somehow emphasized by the hooting of the owl that swooped over the open spaces. The mule that his father had ridden up the hill nervously shifted his feet, pulling on the braided leather rope that Soterios had fastened to an olive tree. The tree shuddered as the gusting wind scattered ashes from the fire pit that mixed with sparks swirling into the mountain sky.

The old man glanced at the mule then continued talking, "It looks just like it did when I was your age. I suspect that at night Greece looks the same now as it did a hundred years ago. I know that I feel closer to history when I sit up here at night beside a burning fire. Well, it's getting late, so let me tell you the story."

However, the story telling was interrupted when the mule pulled against the tether, helped the wind win its battle with the tree. The falling branches drowned out Vasilios' voice. Soterios leapt to his father's side when he heard the creak of the old tree suddenly turn into a shriek. The tree struggled then teetered and crashed across the back of the old mule, snapping the vertebrae just behind the shoulders and driving the gentle animal face down into the rocky soil. The old tree's concession to gravity stirred hot dust and embers as a branch that had hung over the fire embedded itself in the hot coals.

Vasilios, who had been sitting upwind to avoid the smoke, cried out in fear. Soterios ran first to the collapsed mule, which brayed in gasps, then he turned and raced the ten paces back to his father. The old man spat out some fire debris with a series of violent coughs of white milky spittle.

"Goddamn this tree and this mule and the bakery. Father, please stop coughing. Are your eyes all right? Why is life so hard?" Soterios lamented.

Vasilios finally regained his breath, and whispered, "Just thank God that he has allowed us to live long enough to feel some pain. Don't blaspheme by using his name as a curse. Be thankful and praise Him. He could have dropped the tree on you instead of the mule. The mule is the only one who has a right to complain."

The mule had begun to cough up foam-filled blood, which slowly disappeared into the moisture-starved earth.

"Calm down son, sit and relax. There isn't anything we can do. I believe the poor brute has a broken back. Help me clean up this mess, when the mule dies we will go home. Besides look who is coming up

the hill. It's Costas your brother. *Yiássou!* Costas sit there beside y
brother. Give me a moment to catch my breath and while we wait ᴎᴏɪ
the mule to die I'll continue with the story of how we won the right
to our name.

᠌᠌᠌᠌ⅎⅎⅎⅎⅎⅎⅎ

"I was born in 1844. That was only a few years after the final cel-
ebrations for independence had taken place. We, those of us who lived
in the villages, did not realize yet what self government meant to us.
The Turks had finally been routed. They had dominated our land,
the land of the Hellenes, for 360 years. The worst times were when
the Turks demanded that one out of every five young boys in each
Greek village would be taken to live with Turkish families until they
were ready to be sent to live in Turkish army barracks. They were
raised and then trained to became part of a most effective army dedicated to the defense of what the Turk called the 'True Faith.' These
troops were known as Janissaries, and because of their outstanding
performance and bravery, they became favorites of the Sultans.

"My grandfather was a Janissary, as was his grandfather, who was
one of the best of them. He was decorated and had been recognized
and rewarded by the Sultan after he had performed bravely in the
Peloponnesian wars against the Venetian general Francesco Morossini.

"I don't know what my grandmother's name was; all I know is
that our family's known history begins in 1687 when my ancestor's
post was to oversee the storage of munitions and arms in Athens. It
was my ancestor who moved the explosives from the ancient temples
on the Acropolis in case the Venetians, who were Christians, shelled
the city.

"It was tragic that Christians took the opportunity to destroy what
they saw as a monument to pagan Gods. The Sultan, who was a Moslem, had given orders to save the architectural miracle of the
Parthenon. His men were removing all munitions so there would not
be a reason for either side to attack the building. The Venetians fired
on it anyway, almost completely destroying the ancient temple.

"Our ancestor, who was, if you remember, a Christian by birth
but a trained Janissary, was hit by artillery fire as he stood on the
shattered ruins. Wounded, he shrieked defiance and waved his fist at
the Venetians. His outstanding service and behavior were noted, and

later reported to the Sultan. However, his injuries made him unfit for further duty. He was pensioned and, as a reward for his loyalty, was given title to land—two small farms located on a plateau overlooking a valley not far from Tripoli.

"The plateau was located at the very top of a mountain, which looked like one of the ancient Gods had cut a piece out of it as if it were a wedge of bread. The sides of the cliff were straight and flat as a board so that, at first glance, it looked from the valley below as though a massive wall three-hundred feet long and seventy-five feet high had been constructed to hold up the farms which were barely visible over the tops of the olive trees."

Vasilios rose, filled his glass with more of the red wine he liked so much, and waited while Costas relieved himself on the trunk of the lemon tree, which was silhouetted against the stone wall.

"I am getting tired, and I don't feel well, but I want to finish the story," Vasilios sighed before he continued. "Anyway, our ancestor was known as a good landlord and employer—probably very forceful, but fair. As you two know, the men in our family have always been strong, and perhaps overly fond and capable, I must add, of satisfying women sexually. Age does not seem to be a major problem for us."

Soterios and Costa looked at each other and together exclaimed, "Yiasou! Patéra," and laughed until tears dripped down Costas' cheek.

"If you two smart-asses are through laughing, I will continue." Vasilios said sternly. "In any event, in spite of his advancing years, your ancestor married one of the local girls and settled in the mountains and blended into the land. It didn't take him long to sire a son in 1690, whom I think would have been my great-great-grandfather. The son was able to avoid being among the youths who were selected to become Janissaries. He married a girl who gave birth to several children before she died at a relatively young age. My great-grandfather remarried and when he was at least sixty years old had a son named Vasilios, who was born in 1750.

"Vasilios was forced to join the Turkish Army. He was also wounded and allowed to return to his father's village. He married and at the age of fifty sired a son, whom he named Soterios, and this is where our story really begins. That son was my father, and your grandfather.

"If you recall, the son's name was Soterios, and you, my eldest son carries his name. Surprisingly enough, however, he was not a tall, handsome, and a powerful person. He was an average man who loved his family and praised the Lord constantly; more than most men. He was never too proud to sing out loud with his strong voice when attending church services and celebrating the Holy Days. Even as a child, he was more apt to take a secondary role in the games in which he participated with the village children. He did not take advantage of his father's position as president of the village. The peasants in the village loved the old man, who quietly supported the growing resentment toward the Turkish led government.

"Remember the Turks had ruled the land for almost four hundred years. In the old man's time, the Turkish empire had begun to crumble, partly because of pressure from the growing empire of Christian Russia. The first agents of Russia to speak to the old warrior knew that he had once been forcefully drafted into the Turkish Army. The agents praised the Russian rulers for their support of the Orthodox Church's struggle with the Moslems. They found a willing listener in the old man, who became more eager to make peace with his God and church as he aged and got closer to death.

"The old man was worried about his son's future. He hired an Orthodox priest to tutor Soterios, who eagerly listened to the priest's wonderful tales of the ancient heroes and the always brave and defiant saints. The tutor, with all the religious intensity of his calling, filled the boy's head with these spellbinding stories.

"Soterios' eighteenth birthday was not a day of celebration. Most of the youths, younger than he, had already been conscripted into the Turkish Army. His father's position and the help of some old friends had been engaged to keep Soterios at home. On the morning of his birthday, Soterios and his father had gone to church. They stopped for a moment under an old twisted olive tree while the old man made a point of inspecting a clump of wild mint in an effort to hide the real reason for stopping their climb. It was to enable him to catch his breath.

"May you have many happy years, my son, four times as many as you have given me. But now we have to face the fact that the Turks will not always allow you to remain here with me. The Turkish bastards want you to betray your lineage and go to war against your Orthodox brothers. Well, curse them! They took me, but they can't have you. I want you to take that little girl, Aphrodite, that you have been making owls' eyes at and go to the mountains with her uncle. You will be safe there. The Turkish pigs don't have men to spare to try to find anyone in the wilderness that lies in the mountains."

"Soterios protested, explaining that he couldn't do that. First of all, her brothers would follow and kill both of them if they ran away without being married. Then he wouldn't leave the old man to face the Turks alone.

"The old man swore by the robes of Christ that Soterios had to listen because the arrangements had been made. Aphrodite's father and the priest had both agreed to waive the need to post banns. Her brother would act as *Koumbáros* and they could be married that afternoon. He assured Soterios that the Turks wouldn't punish him, especially when he lied to them and told them that Soterios had left without his father's permission. In any event, Soterios did not have any choice. His father was ordering him to leave.

"That is how it happened that Soterios left his father and village. Shortly after Soterios disappeared, the old man was evicted and his house turned over to a collaborator. Soterios periodically sneaked into the village at night and pleaded with the old man to escape with him to the mountains, where the weakened Turks did not dare to go. The old warrior refused to leave what he regarded as his post. His defiance served to keep the growing flames of resistance and revolt alive and burning in the district where the village was. The Turkish police kept him in the cellar room that he had used to house the animals. He had not been allowed to leave the grounds and had to suffer the indignity of watching someone else use all of his possessions. Six years later, the old man died.

"The Turkish forces were constantly being harassed by the guerrillas. As the revolt grew stronger the Turks began to consolidate their troops, and withdrew from the smaller villages. When the main Turkish garrison left, Soterios' family, one son and two daughters as well as his beloved Aphrodite, quietly returned to the village. Soterios' family moved into Aphrodite's mother's home, where the old woman lived alone since her husband had died and her sons had left to live in the mountains near Sparta.

"Then, his fathers house mysteriously caught fire. The collaborator who had been living there wisely saved what he could from the ashes and moved away.

"Soterios went from village to village making speeches that preached resistance and seeking assistance for the guerrilla forces (kléphtai) living in the mountains.

"When the main Turkish garrison left the village, they turned over the policing and enforcing of policies to the Armatóli. The Armatóli was a police force consisting of Greek collaborators and Moslem Albanians, led by brutal Turkish officers.

"Aphrodite, Soterios' wife had always been one of the prettiest girls in the village. At Easter, the Priests always asked her to carry the silver icon and lead the procession that wound around the churchyard. Her second cousin, Eugenia, deeply resented that she was never chosen and became unreasonably jealous of Aphrodite.

"Eugenia found her revenge by eventually betraying Soterios to the Armatóli by giving information regarding Soterios' movements. The Armatóli set a number of traps that did succeed in capturing a number of guerrillas and even ambushed a supply train of mules, but Soterios' luck held out. The Armatóli began to doubt that the information Eugenia had given them was accurate. One evening from the front door of the cafenion a drunken Albanian accused her of lying to them. The Albanian's words seeped through the walls of the building and seemed to hang in the air long enough for the women drawing water at the well to hear them. The women were dressed in their old and tattered wool dresses, most of which had recently been dyed black.

"One by one, like a chorus line, the women turned and stared at the terrified, wide-eyed girl. She twisted to one side, shrieked in fear, and ran toward the building that served as a police headquarters, hoping to find refuge there. A week later a tinker found her body, stripped naked and bloody, with her head scraped smooth of any hair and her throat cut. When she had gone to the Armatóli asking for protection, they had told her to go home, assuring the terrified girl there weren't any men left who were bold enough to harm her. They may have been right, but they forgot about the women.

"The weather turned cold with the arrival of winter. It was the coldest winter that anyone could remember. Winds from the North blew incessantly. Snow buried the hills, and the sheep the livelihood of so many people, froze to death. The entire village—children, grand-parents, women, as well as the animals—were driven out by the *Armatóli* into the snow and cold, where they instinctively herded to-gether. They were pushed beyond the frozen olive trees onto the flat circular section of land where the wheat would be separated from its stalk at harvest time. The *Armatóli* had picked this spot because it was in plain view from the mountain peaks.

"The Turks waited, themselves protected from the cold. They waited, knowing that the *kléphtai* would eventually come down from the mountains to rescue their families. By the end of the third day, the extreme cold killed the weakened women and children. No one was left alive. They died in frozen clumps with arms and legs clutch-ing one another. Every face was turned toward the mountains look-ing for the help that never came. The Turks departed, leaving the dead where they lay.

"The guerrillas had been on a raid, unaware of the plight of their village. Two men were wounded and needed assistance. They planned to hide them in the village storage shed where the women would care for them. Soterios looked forward to spending a few hours with his children before returning to the wars. The guerrillas were half-blinded by the wind-driven snow when they came down from the mountain. The village was deserted; No sounds drifted up into the hills where the men had stopped to let the forward scouts search the area. When the youngest of the scouts returned to the huddled men who had scattered amongst the rocks, he couldn't talk. He was crying and shak-ing; All he could do was hug Soterios and point to the field where his own mother and baby sister were frozen into the earth. Parts of the bodies had been eaten by wild dogs and wolves that had been driven out of the mountains by the bitter cold and lack of food.

"Soterios and his men retched and cried as they buried their dead. They had to bury what remained of two corpses together because the animals had torn the bodies and scattered the parts. Soterios buried his own son without his right arm. He screamed at the sky.

"Holy Jesus, Mary, mother of God, how could you let this hap-pen? What kind of animals have you created? Look at my soul, my son, my children, my sainted wife. Look at them! You up there in the sky, look down here and see what the Turks have done. Never again ask me to love and understand. Don't ask me to give even one piece of mercy to these Turkish animals. I swear to you that anyone I find who has one drop of Turkish or Albanian blood in them will pay for this. I don't care if they are adult or child, man or woman. They must pay!"

"Soterios fell to his knees and ground his fist onto a sharp piece of granite. Blood poured through his fingers from the gash. He slapped his face with his bloodied fingers, splattering blood droplets as he shrieked at the wind. Some of his comrades hesitated in the collection of their loved ones' body parts as the crazed Soterios continued to bleed and blaspheme the Holy Ones above.

"Soterios' first cousin, Athanassis, frantically tore at the frozen body of his mother, trying to pry it loose from where it had frozen solidly into the earth. When he tried to take the hand-carved prayer beads from her hand, two fingers broke off and fell on the stained earth. Athanassis, sobbing and screaming at the same time, tried to push the fingers back on, but they kept falling to the ground.

"The grief-stricken men burned the village houses and the church. When the embers from the place of worship died down, the men dug graves in the fire-softened earth and buried their dead.

"The massacre turned the men into Godless creatures who showed no mercy to anyone. The memories of all those torn and mutilated bodies fed their grief and caused them to reject any thought of mercy and forgiveness. Any captured Turks, including women and children as well as suspected traitors, were executed.

"Soterios, as the band's chief, acted as the judge whenever someone was caught and brought before the guerillas' ad-hoc court. He showed the accused a face as unemotional as the granite rocks of the hills. He was no longer capable of mercy or kindness. His judgments were instant and final. There was no appeal.

"The Turks as well as the Greeks started to call him Douros, 'The Hard One.' The Turks offered many rewards and promised protection to anyone who would help capture the Hard One, but no one dared turn him in again. He became the ultimate symbol of resistance. Greeks who did not have the courage to oppose the Turks joined the revolt because they were more afraid of the Hard One than they were of the Turks. Don't forget that our ancestors suffered terribly. They saw members of their family butchered and violated by the Turks. The survivors took their vengeance on many people, Turks and Albanians alike, but I admit that they should not have been so cruel. In order to understand the truth of it you must know the circumstances that caused the tragedy. These circumstances are so important that I waited until you were both old enough to understand the facts."

The old man stopped talking, and pointed at another figure coming toward them.

"Ha! Look at that. Look who else is coming to join us. It's your brother Angelo. The slut that he is always chasing must have been too tired to satisfy him."

Costas whispered to his father, "Come on now father take it easy on him, see, he has made the effort to be with us tonight. Perhaps you are too hard on him." Before the old man had a chance to reply the two brothers, Soterios and Costas rose and cheerfully greeted their wayward younger brother. Angelo quietly sat on a rock between the two, nodding to his father.

Costas quickly brought Angelo up to date, retelling the story about their infamous ancestor while the old man stared at the now dead mule through the flickering flames of the dying fire. Soterios broke some of the smaller branches from the shattered olive tree and threw them carefully into the fire-pit causing the flames to reach upward.

When Costas had finished, the old man poured half a measure of wine for each of them into bowl like cups and began once again.

"If you recall, I stopped at the point where the local villagers were more terrified of our ancestor Soterios, than they were of the Turks. They had reason to be, as his methods of getting revenge became more cruel with each day. He became very bold and somehow evaded every trap that the police set. The Armartoli (who, if you remember, were the police force made up of collaborators and Albanians) became embarrassed. The Greeks began to nail signs to the trees late at night mocking the police because they could not catch one man. Little peasant children began to act out the stories that they heard their parents tell of how the bandits were evading the police. It was especially galling when the police noted that the children who took the part of the Turkish forces were always the youngest or the idiot, simpleminded ones.

"Your ancestor had become a hero. The Turks feared if he was not captured he would become a legend. Soon stories began to circulate that he had been visited by the great patriot, General Kolokotronis, and had taken part in the battle that eventually recaptured Argos.

"The liberation of Argos was a major victory for the patriots. Hundreds of years ago, when the Turks had initially conquered the Peleponnesos, the two towns Argos and Tripoli were burnt to the ground. All of the inhabitants were killed or forced to move elsewhere, and the towns were repopulated by Albanians. Once we recaptured it and took our revenge, may God forgive us, the town of Argos became the headquarters for the continuing rebellion.

"The guerrilla troops under your ancestor's command attacked the Turks at every opportunity, but their secondary mission was to find a way to keep the villagers and peasants informed of the victories of the revolt.

"The Turks began to circulate stories that they had killed the bandit leader (they refused to consider him a guerrilla) known as the 'Hard One.' They even put the body of a patriot that they had killed into a large wire cage that was hung from the top beam of a specially constructed gallows, mounted on a flat wooden cart pulled by a team of oxen. The body was bloodied and mutilated until the only thing recognizable was that once it had been human. Four villagers, three women, and one old man accompanied the cart, swearing to anyone who asked that the body was that of the notorious bandit called 'The Hard One' and that they had known him from the time he was a little boy. The cart was hauled from village to village until finally the body decomposed so much that the odor became more than anyone could stand. The damage had been done. Some of the peasants believed that the legendary Hard One had been captured and killed.

"Then, they received messages from the guerrillas that said, "He is alive! The Turk cannot kill him. Watch the mountains and he will send you a sign."

"One day the peasants in his old village looked up at the flat wall of the mountain and saw a man dangling like a spider, suspended from a rope. He was cutting into the rocky face of the wall with a chisel, and a monstrous wooden-headed mallet. He chiseled and carved for two days (and, some said, two nights) while a battle took place during which the Turks tried to reach him. People said he didn't sleep for three nights; it seemed as if he were there continuously. When he finished, the message was there for all the Turks to see and for everyone to know. The Hard One was alive. The message also served as a reminder, for anyone who collaborated with the oppressor, that retribution would be swift. There it was, his name: Douros, which means The Hard One.

"It took the Turks two months before they were able to dynamite the mountain and obliterate his message, carved into the stone face of the mountain but they were too late. Everyone saw his name and knew what it signified.

"When men spoke of him, it was as Douros. He married again and his new wife gave him a son.

He tried to make his peace with God, although he never quite forgave God for allowing the massacre of his first family. His son and all the descendants that followed him proudly added the word Poulos, which translates to "Son of." So my sons our name, Douropoulos, means Son of the Hard One."

When the old man finished, it was Angelo who, with tears in his eyes, said, "Raise your glasses brothers, and let's toast them all. It is over a hundred years since the first Soterios blessed and kissed his sons."

The four men emptied their glasses and hugged one another. Then, with arms around each other's shoulders to form a ring, they moved slowly around an invisible ancestor who stared up at them from the center of the circle.

CHAPTER 2

THE PROMISE

The príka *(dowry) was intended for the bride's benefit so she would not have to go to her husband empty-handed. In truth, however, it served as a bribe, in some cases payment designed to placate the groom's mother for inserting another female into the household. Even though the new wife assumed most of the workload when she moved into her new home, the mother-in-law knew it was only a matter of time before the bride would exert more and more influence on her husband and eventually relegate the older woman to second-class status. The size of the* príka *varied greatly, depending on the quality of the merchandise, the beauty and talents of the bride, and the skill of the negotiator. An anxious groom usually received a smaller dowry.*

Tripoli was a fairly large town for its part of the world. The inhabitants boasted that it had four churches—real churches. Each was more than just a larger version of the peasants' homes, as were the churches in most villages.

The church favored by the two young men who had just crossed the dirt street was a magnificent structure. The Greek Cross atop its domed roof thrust itself into God's own sky. The cross, once white, stood out in stark contrast to the deep blue of the roof tiles. One of the men, once named Yiannis Vanzegos, was now known as Papa Yiannis since he had graduated from the seminary and was ordained as a priest. He lived with his mother and wife in the house in which he had been born. Each morning before he rose from his sleeping rug, he prayed to God to relieve his burden of living in a household with two women who hated each other.

It was difficult for the other young man, Soterios, to think of the priest as anything other than Yiannis. Born only a day apart, the two had grown up together, spent many hours talking, and once speculated on emigrating together to America, as more and more young Greeks were doing. After all, it was 1906 and the mass exodus to the land of "Golden Dreams" was in full force. But Yiannis' plan to go to America with Soterios had been postponed when he promised his dying father that he would stay until he had solved his father's greatest problem.

The problem Yiannis had acquired was his sister, Maria. It was clear by looking at Maria that she would never find a man to marry her unless she had a large dowry, or *príka*. Yiannis' family was too poor to hope they could attract a man to marry Maria. Occasionally, a girl who was poor but was an exceptional beauty would find a willing husband. Yiannis, however, faced an impossible task since his farm was a small group of worn-out fields, a few sheep, one Judas goat, and a hobbling, incorrigible mule. The fields produced barely enough food and income for the family to exist on. He had nothing with which to "sweeten the wine."

Soterios also had a sister who needed a husband, but he was not concerned. Martha was not a raving beauty, but she was known as a diligent and pleasant girl. Her *príka* was reputed to be ample enough that the marriage brokers were eager to add her as a client.

Soterios turned to his boyhood friend and said, "I postponed my trip for a day—or until I am sure that my father will recover from the coughing spasms."

"You know that I will both pray for him and watch him closely," the young priest replied.

"Yes, I know you will, but you haven't had much experience with that praying business. I can still remember when you and I were trying to steal fruit from the peddler's wagon," Soterios teased. Then he suddenly became serious. "Before the old man got hurt he was telling me the story about that bandit who gave us our name. He is concerned that he may remember something that he forgot to tell because of all the excitement. He never learned how to write so he directed me to ask you to put it in writing. He will see that it gets mailed to me in America. It is very important to him that the story is not forgotten."

The young priest scratched his scraggly beard and smiled, "Of course I will help. It will give me the illusion of talking to you and being with you. As you know, I still want to go to America as we planned, but now I can't."

Soterios interrupted, "By the way, I never did learn exactly how you got into this situation. Your father died at the same time I was helping get my brother Angelo out of another mess he was in. You were so sad over your father dying that I never asked you about the details. I would like to know. Maybe it will help you to talk about it. Come on! Sit down and let's talk about things and life like we used to." Yiannis shrugged his shoulders, and cleared some twigs from a level spot on the ground.

"My father's eyes were beginning to get milky, and he could speak only when he wasn't opening his mouth to breathe," the young priest said, settling down under a tree. "Of course, at that time I was still planning on going to America with you. My father was dying and Papa Andreas was saying the last prayers when I made the commitment. I promised my father that I would take care of my mother and would see to it that my sister got married. That is not an unusual request for a dying man to make, but as everyone can see, my sister is a real burden. The only way to get her married off will be to find a pot of gold somewhere."

Soterios smiled, but Yiannis continued in a sober tone. "I wanted to do the right thing, but to tell you the truth, I did not know how to solve the problem. It was Papa Andreas who came to me with the solution which, by the way, will make life a lot easier for him too.

"Papa Andreas comes from a long line of men who had dedicated their lives to the Church. His father and grandfather had both been priests and they decided long ago, when Andreas was just a boy, that he too would join Holy Mother Church. He was to be the one who would elevate the family beyond the status of parish priest. Papa Andreas would sacrifice the most. He would not marry before he was ordained and thus would become eligible to become a Bishop at the very least. God willing, he would bring glory to the family.

"Two months before his ordination the devil found Andreas and stole his soul. As you and I both know, the magical nights in Greece are made for lovers. Andreas fell like a apple from a tree when the beautiful Toula bewitched him. He told me that he was sitting under a golden moon balancing himself on a round boulder that overlooked the valley below. He had used this as a place of refuge for as long as he could remember, and went there whenever he had a problem.

"He had been troubled ever since he had watched Toula bare her arms as she scrubbed her face in the spring by the Shrine dedicated to St. Nicholas.

"Papa Andreas told me the water dripped onto her light summer garment and outlined her breasts. She breathed deeply when the cold water soaked through the cloth. He said she looked at him and smiled openly when she saw that his eyes were locked onto the cloth that covered her wet breasts. He turned and stumbled over a water jug, dragging the hem of his black gown through a puddle. He could not think because he was so embarrassed and confused. The swelling in his groin pounded so much that he was certain every villager could see it. He had dedicated so many hours to prayer and had been spared unwanted dreams for so long that he believed he was immune to woman lust. After seeing her, he came directly to his thinking place where he prayed and beat his hands on the rocks in frustration. Still, Toula continued to invade his thoughts, and no matter how he tried, the image of her breasts lifting that wet cloth forced itself into the forefront of his mind."

Soterios couldn't hold back any longer. He slapped his leg and whooped with laughter—the thought of the severe and holier-than-thou old priest running around with an erection was more that he could bear.

"Now wait, let me finish, you damned atheist," Yiannis protested.

"I am sorry, my friend. I will try to control myself. Please go on," Soterios urged.

"Well, she followed him up the hill, swinging her hands and humming a tune. When she skipped over a rock, her bare ankles flashed in the moonlight. Andreas just sat on his rock and stared at her. Toula swung around an olive tree by grasping the trunk with one hand while pushing her hair back with the other. The movement arched her back, pushing her breasts forward like little trapped animals. She did not say a word, not even when she stood on her tiptoes and melted her body into his, pulling his head down to kiss his sweat-covered lips.

"Of course, the inevitable happened. She told him she was pregnant two weeks before Andreas was to be ordained. The marriage took place. There wasn't enough time to post the banns properly, so the bride's father was disgraced. The entire population knew the truth. The dream of a Bishop seat for Andreas' family was gone. It was only because of the long record of his family's service to the Church that Andreas was allowed to join the priesthood at all. It was rumored that a substantial donation had been made to the Bishop by a mysterious friend at the same time the decision was made.

"Once ordained, Papa Andreas was designated to be a roving priest affiliated with the church in Tripoli. His job was to visit the various small villages that were too little to have a full-time priest assigned to their tiny churches.

Sultry and seductive, Toula produced a daughter who began her life squalling and screaming. They named her Anna. The infant suffered colic spasms, which didn't stop until she somehow managed to become infected with chicken pox, which evolved into a never-ending series of afflictions. As the years progressed, the child seemed to be forever crying, getting ready to cry, or moaning from the exhaustion of her last cry. At the time no one thought it unusual for her to experience terrible stomach cramps when her menstrual flow finally began when she was thirteen. When her wisdom teeth finally pushed through her bleeding gums, the teeth had cavities. The girl understandably developed a bad attitude. Since life treated her so cruelly, it was only fair that her mother, Toula, should suffer also. The squalling and demands for service and ministrations filled every waking hour of Toula's day and night. Her husband escaped by spending more and more time visiting the small outlying village churches. Finally, the exhausted Toula seemed to give up. She withdrew into herself like a tortoise and, when her daughter was sixteen years old, Toula quietly died, with a sigh of gratitude.

"In order to have some peace, Papa Andreas now had to find a husband for his daughter. Anna badgered him and nagged at him day and night. What made it even worse was that she insisted that not just any man would do. The prospective husband must be someone of quality, a teacher perhaps, or a priest. Her agitated father tried to point out that it would be difficult to find someone who would be sensitive enough to understand that she had special needs—one who was also intelligent enough to be an educated man, and who was also honest, hard-working, rich, and worthy of her. Anna had made up a list of qualities that her husband must have and kept adding to it as a new thought popped into her head. The list was pinned to the wall and the poor terrified father checked it each day. It grew longer and longer. Time was his enemy.

"Anna loudly complained that she was tired of doing his washing, and she was disgusted with the dirty habit he had of spitting into his handkerchief. Her father tried to explain that his lungs sometimes filled with mucus and it was unseemly for a priest to be seen spitting phlegm into the streets or, worse yet, on the Church floor. She didn't care about the condition of his lungs nor that the neighbors could easily hear her insulting and screaming at her father.

"When a year went by, Anna was still unmarried and the neighbors could hear her shrill voice beating at her father in endless waves. The gossips told all potential suitors that Anna was a shrew. She did not have one single prospect. The good priest would plead with her: 'Daughter, you have filled my brains with so much anger that I do not have room to do any of God's work. There is not enough room for a fat fly in my poor brain. Please give me some peace.'"

Yiannis shifted his weight and swatted at a pesky fly as he continued, "If you remember, Papa Andreas was giving my father the last blessings when he realized that our family also had a unmarried female. He heard my father's death wish that I would see to it that my sister would find a husband.

"He heard me promise my dying father during the final prayers intended to help the Soul avoid the Devil, 'I promise you, Father, that I will not go to America until my sister is married. I promise that I will find a way to raise the money to provide her with a *prïka.*' Papa Andreas almost forgot to place the silver cross on my father's lips when he heard my pledge over his mumblings. He got an idea. The idea immediately expanded and in an instant he had a plan.

"If his plan worked, he could recruit another worker for the Church, help me find a husband for my sister, and, most importantly, get some peace and quiet by marrying off his own daughter. The solution was an example of Byzantine simplicity: Complicated but simple.

"I would marry the priest's daughter, Anna, and would immediately apply for entrance to the seminary. Papa Andrea would use his influence to ensure that I was accepted. Once I married Anna, then Papa Andrea would give me enough money to provide an ample dowry for my sister, Maria. We would hire a matchmaker to find Maria's husband in another village. The end result would be that both girls would be married, the Church would have a new recruit, and Papa Andrea would be at peace."

Soterios interrupted: "I was arranging the winter purchase of wheat for the bread flour that we use in the bakery. It wasn't until I got back from Doliana that I heard about your father's death. If I had been here, perhaps I could have helped you. Even so, how did it happen that you agreed to such a thing?"

Yiannis looked at him and replied, "Let me tell you the rest of the tale, and you'll see that sometimes fate and circumstances determine the path we will follow.

"The morning of my father's funeral the sun was hot and seemed to burn a hole in the cloudless sky as the long line of mourners left the church. The procession wound its way down the hill, only to struggle up that other small hill to the rear of the Church where the cemetery was. The entire village was there, for in the ceaseless repetition of work, heat, and boredom, a funeral is an event not to be missed. People who lived in the next village, who were lucky enough to have heard the news, came to mourn the dead.

"Marriageable daughters and the official matchmakers had a problem. As you know when they go to a funeral they dress in plain black gowns, yet girls not married need to be noticed. All the women wore a scarf wrapped around their head and face. It is all that is left of the centuries-old custom of wearing veils that the Moslems had introduced.

"The men wore balloon-type pants fastened tightly at the ankles and rough cotton shirts covered with the embroidered vests they saved for special occasions, festivals, and holy days. Some of the men had daggers tucked into their belts as a reminder that their ancestors had been involved as *klephtes* (rebels) in the struggle against the Turks. The older men tried to hurry the procession along so they could return to the coffeehouse in the middle of the village where, ironically, the cups of thick Turkish coffee were waiting.

"As the casket was lowered into the ground, my mother, the widow Katerina, wailed and tore at her hair. She would be a widow for the rest of her life. Custom won't allow her to soil her husband's memory by remarrying. If my father had had a brother not married, then he would have been obligated to marry her and become a father to the children. Since my father had no brother, my mother will live out her life dressed in black.

"My mother pleaded with my sister earlier that morning: 'We must cry loudly today so that the women who fill their water barrels at the well will not be able to gossip and suggest that we won't miss him because he wasn't all that he should have been.' She respected my father and, in her own way, had loved him.

"She will miss him, but her anguish is for the future. She can't ever wear anything except black. Her dress, blouse, scarf, kerchief, even stockings must be black. She can't ever dance again or appear to enjoy life. She has to keep up the pretense that the rest of her life will be spent mourning her husband or risk ridicule and the anger of the Church. As her only son, I would be the one to assume the role as ruler of the house. She knows, too, that when I married, my new wife would not want a mother-in-law underfoot. Mother wailed and bit her knuckled finger. She complained that she was cheated, because usually it is the women who die first. I watched my mother and sister mourn. My face itched where the new, growing beard pricked at my skin. I wouldn't shave for sixty days as a sign of respect to my dead father."

Soterios tried to imagine the funeral as he listened. Yiannis interrupted his thinking. "I told my mother and sister how I had promised my father before he died that I would not go to America until my sister was married. I would live with them in the village until they were both provided for. I noticed that the priest Papa Andreas was listening. He was swinging the incense burner for the third time to the four corners of the graveyard. The incense drifting over the coffin does not let the Devil compete for the dead man's soul. His monotone chanting continued, but he almost dropped the burning incense. His hands were trembling so much that the chain holding the burner almost slipped through his fingers.

"I'm sure he was preoccupied with reviewing the plan he had formulated at my father's deathbed. He looked at me with a look of hope and a gleam in his eye and that confused me. I swear to you that it appeared to me that the priest was smiling at me. In an effort to verify what I saw, I turned to my sister and was shocked to see her looking at me with a smile very much like the priest's. I don't know why, but I swear to you that somehow—in spite of the priest's prayers and the incense, in spite of the cross that my mother and I held jointly—I believed the devil ... Oh, I don't know what I believed! I thought they were laughing at me. I got angry and confused all at the same time, so I bolted and ran out of the cemetery. I could see and hear the villagers asking what was going on as I ran as fast as I could all the way down the hill.

"You, Soterios, were the only one who came after me trying to help. I will never forget how you found me huddled in the little stone shelter that overlooks the orchard. I can still see you as you swung both legs over the wall, kicking the goat in the process. The goat bleated at you and spun away with her teats swinging. You told me that I needed to go to the Church, offer the final prayers, and light a candle. You wouldn't even let me tell you why I ran out of the cemetery. That's why you don't know all these details. Your only concern was to help me set things straight. I thank you for that.

"When I got back, the only people still in the cemetery were my mother and sister. They were talking to the priest. That's when I found out what all the unsettling smiling was about. Of course, my mother's main concern was what her neighbors would say about my running out of the cemetery. She seemed more bothered by what other people would think about her than anything else. She didn't care what my motivation for escape was. All she wanted to do was complain as she shuffled her beads through her fingers. My sister swore that she wasn't smiling and I must have misread her expression, though she admitted that she felt good knowing that our dead father would have been happy to know she would be getting married soon.

"The priest was the one, though, who gave me some peace of mind. He explained that the smiles of joy I saw could only have been a sign. 'Our Holy Father is blessing us all,' he told me."

Soterios stared in disbelief at his friend and started to speak when Yiannis, his face shining with sweat, continued. "It was a sign that God had heard all my prayers. As you know, I have always wanted to learn. I knew that I wanted to get as much education as possible when we were little boys together. You also knew I had wanted to be a teacher. I just never put teaching and the priesthood together. In these days, as you are aware, only the priests and teachers receive any education beyond the first few years. The priests are the most respected members of any community. The only way out of poverty and ignorance is through the Church. I knew I wanted to be a teacher. I just never knew that I wanted to be a priest."

Yiannis made the sign of the cross using three fingers, touching his forehead, the center of his chest, then the right and finally the left shoulder. He muttered a statement of thanks, and explained to his startled friend that it was true that God did work in mysterious ways. He could find a husband for his sister and fulfill his desire to become an educated man. Of course, he had to marry the priest's daughter, but that was a small price to pay.

"Soterios, my friend, do not be alarmed. Remember that in order to pick a rose, you must endure the thorns. By taking this offer, it is possible that in a few years—with some luck as well—I can get a lucrative posting. I will bet you that I can convince Papa Andreas to apply for another job—perhaps the priest of a small village like Doliana or Kaparelli, both of which are just over the mountain. I will take over the visiting priest's job for a while. That will get me out of the house for days at a time."

Soterios shrugged and embraced his friend. The two friends shook hands solemnly and wished one another the best of luck in achieving their plans for the future. As he walked away, Soterios turned around and called out to Yiannis, "Remember your promise to write to me."

Yiannis replied, "I never forget my promises."

CHAPTER 3

THE SMUGGLER

Two of the Douropoulos brothers returned from the top of the hill and walked through the narrow twisting roads lined with stone walls. Only a few feet beyond were the whitewashed walls of the "long-lived-in" homes of the residents of the small city of Tripoli, where all three brothers lived with their parents and sister Martha. The brothers rehashed their plan in which Angelo, the youngest, would go part of the way with Soterios, the eldest. The middle brother, Costas, would take Soterios' place in the bakery.

Soterios had purchased a handsome pair of black shoes with thick heavy soles. He had never owned such shoes before and knew they had to last him until he made his fortune in America. The shoes were carefully packed into a cloth satchel, along with his spare shirts and pants. He would not wear the shoes until he was on the ship, ready to leave for America. After all, he could not walk on streets paved with gold without the proper shoes.

Soterios and Angelo left the morning after the priest had blessed them and invoked their patron saints to watch over them. The priest gave Soterios a small icon that bore the likeness of Holy Mother Mary. The priest hated to part with the icon, but Soterios would have a greater need for it if it were true that there probably wasn't a Greek Orthodox Church in the entire country of America. He made Soterios promise to return the icon once he had become wealthy enough to buy a new icon for himself. The priest would then re-hang it behind the altar in the Church.

It seemed as if the entire population of Tripoli had turned out to cheer the brothers on their way. The women, dressed in homespun, dark-colored dresses with kerchiefs pulled low over their heads, were especially vocal as they called upon God and the Saints to watch over the young men. Soterios was just twenty years old. He carried his extra shirts, his grandfather's pocket-watch, 700 drachmas, a loaf of bread, some white goat's cheese, and a flagon of wine. Angelo and Soterios moved briskly as they walked into the first rays of sunlight peeking over the mountains. They were headed toward Argos, an ancient city that had once lay at the top of an enormous bay from which its name was derived. The city was now located six miles from the ancient port, but was still an important way-station at which travelers could obtain information about what ships were leaving from what ports to which destinations.

It was almost noon when the two brothers decided to stop for lunch before they began the climb that would lead them to the city. Angelo opened the kerchief in which the cheese was wrapped while his brother sliced the bread. They drank water from a spring that bubbled up between two rocks. The water tasted slightly of the wild oregano that surrounded the rocks, and their bare feet crushed the plants that grew by the path, filling the air with the aroma of fresh mint. It was difficult for Soterios to look at his brother, and he could not turn back to gaze at the village in which his home lay without showing his tears and anguish. Angelo, however, was so excited about the coming adventure that he could not stand still. He turned and laughed.

"I know I will get another beating when I get home and mother will remind me that my wild and crazy ways are inherited from our ancestor, the bandit; but it will be worth it. I don't want to be a baker. I don't want to ever settle down. It is the life of adventure for me! I may not go with you now, but you will look up someday and see me in America, and somehow I will get rich."

When Soterios asked why his brother expected to be beaten when he got home, Angelo revealed that their parents had agreed that he should go only to the city limits and then should return home. Soterios' brow dropped closer to his eyes as his face turned dark and angry. In a voice barely above a whisper, he hissed at his brother through clenched teeth.

"It's difficult enough as it is without having to know that our parents are worried because you won't return home on time. It was hard enough for me to leave, knowing that the old man was sick. I don't want them troubled any more than necessary. They know that the roads are still dangerous, and if you are late, they will be concerned. It is time for you to stop thinking only of yourself. You can be a jackass sometimes," he muttered, then warned. "I am telling you, for the last time, to stop associating with those wild bastard friends of yours. Remember, if you run with dogs, you too will be covered with fleas. In fact, go back! You can't continue with me. Be careful you don't anger me any more than you already have."

Angelo was stunned. His oldest brother almost never lost his temper. He had always been so kind and generous that Angelo often took advantage of him.

"All right, I'll go back, but I was counting on seeing the city. I've been thinking about it for a long time. It won't make a lot of difference to anyone whether I am home or not. If it will make you feel better, though, I'll go home; but I'll make you a deal since I am giving up this trip. It is only fair that the one you help get to America first is me, and then Costas can go later."

"Your brother Costas is used to having you crap all over him, so I guess he won't be surprised if it happens again. It's a deal," Soterios answered with a shrug.

A government transport wagon, pulled by two tired-looking, sweat-covered horses, lumbered up the hill. The driver was bleary-eyed, and his unshaven chin and drooping mustache filtered the smoke from the hand-rolled Turkish cigarette that stuck to his bottom lip.

He shouted, "Hey, if you want to ride in back, get on, but you have to jump on while I am still moving. I'm not going to stop for you."

Soterios tossed Angelo the satchel and tried to jump into the wagon bed while the wagon climbed slowly up the hill. After a series of little testing hops, he flopped sideways into the wagon while the canvas slapped at him. Angelo tossed the satchel up into his brother's outstretched arms, laughed, and waved a final good-bye.

Clouds of dust swirled around the wagon as it wound around the narrow rock-faced curves. It became more and more difficult to see Angelo. Soterios panicked until he reminded himself that, after all, this was the way it had to be. He was to continue on alone.

He tried to focus on something, anything except the fact that he was alone and frightened. He concentrated on the argument that the priest and the local school teacher had extended just before he left. The two often had different points of view, but it was surprising how vehement their arguments got whenever they discussed the history of Greece. All the old men seemed to consider themselves experts in Greek history. Most of the discussions of the men sipping steaming cups of thick Turkish coffee in the *cafenion* were about the heroes of the past. The teacher was leader of the group that seemed to favor the opinion that social injustice was the main cause of the misery that seemed so much a part of Greek life. Another group, led by the priest, argued that the morals and the values demonstrated by the heroes were in decline because people were turning away from God and the Church. The young were being corrupted by all the new ideas. How, they would ask one another, could Greece ever return to greatness if its youth kept leaving the homeland?

Soterios kept concentrating on the meeting he had with the priest and the teacher so he wouldn't think about turning back. Surprisingly, the priest had not argued as the teacher rambled on, espousing his ideas. When it was his turn to talk, the priest seemed worried. He babbled on about how the Church was having a difficult time convincing people that God would provide if only they had faith and would go to Church on Sundays. He said that only the old women and men came to mass on Sundays. The priest especially bemoaned the lack of good, honest, church-going God-fearing people in Argos, and warned Soterios to be careful.

The teacher did, however, add this thought: "The citizens of Argos are prosperous and seem to be progressing. They seem to know how to deal with the tangle of administrative laws and the bureaucracy that is destroying Greece. If you were listening in class the day we spoke of the 'Gordian Knot,' you will remember that the task was to unravel the knot. The knot was so immense, though, that no one was able to unravel it, until one man—some say it was Aeneas—solved the problem. He took his sword and cut the knot in half, effectively eliminating the problem knot."

The priest interjected, "Later historians said that the man was Alexander the Great."

"Who he was is not important; what is important is the lesson. The people of Argos are the ones who can cut through all of the foolish laws and rules that are choking commerce and our country, they are the ones who can get things done."

The priest suddenly popped from his chair and hurriedly left the room, walking on stiffened legs in the direction of the outhouse. The teacher was able to continue unchallenged.

"While the priest is gone, let me remind you that his first cousin is the Bishop in Argos. He also has a second-cousin who is a merchant and is known to be involved in the resale of smuggled goods. I am certain that Papa Andreas gave you a letter of introduction for the Bishop, but you can use it to meet the smuggler if you want. One more thing: whether you meet the Bishop or the smuggler, there will be a price to pay in return for any kindness they do for you. Remember, when one gets into a dance, he must dance to the music."

Since the priest had been busy taking care of his own affairs, Soterios never had opportunity to get the cleric's final advice. Soterios decided that the first person he would attempt to see when he got to Argos would be the resourceful smuggler-merchant.

In Argos Soterios made his third visit to the coffeehouse located at the top of the hill that marked the beginning of Othon Boulevard. The smuggler was known to frequent the place.

As Soterios saw the street sign 'Othon Boulevard,' he found himself shaking his head in disgust as he thought, "Another great example of how we Greeks love to argue, and because of it spend more time arguing 'how' than it would take to actually solve a problem. No wonder foreigners rule us!"

The street was named after the deposed Bavarian who had been selected by European leaders to be the king of Greece. French and British authorities picked Othon when they got tired of waiting for the patriots Kolokotronis and Kolettis, who had led the Greeks to independence from the Turks, to agree on their own leader. After Othon had been deposed as the king of the Hellenes, the seventeen-year-old Danish Prince William had become king, taking the name of King George I.

As Soterios climbed the last stair upward to the *cafenion*, the first thing he could see as his eyes passed the last cobblestone step were the legs of the smuggler's favorite chair and the enormous legs belonging to the human who occupied it. The chair legs looked like toothpicks compared to the two tree trunks of brown cloth that straddled them. Soterios was amazed that the mass of muscle and fat

43

attached to the giant thighs hadn't squashed the chair flat. The smuggler's legs were covered with European-looking trousers that ended above the bare ankles that emerged from the Turkish-type, green silk slippers with curved toe tips. Soterios gaped and his eyes widened as they traveled upward to the face of the biggest man he had ever seen. To call this man huge was an understatement, Soterios thought. You couldn't say the smuggler was fat because so much meat made it impossible to distinguish between the fat and muscle.

He was dressed in the fashion of the French, a once-white suit with a necktie that seemed to squeeze his Adam's apple so that his drooping mustache quivered with the effort to keep his wide pink lips open and pumping to bring air into his open mouth. He was sweating in the heat, even though a young and nicely dressed boy with huge eyes and curly black hair waved a long-handled, oval-shaped fan so that a breeze of some sort traveled over the tabletop.

Lowering a large glass of water whitened with *ouzo* to the tabletop, the smuggler looked at the astonished Soterios and questioned in a high-pitched voice, "Are you the person who has been looking for me? If you are, you had better have a good reason. It is not polite to be bothering my friends with questions, asking directions on how to find me."

He stared, waiting for some response from the terrified and confused Soterios, who finally managed to explain that he had come from Tripoli and had brought messages of respect from Papa Andreas, the smuggler's cousin, and a request for assistance.

Once it was clear that Soterios was a prospective customer who needed assistance to travel, not only to the port of Pireaus but even beyond to America, the smuggler relaxed and even seemed to smile at his visitor.

"Just exactly what is it you require of me?" he said as he sipped his drink and looked at the fan waving overhead.

Soterios explained, "My father has decided that I should go to America since I am the oldest son. As soon as I can, I will send for my two brothers. Together we will be able to get a good husband for our sister and then send for our parents. I am in a hurry to do all of these things because I can't think about starting my own family until all this is done."

While Soterios talked, he was uncomfortably aware that the few *drachmas* he had would not be enough to sustain him in the great city of Athens, or even Pireaus—not to mention during the trip across the ocean. He needed to find work as quickly as possible.

"I am willing to work, and in fact have been trained in my father's bakery. I can and will work at anything that needs to be done," he explained, and then interrupted the silence that followed his own remarks. "I want you to understand, though, that I won't do anything dishonest, but I will work hard." When the silence continued, he added in a loud and angry voice, "But I won't beg either." Meanwhile, his eyebrows drew together as they always did when he began to lose his temper. He was embarrassed, hungry, and, most of all, frustrated that the gross, sweating mass of flesh he faced had control over his future. Soterios felt rage building inside him, and he began to lose control.

Such emotional upheaval happened rarely with him, though it was a common occurrence with his brothers Angelo and Costas. The smuggler noticed Soterios' darkening skin and the slight trembling of the fingertips and instinctively drew back in the chair.

"Now wait a minute," he said, "what the hell are you mad about? Don't let your brains get away from you. In order to get to America, you will need a thousand dollars in American money. Where do you think you will get it? Are you foolish enough to think you can save a thousand dollars out of some piss-ant salary you may get? Do you realize what a thousand dollars is? Let me give you two pieces of advice that will help you for the rest of your life. Drink a glass of water, calm down, and—when you are ready to listen and learn—come back and see me."

Twenty minutes passed before the two faced each other again. Embarrassed by his behavior, Soterios looked up and listened respectfully as the smuggler rose from his trembling chair, stretched, and said, "First of all, when you want to get something from another person for free, or even if you are going to buy it, never get angry or show emotion until you have gotten what you want. Until you have what you require, remember that your opponent has the upper hand. Let him say whatever he wishes until you have fulfilled your objective. Secondly, you will never get rich as long as you work for someone else. As long as you work for others, you are working to make them rich. Jobs were not created for your benefit. Now, go away and come back tomorrow; and we will talk some more of the opportunities that exist. We will see whether you are strong enough or are hungry enough to reach out and grab them."

When the fleshy smuggler finished talking, he turned and walked between the rows of chairs and tables until he reached the sliver of sunlight that slipped through the shutters at the rear of the coffee-house. He managed to squeeze through the opening created by the large amphora floor vases and the wall, then slid onto a low, cushioned couch where he was joined by the pretty boy who had been waving the fan during the hot afternoon. The boy handed him a long hose attached to a water pipe. He lay back on the cushions, closed his eyes, and inhaled the smoke.

Soterios turned and again descended the stairs. He had just reached the street when he felt someone pulling on his sleeve.

"Please wait a minute. He wants to talk to you again," said the boy, who moments ago had been flapping the hot air away from the smuggler.

Reluctantly, Soterios returned to the stifling room where the smuggler kept Soterios waiting for a moment before he turned to him and asked, "Did my cousin give you a letter for me? It seems to me, now that I know you a little better, that your nature and upbringing does not mix well with my business. Why would the pious fool send you to me?"

Soterios explained that he did have a choice. He handed the crumpled letter to the smuggler.

"I could have gone to your uncle the Bishop, but I decided to come to you first. It just seemed to me that I had a better chance of accomplishing something with a more practical person like yourself. I am sure that the Bishop is a good man and all that, but priests talk a lot yet don't accomplish much."

"Well well, maybe there is some good stuff in you after all. Come on back in the morning and maybe I can set you up in a little business of your own." The smuggler unsuccessfully swatted at a fly, using the envelope like a club. "Don't worry. I will be the main partner. You have to realize, though, that I may ask you to do some things which are just a little bit unlawful. Think about it, and if you are willing to take some risks, then come back in the morning." The smuggler squashed the careless fly, then looked with disgust at the yellow, oozing corpse plastered to the envelope flap and threw Papa Andreas' letter on the floor.

Soterios turned without saying a word, then went out into the street beneath the scorching afternoon sun. He dodged a donkey that walked slowly by, his head hanging while his owner rode sidesaddle, idly tapping the beast's flank with a limber stick. The donkey's rider looked just like his 'almost' uncle Panayiotis, and a lump of homesickness grew in Soterios' throat. He struggled to regain his composure and hurried down the hill, walking in a northerly direction toward Athens. He was leaving Argos. As he walked he made a promise to himself that he would not stop until he was certain that temptation and loneliness would not cause him to return to Argos.

Soterios kept reliving his bothersome confrontation with the smuggler as he walked the rock-filled, dusty roads. He spent the first night huddled against some boulders next to a spring that bubbled up by the road. A wooden cross and an icon created a shrine of sorts, and a metal cup dangled from a thorny bush next to the spring. He felt that he might be safer next to the holy images than anywhere else on the road.

The next day, in late afternoon, he looked down from the bridge at the Corinthian Canal and wondered how man could have cut such a gap in the earth. The canal separated the mainland of Greece from the Peloponnesos. As he looked down over the railing, a freighter steamed westward on its way to the port of Patras on the Ionian Sea. The distance from the bridge to the water was so great that the freighter didn't seem any longer than his shoe-covered foot. He wanted to ask someone. Who built the canal? How did they dig all that earth out? How long did it take? His own education had stopped in the fourth grade and he was too ashamed to ask. He wondered if perhaps he should have lied years ago and said that he too wanted to be a teacher. Then he might have been eligible for more education, which would have been a great honor for his family.

His father's family, he knew, had once been important and were still of a slightly higher station than ordinary peasants. After all, his father was a businessman. Now that he knew the story about his ancestors, he would have something to tell the brothers of a prospective bride in America. He was not just an ignorant peasant; he was, after all, a Douropoulos.

One thing he was sure of, though, was that he did not want any son of his to become a priest. He had seen too many of them living off people poorer than themselves. He knew that his mother and the other women of the village were deeply religious and superstitious, fearing both God and the Devil. He noticed that the men were less prone to following the myriad laws and rules of the Church until they became old enough to begin thinking about death. Maybe the Church was needed more by the weak and the vulnerable. He also knew that if the priests could see into his thoughts, he would be considered guilty of the most heinous of sacrilegious crimes. He hoped God was too busy to listen to what he was thinking.

The cheese and bread that he had when he started his journey were gone, and his growling stomach reminded him that he had to think about getting something to eat fairly soon. He remembered the smells of the bakery, especially the fragrance of the special bread that was made at Easter. The warm sweet-smelling yeast mixed with the aromas of allspice, cinnamon, and anise enriched by the butter-melted sugar would fill the entire bakery and drift out into the street. He could almost taste it.

Once he reached the other side of the gulf, he knew he would find the town of Corinth where he would get work if he could find a bakery, possibly cleaning out ovens. He was desperate enough to take on the dirtiest job in any bakery that heated its ovens with coal or charcoal—scraping off the sides and bottoms of the oven. The hard carbon almost crystallized into thick sheets and chunks.

The next morning Soterios walked through the ruins of the old city of Corinth. In ancient times, the city had been a sensuous center where the most beautiful prostitutes gathered to worship at the temples honoring the goddess of love. The only thing that remained were piles of marble and granite slabs that fell when the temples were destroyed. The marble columns that supported the temple roofs had been constructed by inserting lead pins between the hand-carved circles, then fastening one on top of the other. During the war for independence, it had been necessary to tear the temples down in order to extract the lead needed to make bullets and cannonballs. All those magnificent buildings had been destroyed so men could kill each other.

It wasn't until Soterios got to the newer section of the city, just before the sun went down, that he found a bakery whose proprietor was willing to hire him to clean a storage shed in which the wheat flour was kept. As payment he received a large bowl of lentil soup that smelled of bay leaves and vinegar. It was thick and brown, just like the soup his mother used to make. He dipped and dunked a large piece of hard-crusted bread into the lentils, inhaled the aroma, and almost fell asleep at the rough table in his host's kitchen. The small, stooped lady, who he knew was someone's grandmother, loaned him her shawl to use as a blanket as he curled up next to the ovens for warmth.

When he awoke the morning of the following day, he lay motionless on the floor with his eyes still closed and listened to the baker whispering to his wife. Soterios heard that he was about to be introduced to the baker's niece.

"I tell you that if we are not careful and as sly as a fox, he will think we are trying to pawn damaged merchandise off on him. She is not a queen, but she is not bad looking. *Yiayiá* is outside talking to her, trying to explain that she has to be more talkative without appearing to be bold. She is too shy now."

The wife's response was interrupted when Soterios sat up and stretched. She quickly shifted her attention to him.

"Good morning, young man. How did you sleep? I hope you are rested because I have some more work for you. First let's have some breakfast, or at least a piece of cheese and bread. We are not wealthy in these parts, but we are famous for our hospitality and our women."

"That's right," the baker added, "The females from this area are famous throughout Greece for their virtue and the bread they bake."

It was the baker's turn to be interrupted by the door opening. The grandmother who had loaned Soterios her shawl came in, pushing a young girl in front of her. The old woman spoke in a loud voice, apparently convinced that the louder she spoke, the more apt others were to understand her.

"Look who came to visit us—your niece Sophia." As she spoke, she nudged the girl with her elbow.

The girl managed to stutter, "Good morning, Uncle. I - I - I wanted to say hello."

Quickly the baker turned to Soterios, "Young man, I want you to say hello to my niece, Sophia. Perhaps we can convince her to share breakfast with us and we can all get better acquainted."

Sophia was a thin, hatchet-faced girl with one brown and one blue eye. Soterios was fascinated by her eyes and sneaked glances when he thought no one was looking. But they were watching. The situation demanded attention. Sophia was not married and unusual-looking. Soterios was handsome, young, healthy, and also not married.

Breakfast was filled with uncomfortable dialogue. It took all of Soterios' tact to avoid all the couple's attempts to convince him to postpone his trip without appearing rude. The baker turned to Soterios as they drained the last drops of tea.

"Come, young man, help me move the bags of flour to a higher shelf."

They left the house and walked to the storage area in silence. Soterios stopped walking and kicked a stone out of his path.

"With all the humility I can manage, I must refuse your offer to stay a while. I am honored that you would consider me for your niece, but I am going to America and I can not let anything slow me down. I hope you understand." He would have gone on to say more, but he was interrupted.

"Now look, we gave you work, fed you, and by accident my niece stopped by. We would not consider having a village bumpkin from Doliana or Tripoli, or wherever you came from, as a possible suitor for her. Everyone knows that people from that part of Greece aren't worth much. I insist that you apologize to me and leave before you insult my family any more."

Startled, the young man looked at the downcast older man, and suddenly understood the pleading expression.

"Please forgive me for being so brash, and thank your wife and mother for their kindness," Soterios said, then turned toward the kitchen to gather his belongings. The baker reached out and caught him by the sleeve.

"You are a good boy even though you are a little impetuous. When you get to Pireaus, I believe my *Koumbáros* can help you out. He lives on Doxina Street, Number 22. He has a cafe. They make a living by feeding the dock workers who handle a lot of the produce coming into Athens. Go now and leave. I am sorry, but it must appear as if I chased you away. I don't want the girl's parents to blame her for losing another prospect. We can't officially shake hands as friends, but if I ever meet your father, I will tell him that he has a good son."

Soterios was able to hitch a few rides on the backs of mule-drawn wagons, but he walked most of the way to Piraeus, the outskirts of

Athens. He finally found the cafe on Doxina Street with Number 22 painted on the window. Adjacent to the window was a door, also numbered 22. The door opened into a courtyard protected by a low wall on one side and the rear wall of the cafe on the other. The living quarters of the cafe's owner made up the other wall of the courtyard. Geranium blossoms and leaves flowed down the grayish white 'piazza' steps. The *Koumbáros* and his wife were shouting at each other. The man's face was dripping with sweat, which beaded up and dripped from his nose every time he shook his head. The woman held both hands over her ears while she shrieked as loudly as she could.

Unnoticed, Soterios watched as the argument seemed to develop into a crisis that threatened to turn into a full-blown tragedy, as many Greek family squabbles did. Apparently the husband, Emmanuel, had a brother who owed him 4,000 drachmas as a share of their father's estate. The misguided brother, a prosperous shoemaker who had two cobblers in his shop, had owed this money for six years. One of the cobblers was Emmanuel's wife's "good-for-nothing" brother who kept telling his sister that business was booming. That information made matters worse, since business in Emmanuel's cafe was not good.

Communists were causing trouble on the docks and interrupting normal activities. The dock workers could not be counted on to buy the little cakes and coffee as well as the other foods sold in the cafe. The 4,000 drachmas would come in handy, but Emmanuel was unwilling to ask his brother for so "trifling an amount." Admitting that he needed the money would cause others to say his older brother was more successful than he.

Emmanuel's wife was furious. Her husband did not understand why she wanted the money so badly. In order to make him understand, she believed she needed to talk and yell as loudly as she could. The more she shrieked at him, the louder he had to yell back to get his point across.

Emmanuel spun on his heel, shoved her out of the way, and escaped into the house. She threw her hands into the air and looked at the heavens as if for validation then pursued the fleeing man into the house, slamming the door behind her. Soterios backed up against the wall as neighbors, attracted by the noise, gathered in the courtyard. The men stood together on one side by an olive barrel scheduled for repair. The women paced back and forth in agitated little groups.

When their own wives were not within hearing distance, the men whispered to each other, "What that woman needs is a good lesson with a stout stick." The women were getting ready to send for the priest. The ongoing, intense argument seemed to be getting out of hand.

Soterios didn't like the prospect of being caught right in the middle of the fiasco. There he was, a complete stranger who needed to ask a favor of two people in the middle of a real Greek tragedy—a family fight with the neighbors listening. He turned on his heel and headed for the wharf. It was at the docks, after all, where most of the jobs would be found, and even though he wasn't a seaman, a stevedore, or a Communist, he was strong and willing to work. At least he didn't think he was a Communist. Of course, he didn't know what a Communist was, except that he heard people saying that they caused a lot of trouble but were willing to share what food they had with each other. As hungry as he was, he would welcome a Communist or two as long as they had some food to share.

Soterios slept on the dock that night, snuggled between two large bales of merchandise wrapped in burlap decorated with the Greek flag and emblem, along with some writing printed on the side. He tied his shoes tightly on his wrists since he could not afford to lose them to some thief. The good black, sturdy leather shoes were a sign of respectability. With a good pair of shoes like that, he could get a job anywhere.

The morning was cold and foggy. The fog seemed so full of water that it felt as if he should push the sheets of fog aside as he walked. An Armenian who operated a produce stall that sold nothing but oranges and lemons gave him a small bag full of oranges in payment for sweeping the floor and moving a huge stack of lemon crates.

Soterios, peeling his third orange, watched the docks come to life. Groups of men, two and three at a time, walked into a "just-opened" warehouse. The workday was beginning, even though the sun was still sleeping. Soterios threw the orange peel into the bay and sucked the juice from the quartered orange.

He was leaning against the corner of a building when a man negotiating the curve bumped into him. Soterios dropped his own bag of oranges, yet somehow managed to catch the tray of pastries the startled man dropped.

"What in hell are you doing standing around bumping into honest people trying to make a living?" the stranger shouted. Soterios recognized the voice of the *koumbaro* from Doxina Street.

"Excuse me, Mister, but how can I be guilty of standing around and bumping into you at the same time? I was standing and you were the one who did the bumping. Don't get excited. No harm was done. After all, you didn't lose your tray of pastries," Soterios reminded the baker and smiled as brightly as he could.

The man, who Soterios had learned last night was called Emmanuel, shook his head.

"Well, of course, you're right. I sometimes talk before I think. Thanks for catching the tray. I would have been in trouble with my wife if I had dropped it and she found out."

"God, who made it possible for me to save the food, must have arranged this meeting. I came to your house to see you yesterday but," Soterios hesitated, then went on, "you were busy, so I left. I have a message from your *koumbaro* in Corinth. I would like your permission to come and see you this evening when you aren't so busy."

Emmanuel looked at him suspiciously. "I hope you aren't trying to mock me, about being busy yesterday. If you are making fun of me, watch out. If you are serious, you may stop at my house this evening and I will talk to you when I have more time. I am a very busy man and have some important things to take care of."

"Thank you. I will come this evening." Soterios almost had to shout as Emmanuel turned and scurried down the street.

"Well, it's good to see he survived yesterday's battle," Soterios smiled, talking to a gull perched on a nearby piling.

Soterios aka Louie

CHAPTER 4

THE COMMUNISTS AND THE COOK

S oterios spent the rest of the morning walking around the busy docks, occasionally stopping to talk to the old men who sat on benches or discarded food crates. He shared his oranges with two old men sitting at the base of a statue. The men stopped twirling strings of blue worry beads between their fingers as they peeled the oranges with little knives that hung from a chain on each of their vests.

"I am not from these parts. Actually, I come from a section of the Peloponnesos where we do not have any Communists. What can you tell me about them?" Soterios asked two men.

"You don't have to tell us that you're a stranger to the big city. We can see that," one of them replied. "We have been watching you walking around looking at everything with your mouth open. As for Communists—well, they are a political bunch who say people who have more than what they need should share what they have with those who don't have enough. Since we old people don't have enough of anything, we think it is a wonderful idea." His friend displayed a toothless grin.

Soterios continued with his questioning. "Do the rich Communists think it's a good idea to share their wealth with the poorer people? If they have to keep sharing, why should they work hard to get rich in the first place? I am going to America so I can get rich. Why should I share that with someone else?"

"Listen to this poor rooster talking about not sharing his wealth. First get wealthy, then we worry about keeping it, you damn fool," the toothless old man snarled.

"I may be a fool, but I am going to America. Before you make too much fun of me, remember that I shared my oranges with you. I had more than I needed. Perhaps the difference is that I shared because I wanted to and not because it was required of me. I don't like it when anyone tells me I have to do something. No! I can tell you this right now: that Communist stuff is not for me!"

Soterios slung the bag containing what remained of the oranges over his shoulder and continued his wandering through the confusion of the port's busy docks. He found his way back to the house inhabited by the warring husband and wife, now reconciled and recommitted to the task of caring for themselves and family. Since Emmanuel had not returned, Soterios introduced himself to the businessman's wife. By the time her husband showed up, the wife was convinced that their visitor was a good, honest person who came highly recommended, truly needed help, and could be counted on to repay any favors or assistance now or in the future.

Soterios sat on a small stool on the veranda that overlooked the enclosed courtyard. Emmanuel, his host, who so recently had been embroiled in a shouting match with his wife, sat opposite him.

"I suppose you were here last night when my wife and I had a little argument. Well, we do have our ups and downs, but she is a good woman. I am sure that a lusty fellow like you will understand when I say that 'an old hen makes the best broth.'" He winked and made a obscene pointy gesture with his ring finger.

Soterios shifted uncomfortably in the straight-backed chair. He ran his fingers through his hair before replying. "Yes, I was here, but I left when I saw it was a bad time to introduce myself. I slept on the dock last night. I was trying to decide what to do next when I bumped into you—that is, you bumped into me!"

Emmanuel continued, "My neighbors were listening and shaking their heads, but if they turned and looked around, they would remember that even the Apostles wept at their own suffering. What I mean to say is that everyone has their own problems. I suppose that in a moment or two you will tell me what yours are and why you came to my house."

Soterios chuckled and said, "Your friend in Corinth felt sorry for me when his niece turned me down. He suggested that I come to see you. I need work to earn enough money so I can get passage to America."

"Ho! That will be the day that fat grows on a fly when he would allow a fancy fellow like you to get away from that homely, skinny, cockeyed niece of his—especially if there was any chance of marrying her off."

Soterios protested, "She isn't cockeyed. One eye is blue and the other brown. And in any event, she was pleasant to me, as was the whole family. I came to you because I am a baker. I want to work and eventually plan to go to America. I hope you will help me. Of course, if you do, I will repay you or your family some day. Now, you can help me if you want to, but I can't let you disparage those who have tried to assist me. As you said, everyone has his own problems. You should be more sympathetic to your cousin's problems."

"There, you see, even strangers tell you that you say too much. I have told you before that you have to learn to think before you talk so much." The voice came from the wife of the now thoroughly chastised man.

"Come in, young fellow. Stay for dinner and a glass of wine. Be assured that anyone who is as thoughtful of others' feelings as you are will find a helping hand in this house. Come in. Come in."

Dinner that night was a heaping bowl of dandelion greens mixed with bits of stewed lamb. The greens had been picked young and tender, then cooked in a mixture of olive oil and lemon juice, and seasoned with garlic and mint. Soterios was soaking the last piece of heavy-crusted, homemade brown bread into what was left of the liquid from the greens when his host suddenly acted as if he had just remembered something.

"Po! Po! Po! I know what can be done. There is a freighter that travels between the islands and the mainland that is lucky enough to have as a cook another member of my family. He is the son of my first cousin. Let's see—that makes him my nephew. How can he be anything else since I am so much older than he is? In any event, he always needs an assistant, someone who will wash pots and pans, clean, and assist in cooking and serving meals to the crewmen—and occasionally to a tourist who is foolish enough to book passage on the boat. It will be perfect. You will not only get a job, but you will have a place to sleep and food to eat while you are trying to find a way to America." And I will not have to feed you, my fine friend, the old rogue thought to himself.

Soterios spent the night with his new found benefactors, and the next day went to the docks where he met Emmanuel's nephew, the cook. He was a short, pugnacious man, wire-thin and balding. He strutted, his head bouncing from side to side, to the table Soterios occupied and smiled.

"I am looking for a fellow called Soterios who comes from a village close to Tripoli. My landlady told me that a relative of mine had left a message saying it would be to my advantage to come here and meet with this Soterios fellow. Is that your name?"

Soterios stood, offering his hand and, at the same time, hooking an empty chair with his foot and pushing it toward the speaker.

"I am Soterios Douropoulos, and I come from Tripoli, though we once lived in Doliana. Your cousin—or perhaps he is your uncle—was supposed to be here so he could introduce us. He and his wife run a café over by the wharf. I met him when his cousin, who has a bakery in Corinth, recommended me."

The cook interrupted him. "Wait! Wait a minute and sit down. Buy me a glass of wine. I think I know who your benefactor is. The first thing I have to know is what advantage I am supposed to gain by meeting with you."

Soterios shrugged, caught the waiter who was laughing at someone else's joke by the sleeve. "Bring us each a glass of *retsina* and some fresh water for me." He again offered his hand to the Emmanuel's nephew. "I thought you were going to be of service to me, but if I am going to be of service to you instead, then at least tell me your name and where you come from."

"Well, at least you are bright enough to have a sense of humor, which is something you mainland Greeks from the mountains seem to have buried under all those rocks you always move around. My name is John Adonis. I was born on the island of Lambros just off the Turkish Coast. I left there when I got tired of trying to figure out whether I was Turkish or Greek. We had been ruled by Turkey for centuries and by Greece for only the last 50 years or so. In order to survive and keep our own Christian faith and churches alive, we had to be as smart as a fox and stubborn as a mule in those years of Turkish domination.

"Now we think like Turks but have the emotions of Greeks, so there is a lot of confusion. The people of Lambros are dirt poor, and I couldn't see anything getting better so I left and came here to the mainland," he said in disgust. "Of course, things aren't a lot better here. The local Greeks sometimes give me a lot of crap about my not really being Greek because my island was Turkish for so long. Screw them all! I am going to go to America. Get another glass of wine for me and, what the hell, get yourself one too. You're paying for them." John Adonis slammed the glass down on the scarred wooden table.

It took two more glasses of wine before John was satisfied that Soterios was the kind of person who would feel obligated for any assistance he received. John also suspected that his companion was running out of money.

The two men left the *cafenion* and walked to the southern end of the *pláka*, or marketplace, for the port of Pireaus. They found the captain of John's ship in his favorite *taverna*. Soterios anxiously waited at a table by the smoke-filled kitchen, while John and the captain sat at a round metal table on the balcony overlooking the busy street below. Every time the captain leaned back, Soterios could see a church's onion-shaped steeple, with a white cross silhouetted against the sky.

The papers that the captain had been looking at were piled neatly on the table. A strong gust from the Aegean winds almost scattered them on the floor. The captain slammed his hands palm down over the moving papers in exasperation.

"Enough, enough. I'll hire him." He turned to Soterios and shouted, "Hey, country boy, come here so I can see what you look like!" As the young man approached, the captain continued, "Your boss will be this friend of yours here, this little Turk masquerading as a Greek. You will do whatever he tells you to do when we are at sea. You can expect to work every day except when we are tied up at the docks, loading or unloading. Then you can get one half day a week to yourself. You will have a bed to sleep in and food to eat. John will teach you how to cook, and if you behave yourself, we will pay you each month.

"John insists that you get the same deal he gets. The deal is that you will not get paid monthly in drachmas, but the purser will see to it that you get paid off in American dollars when you need money. You will receive twenty-five dollars in American money each month."

They left the captain in the smoky *taverna*. Soterios turned to John. "I don't understand why I am going to get paid in American dollars instead of drachmas."

John looked up at the much taller young man and said, "I hope you are not going to be asking me 'why' all the time. You farm people are like little kids, always wanting to know why. If you spent a few minutes trying to think things through, you would be a lot smarter. All I am going to tell you now is that you've got a job, and if you are not too raunchy and don't spend too much on the whores in town, you can save enough American dollars for your fare to America. What the captain does to get enough money to pay a crew of misfits who do not have merchant sailor's papers is his business and to your advantage. Christ! I thought that since your nose is so big maybe you would have some brains." He muttered all the way back to the ship. Soterios got tired of trying to decipher John Adonis' mumblings and instead looked at all the new sights.

The ship left the next morning. It was scheduled to make the long run to Crete then westward to Malta, returning through the islands in the Ionian Sea where they hoped to pick up cargo and freight before they had to return home. Soterios cooked, washed pots, and cleaned up after the sailors. He fetched and carried for the diminutive cook who shouted and demanded that Soterios stop what he was doing and reach up to get something he could not reach. "Hey, farm boy, remember a tall man is always a short man's ladder."

It took six months before Soterios' hard work and courtesy finally wore John down. He began to share some of his own emotions and frustrated dreams.

"Hey, Soter, if you do not do some heavy and serious planning, you will never get enough passage money together. You'll end up just like me—full of dreams but no prospects. How much money do you have saved? Where do you keep it?"

The Turkish cigarette dangling from his lower lip made it difficult for Soterios to answer. He pursed his lips, shoved his jaw forward, and blew the cigarette out and over the rail.

"I'm glad you brought this up because we haven't talked about it before. I only have fifty dollars saved and I have it hidden in a safe place. Someone else besides me, though, should know where it is in case something happens to me. I would want my savings sent home. The only person I trust, John, is you, but I didn't know if it was fair to give you additional responsibility."

"By the holy robes of the Virgin Mary, of course I accept the responsibility. In addition, let's figure out how we can invest that money in some kind of a business deal. Legally, of course," he said with a chuckle. "Christ! Here we are on a boat that does nothing else but move stuff around. Each time it gets moved, somebody makes money. Why can't we get some of it too?"

The world became more interesting once the decision had been made to find a business venture instead of depending on the generosity of an employer. The advice given to him by the disreputable but wealthy smuggler in Argos kept coming back to Soterios: Jobs weren't created for your benefit. Now, when he looked at a tree, he no longer saw just twigs and branches but saw firewood that he could possibly sell. Dead fish became fertilizer; bales of tobacco became cigarettes. Even John started to get tired of hearing Soterios say as each idea came up, "We can make a lot of money if we can ... "

And one by one, his propositions were rejected. The lack of money to begin the proposed venture was a continual deterrent.

Six more months passed, and by then Soterios was doing most of the cooking as well as the cleaning. John had developed a paralyzing cough that shook his body and forced his lungs to expel the phlegm that clogged his air passages. The two men spent as much time hiding John's sickness from the captain as they did continue the quest for riches. The crew members noticed that the quality of the meals had improved greatly and generally acknowledged that the credit belonged to Soterios, even though he denied it.

It was during a trip to the straits that led to the interior of Russia and separated Turkey from Greece when the captain found John gasping for breath and ordered him to bed. The quality of the meals did not deteriorate, and as a matter of fact, the two German tourists who had joined them in Istanbul were ecstatic about the variety of flavors and aromas that came from the galley. It did not take long for the captain and the owners of the ship to realize that they had a valuable asset in Soterios.

The ship was docked in port when the captain made the mistake of drinking too much *raki* in his favorite *taverna* in Pireaus. He boasted of the wonderful cook and the fabulous meals served on his ship. The purser of a small tourist steamship company that regularly made the trip across the Atlantic to Norfolk, Virginia, and ultimately to Boston was sitting at the next table. The purser was getting closer and closer to the magnificent breasts of the Bulgarian prostitute sitting next to him when he was distracted by the captain's oratory. Only his devotion to stuffing his belly had a higher priority than satisfying his groin.

The purser reported what he heard to the captain of his ship. The captain personally went to the tavern. He bought a few rounds of drinks for Soterios' shipmates, and asked a few cautious questions. John, who was sitting at the table when the captain bought the first round of drinks, turned to his right and asked his companion, "Why do you think that peacock with all his fancy talk and gold braids wants to buy us free drinks? He knows most of us don't have legitimate papers. In my village we say, 'When you care to learn, listen; don't speak.' Let's have as many free drinks as we can get. If we can find out what he is after, we will get even more out of him."

The captain bought another round of drinks and asked three more questions about the quality of the food and the name of the cook before John spoke up.

"The ship itself is a rotten tub. The captain and the first mate are so bad that we would all jump ship except that the good, kind Christ gave us an angel to cook for us. This angel is able to take old fish that the company provides and turn it into a delicious stew with plump raisins, celery, and onions swimming in a tomato sauce. He makes chowder and soups that even the fat German tourists can't get enough of. His galley is so clean that not even starving, skinny flies exist on our ship."

The captain ordered another round and asked again about the cook. John knew he had him!

"Captain, this cook is a good friend of mine," he said, as he purposely slurred his words. "I will be happy to introduce him to you. If I ask him to, I am sure he will speak to you. He always listens to me—even when that stinking Italian purser from that fancy cruise ship wanted to hire him. I told Soterios he was better off with his old friends. Buy me another drink and, if you want to see him, I will arrange it."

The waiter brought the drink and John promised to bring Soterios to the house where the Captain lived with his Pireaus woman. The meeting was set for the next day, when most people would be taking their afternoon nap. John suggested that two o'clock would be perfect.

ᔕᔕᔕᔕᔕᔕᔕᔕ_____

"Wake up! Wake up! The eggs are on the table and the cock is in the sack. Wake up! For the love of Christ, listen to me!" John cried as he burst into the room.

Soterios was asleep on the bed, wearing a sleeveless, soiled undershirt and a pair of under- shorts. The dark overnight stubble of his beard glistened in the harsh light of the bare bulb that hung from a wire. "If the fancy-dancy Captain saw you now, he would wonder if all Greeks were liars."

"Captain? Liars? What the hell are you talking about?" Soterios managed to stutter, reaching for a cigarette. John explained what had happened.

"Listen to me! Do exactly as I say. If you do, we will both go to America, make a lot of money, and you can become famous. It is time for you to learn how to be a little bit crooked. You cannot be a good businessman and a good dealmaker unless you are at least just a little bit crooked."

The three men sat at a small table on straight-backed iron chairs in the courtyard of the Captain's lady friend. Her two bright yellow canaries sang and fluffed their golden wings, contrasting with the bright red, popcorn geraniums in the clay pots on the low wall protecting the courtyard. The captain hawked loudly to recapture Soterios' attention, which had been diverted by the colorful antics of the birds.

"I am willing to make you the first assistant cook, but because you aren't a licensed seaman, I can't pay you the full rate. You can gain a lot of experience, and I will promise to help you get your papers if you come to work for me."

John looked at Soterios, smiled, and pleaded with his eyes. Soterios stared at the cruise-ship captain and replied, "Thank you for your offer. I am sure it is a generous one, but I have sort of agreed to work for the Italians. They need cooks so much that they are willing to hire my friend John as an assistant cook also. They will give us papers when we arrive in America." He took a deep breath, avoided John's eyes, and continued.

"They are willing to give me five hundred drachmas so I can visit my parents before the ship leaves for America in one week."

"Turk, that is what you are. Two Turks! Greeks would not work for Italians when they have a chance to work for their own kind. You're trying to force me to meet the Italian's offer. Have you no shame? Because of national pride, I'll agree to everything you asked for except," he hesitated and then continued, "Four hundred drachmas is all I will give you to visit your family."

"We will reluctantly accept your offer," John interjected then shook the captain's hand and shoved Soterios out the door.

Soterios waited outside while John finalized the deal. John pocketed the four-hundred *drachmas* and agreed that Soterios would go back to their old ship and say good-bye to his shipmates. He would pick up John's possessions as well as his own, and drop them off at their new ship where John and the captain would meet him. John was to remain a hostage, unable to leave the ship until Soterios returned from visiting his parents. John explained the details of the agreement to Soterios as he counted the *drachmas* into Soterios' hand. The young man first turned away and then again faced John, who was surprised to see Soterios' eyebrows drawing together, a sure sign that he was angry.

"John, I don't understand why you gave up one hundred *drachmas*. I am sure we could have squeezed it out of him."

John coughed, then chuckled as he replied, "Before you start crowing like a barnyard rooster, learn one more thing. Any time you are winning an argument or negotiating a business deal, and you have gotten what you want, always allow your opponent to win something. You don't need to win everything. Give a little when you win a lot."

zjzr

CHAPTER 5
THE FUGITIVE

The road dust clung to his unshaven face as he limped around the last corner, blocking his view of the city. He stumbled and almost fell, dropping the bundle as he grabbed at the gnarled olive tree branch that jutted into the path. Soterios had been walking for almost twenty-four hours and had nearly reached his destination. He left his bundle where it fell and climbed to the crest of the hill so he could view the growing city of Tripoli.

Suddenly, without warning, he started to cry. He sobbed as the tears ran down his cheeks, creating twisting paths through the dust-covered whiskers. He couldn't remember ever being as happy as he was that moment. He retrieved the bundle of gifts that now seemed weightless and, almost running, hurried homeward, crying and sobbing as he came to each landmark.

When he reached his home, his entire family greeted him with surprised cries. His father looked pale, and his mother even more stooped than he remembered. She stood in the street, her brown skirt skimming the road, holding a kerchief to her mouth as she wept uncontrollably. She didn't move until he disentangled himself from his father's embrace. After Soterios kissed her, she took the great silver cross that hung on her chest, kissed it, and raised it to the heavens as if to say thank you. Costas and Angelo didn't look any different than they had when he left. He had a second to wonder at the impact that a year or so has on the older ones before they surrounded him again.

His father sent Angelo scurrying to get Martha, who was at her cousin's house.

The next few days seemed to fly by so quickly that Soterios was surprised when his father said to him, "Tonight is the last time that we will have to discuss the story of your ancestors.

Vasilios sipped the homemade red wine that he stored in a barrel in the basement. He turned to Soterios and asked him to retell the story in his own words. It took Soterios over an hour to finish his rendition as his father interrupted him correcting and emphasizing repeatedly.

Eventually being satisfied, Vasilios left the room to relieve himself by the lemon tree in the front yard. As he lowered his head to enter the room he said with a sigh, "I'm just like that old tree I just pissed on, all used up and waiting to die. The old tree and I never accomplished much but we kept trying to produce a little more each year."

Soterios gasped and replied, "Father, don't be foolish. We have always been proud to be your sons. Everybody knows how hard you have worked. All of us love you and respect you for what you have accomplished. That's more important than any story about the heroes of history."

The old man's eyes glistened and shone like wet green pebbles as his son continued. "I know how much you grieved and how difficult it was when your first wife, my mother, died. I know how lonely you were until another good woman agreed to marry you and to raise not only her own children, but me as well. You have been a wonderful father. No one ever accomplished more.

"I went to church today, and as I sat there in the silence, I thought about staying in Greece instead of leaving. I wondered if the reason that you got sick and the mule died when you began the story was a signal from God that I should not go. But I decided that my future contribution to our family depends on my going to America, and accepting responsibility for my brothers and sister. I'm the oldest, and I'll go to America because that is my destiny."

Angelo, listening at the door, entered the room and, with an effort to be lighthearted, said, "I will be the next one to go to America and I promise not to leave until I can tell the story backwards and forward. That's enough story-telling to make me stay home more in the evenings. I will go to America with my head so full of our past that I won't have room for even the names of any loose women I might bump into. So you see, some good will come of all this crying and soul searching"

The next morning Soterios left home, knowing he would never see his father, or mother again. The trip back to the ship was uneventful. He and John had settled into a new routine of shipboard life before they had their first major argument. Soterios loaned a hundred *drachmas* and his new jacket to the seaman who was in charge of greasing and splicing the ropes that held the lifeboats in place.

John was furious. "How in God's name are we ever going to save enough money if every time some jackass says he needs help, you reach into your pocket? You barely know this guy and you not only let him borrow money, but you give him your new jacket to wear. What the hell are you going to wear when it gets cold tonight? You will freeze your ass."

Soterios flipped both hands, palm up, into the air. "I still have that heavy sweater to wear. Besides, I'm not going anywhere tonight and he promised to pay me back as soon as he gets paid."

"Who is this guy? How do you know he can be trusted? For Christ sake, Soterios, smarten up. You can't trust everybody just because you met them and like them. Christ! You like everybody."

John slumped, frustrated, into a chair, only to jump to his feet choking with rage when Soterios argued back. "Come on, John, this guy is a good person. He comes from a village near my home. He knows that I will need the money when we jump ship in America."

John stared at his friend in disbelief. "What do you mean he knows we are going to jump ship? I don't believe that you would be foolish enough to tell somebody who owes you money that you're going to jump ship! Not only does he owe you money, but he probably is going to be so jealous of you that he will squeal to the first person of authority he meets that could do him some good. Soterios, most people in this world aren't honest, and if they are honest, they are honest only most of the time. Nobody is honest or ethical all of the time. How can I make you understand that honesty, just like ethics, is a matter of circumstance?"

John was so upset that he forgot to swallow at the right moment and choked on his next words. After coughing and finally spitting out phlegm, he continued, "There is a story that we tell back home that might make some sense to you. Settle down and let me tell you about a fox, a bear, and a dog.

"Long ago a strange friendship had developed between a wily gray fox and a half-wild dog who lived in the hills above a muddy pond. One day they were traveling together and were just about to head up the crest of a hill when a loud smashing of branches prompted them to look up. They saw a hungry-looking bear forcing his way through some old dead branches, heading straight at them. The dog became so frightened that he fainted and fell unconscious, rolled down the hill, and into the mud of the pond. The fox jumped down beside the unconscious dog, quickly rubbing mud all over the dog and himself so that they looked like two great lumps. The bear looked at the pond, saw nothing but mud, and continued down the trail where he was sure his prey must have gone. As soon as the bear was gone, the fox quickly washed the mud off the dog. The dog recovered and asked how the fox had saved them from the bear. The fox merely smiled as foxes do and trotted off. Whenever the fox was asked why he did not tell his friend, the dog, how he had tricked the bear, the fox would say, 'If you never tell your friends your secrets, they cannot use them against you if and when they become *your* enemy.'"

Soterios sat quietly with his head bent, staring at his knees. One leg pumped up and down as it crossed over the other leg. Eventually he raised his head and spoke. "John, I understand the story and I know you are right. I can't help but wonder, though, how many times you have played the fox with me. What secrets haven't you told me? Wait a minute! Don't tell me. It doesn't matter. I understand the message that the story tells. But, I can't accept your belief that ethics and honesty are a matter of circumstance."

"Soterios, old friend, our relationship is something special. The way I deal with the world is completely different from the way we deal with each other. Circumstances, my friend, circumstances."

The two friends spent the next two days going about their duties quietly. John purchased five heavy wool sweaters and quietly stored them away.

"Maybe we can sell these extra sweaters to our shipmates for a nice profit. We have to take advantage of every situation," John explained to Soterios.

"I can't believe we are finally going," Soterios said as they boarded the ship on the third day. They had just returned from the government post office after sending a letter to Tripoli with a money order for 300 *drachmas.*

Every one of the four letters he had sent included money as well as the names and locations of anyone who had helped him. Soterios was now obligated to them and wanted to transfer the commitments to his brothers.

The ship cruised through the straits of Gibraltar and out into the Atlantic. The two Greeks soon discovered that, even though their country had always been a seafaring nation, there was a difference between sailing the Atlantic and the Mediterranean Sea.

The ship's passengers were divided and housed in three separate groups: First Class, Tourist, and then the immigrants, who were considered Third Class. First Class passengers had a window or porthole and were located in the center of the ship, usually just below the top deck. The Tourist section, which included some cabins with portholes, was located on the same deck but closer to the front or bow. The immigrants got what was left: the bottom deck, which had no portholes. The cramped quarters were always up front where the rising and falling motion from the bow was felt most. Not even the crew were bunked there. The crew had cabins on the lower decks but was located back toward the center of the ship. The cooks were important enough to receive the best of these quarters.

Most of the immigrants were ill during the entire voyage. Their skin took on the green and yellow tinges that comes from seasickness as well as from being cooped up without fresh air. Watching the children especially motivated some seamen to want to help the immigrants. The children's eyes seemed to get larger and larger as they lost weight from the constant retching and dehydration. Some of the children seemed to have lost the ability to close their eyes even when crying. The large, staring eyes haunted Soterios as he struggled to keep the soup pot's full and boiling while the sea continued to toss the ship about. The chef, Soterios' boss, had left two children at home with his wife, and missed them all terribly. He spent a lot of time trying to ease the children's seasickness by giving them strips of cloth soaked in a sugar water mixture to suck on.

After the voyagers passed the Azores, the seas calmed down for a day, then another storm hit and lasted until they landed in Norfolk, Virginia. Soterios and John were planning to jump ship in Norfolk.

It had been less than fifty years since the end of the Civil War. During that time, the port and the warehouses had been rebuilt. The city had grown over the bones of its past, memories of which spawned the Ku Klux Klan. Many veterans of the war still lived and sons still listened to their fathers tell of the horrors as well as the glory of war. Because the young people loved their parents, they listened to the stories, and adopted the prejudices of their forebears. Time and the natural gentleness of youth would slowly shrink the tumors of hate and bigotry, but not enough time had elapsed.

The ship slipped into the pier during the night, and huge ropes were thrown to the men waiting in the brightness caused by the newly installed electric spotlights. Soterios had just finished putting away the last of the utensils from the previous meal when the steward called and told him to report to the chef in the storage room where dried foods such as beans and macaronis were kept.

The chef was a huge man who had been a professional wrestler in his youth. He had dreamed of being a champion but had never had the talent to overcome the streak of kindness and sympathy for his opponents that prevented him from smashing them into total defeat. He had a huge nose that not only jutted out but was thick at its base and bent in the middle from being broken too many times. Thick wire-rimmed glasses perched on his nose but always slipped forward, waiting for a thick finger to push them back where they belonged before they dropped off the end of his nose.

"Come on in, Soter, and close the door. I want you to help me find out where all of the macaroni disappeared to. I gave that shoemaker of a steward the list of supplies we need to buy here in Virginia. He wants me to give him an inventory of what we have on hand. His boss went to college and insists that we follow some damned system that he learned there. It isn't enough that good honest people like us just say we need something; we have to prove it." He said this loudly and, when the door was closed, he dropped his pencil and paper on a sack as he whispered.

"Quiet now, I have to tell you something in confidence. You have worked hard for me and never gave me a lot of guff. I owe you. What I am going to tell you is partial payment. I do not believe that the ship's officers will do anything to get you your papers or those of your friend John. They always make promises but don't follow through," he said, shaking his head in disgust. "If the immigration people find out you don't have the right papers, they will take you off the ship unless you agree to stay on board until the ship returns to

Greece. They will make the captain agree to post a guard so you can't get off. In the event that you and your friend plan to jump ship, you'll have to do so before all these things happen. I'll miss you, but I want to help you get away. Those bastards have to get outsmarted once in a while. In any event, decide what to do. Be sure no one knows I told you anything."

"Thank you for telling me. I didn't know what might happen. To be honest with you, I was worrying about how I could jump ship without talking to you. You have taught me a lot. I am indebted. John had told me not to worry because you would understand and, if not, what the hell? I would never see you again anyhow."

"Soterios, my boy, that Turk in disguise may be a good friend of yours and he is pretty canny, but don't let him confuse you with his sense of morals and values. His ancestors had to be as slippery as wet fish to survive until we real Greeks could rescue them from their masters in Turkey. They have become so sneaky and mistrusting of others that no one completely trusts them either. Their children have picked up the same traits. After all, you do not get figs from an olive tree. Your values have been taught to you by good strong God-fearing people, and even though the values sometimes appear to be naive, do not discard them. The values of commitment to friends as well as family should not be overpowered by the acts of a few strangers devoted only to their own comfort. Do not forget your upbringing; instead, build on it by learning from your experiences."

That very evening John and Soterios formulated the plan that would allow them to get their few belongings off the ship so they could sneak ashore when the time was right. The next morning John went ashore with a large bundle. He told the guard at the gangplank that his dirty clothes were going to be washed by the Chinese grandmother, who waited patiently under a sign that proclaimed her honesty by guaranteeing to return all clothes in a clean condition.

Soterios had been concerned that the bundle would be inspected until John pointed out that the authorities were now only concerned with what was being brought onto the ship by the sailors. That night the two crept down the gangplank that had been used to load food supplies to the forward storerooms. Soterios had been the one who had helped the steward receive the shipment and had kept the key to the gate for the gangplank when the steward was signing the delivery sheet. John retrieved their belongings from the Chinese grandmother, who smiled at them while speaking rapidly in an excited blend of what must have been English and Chinese.

The impact of what they had done and of the little chance they had of getting away without being caught began to set in. The two walked out of town quietly, hoping no one would attempt to talk to them. The only words they knew in English were 'ham and eggs,' which Soterios had learned from a tourist on the ship who insisted that the only breakfast he would eat was ham and eggs. The repetition of the words with a visible pointing of fingers began Soterios' introduction to the language that he was to adopt for the rest of his life.

CHAPTER 6

SOTERIOS BECOMES LOUIE

"Soterios, my boy, we are going to be living like Pashas pretty soon. We are in America! We have money in our pockets and shoes on our feet. I stole some food and stored it with my underwear—my clean underwear of course. And best of all, you have me," John clapped Soterios on the back and continued.

"With your good looks and strong back coupled with my brains and wisdom, we will be rich in no time."

"For the love of Christ, John, keep your voice down. Sometimes with all your brains, you have as much common sense as there is fat on a fly. We don't want anyone to notice us. We have to get away from here and find some countrymen who are be willing to help us."

The black shadows cast by the trees on the gravel-covered back road began to assume shades of gray that would gradually pale as the morning light began to break through the overcast.

"We have to hurry before it gets too light," Soterios said as he picked up the pace.

"Bah! Why should we hurry to get someplace soon when we don't know where we are going?" John stopped muttering when he saw his partner double over with laughter. Then he, too, started to laugh until he began to cough and gasp.

"Well, my old friend, I guess it is funny when you stop and think about it, but we do have to hurry," Soterios said.

The road they traveled joined a well-paved highway. The two walked quickly on the soft shoulder as trucks carrying freight rolled by. An occasional wagon pulled by large draft horses slowed the flow of traffic. The number of auto vehicles was so great that John was inspired to comment that there were more trucks on that road than in the whole of Greece.

As they hurried along, Soterios mentioned that some of the truck drivers were not only staring at them but some were openly hostile as they drove by.

"John, something is wrong here. The men driving the trucks look at us as if we were dirty gypsies. They keep looking at us and snarling like dogs!" John shrugged and hurried along with his eyes pointed directly at the toes of his shoes.

Soon, other people could be seen walking in the same direction they were going, The walkers were mostly black men. Soterios had seen his first black man on the docks in Pireaus. He had very little contact with any since then. He was still intensely curious about them so watched them closely, trying not to draw attention. Still, he could not help but stare at them as he walked along. They seemed to be happy and cheerfully talked and waved to each other, but as soon as John or he got close to them, they gave way and quickly moved over. John kept his head down and muttered as he walked.

"I've noticed that these black men seem to be afraid of us. They jump every time we come near them. The truck drivers look at them the same way you said that they look at us. Everybody seems really nervous. We better be careful that we don't get in the middle of something." Suddenly John stopped walking as the realization froze his steps.

"Christ! The reason that these men are behaving this way isn't because they know we are Greeks. It isn't because we are dressed differently or because we are dusty and dirty. They couldn't have heard us talking in Greek because we have been careful. Christ! Soter, they are afraid of us because we are white. You've heard the talk on the docks that the white man is superior to the black. I haven't thought about it and, what the hell, it didn't make any difference to me either way. What this means is that for the first time in our lives we are better than someone else. In the old country the Turks treated us like dog shit for so long that we began to believe it. We were all dog shit. Sure there was always someone poorer than us or somebody who was touched in the head, but here is a whole race of people who are inferior to us."

Soterios looked at him and shook his head. "I don't know what the hell you are talking about. My head is spinning. I am tired, and haven't slept for a long time. You said there was always someone poorer or who was 'touched in the head,' but that was an individual—not a whole race. A whole race of people who were inferior—now that is something to think about."

Both men resumed walking. After Soterios stumbled, he realized his head was spinning from lack of sleep. It had been a long time between meals. A flatbed truck lumbered by and slowed as it climbed a small hill. John and Soterios bent over to shuffle up the slope. Soterios looked up as the truck passed him. He let out a breath then gasped.

"Look! See those bales wrapped in burlap, the ones with the Greek flag on them? I slept next to some that had the same markings when I first got to Pireaus. Do you think that they are being shipped to one of our countrymen?"

"It makes sense that a Greek would be buying Greek stuff. Besides, what do we have to lose? Come on! Let's take a chance, jump on the truck, and see. I am too tired to go much farther anyhow."

The truck slowed enough so that the two men were able to jump and flip themselves onto the back. Soterios quickly draped some loose canvas over them, slapped John on the shoulder, and pointed, "Look, John, notice that the black men are turning away. They are making believe that they don't see anything. Not bad, eh?"

Soterios leaned his head against one of the bales and inhaled deeply. For a moment he thought he could smell the patch of mint that grew outside his mother's window. Just as he dropped off to sleep, he realized that the smell was coming from one of the bales. John stretched his leg, which was bent under the other, looked at the bales that had some Greek letters stenciled on the burlap then at the rolls of barbed wire and farm equipment. He hunched over to wait for whatever was to happen next.

The truck stopped outside of a decrepit-looking house built next to a large oak tree at a dusty crossroad. John heard the truck door close, then a woman's voice shouted a greeting over the sound of a man and woman singing. The door opened again and John could feel the truck move in slow motion. By peeking from under the canvas, he could see they were under a shade tree behind the house. The door of the truck slammed again, the driver left the truck, and John waited. The oak tree provided shade, but the heat and the long hours without sleep finally caught up with him, and he fell asleep.

Both men awoke at the same time, as the truck moved again. John yawned.

"I fell asleep. I think I slept about six hours. I remember we stopped in front of a house—a whorehouse, I think. Anyhow, there was a party going on. Look at the sun. It has moved over to the west. Anyhow, here we are waiting for the truck to stop somewhere and we don't know where. The best we can hope for is that a fellow Greek may be waiting for a delivery. What a mess. Besides, I am hungry and pretty soon I am going to have to piss somewhere."

John and then Soterios struggled to maintain their balance as they urinated off the back of the bouncing truck when they thought no one was looking. As John readjusted his trousers, he looked up and saw a black man sitting on a broken wooden plow by the side of the road. The man averted his eyes as the truck passed by, and John thought for a moment that he was laughing.

It was dark when the truck finally stopped in front of a rickety warehouse. A light went out in an upstairs window that fronted the street. They heard a high-pitched voice whisper a question in Greek. The answer came back through the darkness and the open window, in a voice so filled with fear that, for a second, the two still hidden on the truck forgot to jump out.

"Be quiet, woman, they may not be after us. Can you see what they are wearing?" The voices they overheard were speaking in Greek.

John and Soterios slipped off the truck and blended into the shadows where the light from the truck's headlights did not reach. The driver climbed the stairs and pounded on the door. Speaking in English, he said, "Hey! Come on, get up and open the door, for Christ's sake! I want to go home and I can't go until I drop off these bales. Hey! Come on, open up!" Then he muttered to himself, "Screw it. I'm going to dump them here. I delivered the bales like I was supposed to. If someone steals them, it's not my fault."

Neither John nor Soterios understood what he was saying, but there wasn't any question that the best thing they could do was stay hidden.

The two bales were dumped onto the ground as the driver snarled and muttered in the direction of the warehouse. "Grease-balls and spicks, goddamn kikes, and black bastards. What do I care if someone steals their stuff?"

The truck pulled out of the lot. As the warehouse door slowly slid open, a tall thin man with a long mustache and small round eyeglasses tried to reach out and grab the bales to pull them into the warehouse. He couldn't quite reach them. Suddenly he was jerked back and a woman's voice said. "Come back inside, fool, before something else happens." She pushed past him to drag the bales in herself.

In a carefully muted voice, John whispered in Greek, "Excuse me, Madam, but we are two Greeks who need help. We do not want to frighten you, and mean no harm."

Startled to hear voices coming out of the night, she stood frozen in place. It was several seconds before the shock wore off and she responded, "What do you mean to do then, hiding in the dark whispering in Greek, if not to frighten my husband? Come on out where we can see you. Better yet, help me get these bales indoors. Hurry now before those white-robed devils come."

Soterios and John scurried out of the night and wrestled the bales from the doorway into the first room of the warehouse. The large unfinished room was lit by single lamp bulbs hanging from various parts of the ceiling in a random pattern. The floor was concrete, though remnants of a wooden floor were visible in places, causing a series of step-ups. Other bales and crates, as well as some rolled-up carpets, were stored on the section of wood flooring. A sign proclaimed the crude establishment to be the 'Aegean Import Company.'

The woman was neither pretty nor homely. Her medium build, brown hair, and mouse-colored eyes left nothing to distinguish her. Still, Soterios could tell already that she was intelligent and coura geous, a woman whose true strength came from her single-mindedness and dedication to improving her family's future. Her actions told him that she was the type who maneuvered her husband as a tool to achieve goals. Soterios guessed she allowed her man the illusion of superiority when she knew that was necessary to implement her plan, and was just as quick to reverse the role when it was called for, as he had just witnessed.

She squared her feet and shoulders to parallel John, the smaller of the men, and said, "Where in the world did you come from?"

John started to cough and shoved his hands against his chest as if trying to push the pain back into his lungs. Her husband poured water from a pitcher into a small bowl and gave it to John, who was now doubled over. He gratefully swallowed some.

While John recovered his breath, Soterios turned to the woman and said, "I'm from Tripoli and he is …,"

"No!" she said with exasperation "I don't care where in Greece you came from. I want to know where you came from now?" Then she smiled, breaking the tension. Everyone started to talk at once. Soon, wine was on the table and a pot of *phakés,* a rich lentil soup, was being reheated for the hungry travelers' meal.

Panayiotis, who wanted them to call him by his new name, Peter, spooned some of the thick brown lentil soup onto a slice of homemade Greek bread, sprinkled crumbs of feta cheese on top, then turned to his wife, whom they now knew as Angela. "Woman, after we finish eating, prepare a place for my friends to sleep."

She began to nod as if in agreement, then stopped and stared at him. "Your friends, your friends? How did they become your friends and not my friends? We have been in this country for over two years now and you still act as if we were back in Greece. I am not going to let you order me around like a servant."

She turned to her guests, "In this country, women are not used as servants who cater to every desire of the men. You may as well begin to learn the new ways from now on. Look at him. He is my husband, and I love him. We will raise a family together, but he must begin to face the truth. He has forgotten that it was my uncle, not his side of the family, who paid our passage over here. I was the one who made my uncle agree to send the money. I was the one who agreed that we would work for my uncle for three years and run this business, which he calls the Aegean Import Company."

Angela turned to face the embarrassed Peter and announced, "I will make them comfortable and cook and wash. I'll do the women's work because I should, but … Ahhh, what's the use?" Her words trailed off, as she left the room muttering to herself.

"Don't pay too much attention to what my wife said. It is true we have new things to worry about, and being a woman, she does not understand the complexity of these events. She talks about her uncle owning the business. Well, the truth is," he leaned forward and dropped his voice almost to a whisper. Soterios and John, without realizing it, leaned forward in their chairs to hear. "Her uncle only owns half of the business. The other half, and in my opinion maybe more than half, is owned by a Jew. He never comes around except when it's really important.

"You see, in this country the white Irish Protestant bastards hate everybody. The Protestants hate the Catholics, too, but not as much as they hate everybody else. The blacks and the Chinese get the most trouble because there are so many of them. You know, I have heard it said that if you mix a Chinese woman with a black man they can produce two babies a year. The blacks have been here for a long time, but since they were slaves once they can not be called real Americans. An American is someone whose family has been here for more than fifty years."

He stopped for a minute, took another mouthful of the lentil soup, and continued. "How can a woman understand these things? Even I have a hard time understanding why a person, for example a German whose parents came here twenty years ago, gets so upset when another German from his ancestral home town emigrates here now? The man who has been here for twenty years may be out of work, but since he considers himself an American, he won't take the low-paying jobs. The newcomers work hard, and they will take any kind of work that is available."

Soterios wondered whether Peter would have work for them.

"All I know is there are some white-robed bastards who beat everybody up. They don't like the Greeks either—even though we are white. We are not considered low-class like the blacks and the Chinese are, or the Indians. I haven't seen any of them, but there are some red people who they say used to be the only people living in this country. Those Indians, by the way, are just like the Turks—terrible people who eat babies."

Soterios glanced at John, who seemed amused by the conversation.

Oblivious, Peter continued, "I have noticed that the other whites like us seem to fight back more—especially the Catholics from Italy. Maybe that is why the American bastards in white robes are picking on us. They are punishing us good Orthodox folks for the sins of the Catholics and the Jews.

"You know the Jew sold Christ to the Romans. And what did the Romans end up as? That's right, Catholics. The Catholics are the ones who secretly negotiated with the Turks to cause the downfall of the Orthodox faith, but I'm sure you already know that."

Angela returned to the room with a blanket over one arm and said to the men, "What really makes the Americans mad is when one of us, especially a Jew or a Greek, ends up owning a business after only being here a few years. What the lazy, spoiled fools don't understand is that we sacrifice ourselves by working hard. We care about our children's future. All this hate and jealously is what makes it easier for the Ku Klux Klan to grow stronger. That's what the white-robed ones call themselves. Sometimes you will see signs in store windows that say, 'Blacks and dogs not allowed. No Greeks, Wops, or Jews.' I know that I am not supposed to understand these things because I am just a woman, but I do know that the Klan hangs people and sometimes puts hot tar and feathers on their naked skin.

"Anyway, it is awfully late. It is time to go to bed. Look at your friend John. The poor fellow has not heard a word anyone said for the last ten minutes. He is sound asleep."

The next morning, after they ate a meager breakfast, John started to cough again.

Soterios questioned him. "John, old friend, I am getting concerned about your coughing. We really should get you to a doctor."

"Soterios, make some sense! First of all, I have a little cough, but I have had a coughing problem for many years. Second, we can't go to a doctor since we don't have papers or money to throw away."

Before Soterios could reply, Angela came into the room from the warehouse. She turned to Soterios and asked him to help her move some carpeting, leaving John to recuperate from his coughing spell. No one noticed when the immigration inspector first came into the building. It was Angela who first smelled the odor of his burning cigar smoke.

"Soterios! Shhh! Pick up that broom and sweep the floor, and don't say a word."

The inspector was a burly man with broad shoulders and a huge neck. If it wasn't for the necktie around his throat pushing against his Adam's apple, it would be hard to notice that he had a neck at all. He had a brown, round fedora with a little American flag stuck in the hatband where a feather would normally be placed. He was preceded by a cloud of smoke from the cigar he held in his left hand. The fingers of his right hand stroked the gold watchchain that crossed his vest. He smiled when he saw Peter, then turned to Angela.

"Angela, I wanna ask you a few questions about an oriental carpet that my wife wants me to buy, unless of course I can buy a carpet from you and that Jew partner of yours for less money."

Before Angela could answer, the inspector saw Soterios, now furiously sweeping the floor.

"Hey! Who are you? What is your name ? Maybe I should take a look at your passport."

Soterios heard the voice and saw the cigar pointing at him like a fat giant finger, but didn't know what the man was saying.

"What is your name?" the inspector repeated.

Quickly, Angela spoke up. "He is my cousin. We have his papers in the other room. I will get them for you later. I am paying him too much for him to stop working. Come over here, and let's look at these low-priced carpets."

She pulled the inspector gently by the sleeve while she kept talking in a softer and softer voice so he had to walk faster in order to stay close enough to hear her. When they reached the other end of the room where the better carpets were kept, he turned to her.

"Okay! Okay! All I want to know is what do I call him the next time I come here and see him? And don't give me any greaseball name."

Angela stammered for a second and then proudly proclaimed, "Louie. His name is Louie." Meanwhile Peter edged John into the other room and quietly closed the door. He walked to Soterios' side and whispered in Greek, "From now on, your name is Louie." He paused a second for emphasis, and said again, "Your name is Louie. Whenever you hear that word, look up because they are talking about you."

Soterios started to protest, but the words trailed off into silence as the inspector stared at him and smiled through the cloud of cigar smoke.

"So your name is Louie? Like hell it is! I'll bet you don't have any papers either. You're a goddamn greaseball who jumped ship and is trying to sneak in."

Then, he turned to Peter. "It's a good thing I came in here today. I'm looking for a good deal. I want to buy a rug for my wife's birthday. She has been raising hell with me because the carpeting in our front parlor is stained and torn. Her damn cat pissed on it, which makes my dog scratch at it. Of course," he sighed, "she says it's my dog that tore it so I have to get her a new rug.

"If I hadn't been here, I wouldn't have met good old Louie here, and you could have been guilty of aiding and abetting a criminal."

Angela quickly intervened. "We don't know what aiding and abetting is, but if we did it we are sorry. All we want to do is to be good American citizens. How can we correct our mistake?"

The inspector encircled Angela's shoulders with one arm and hugged Peter with the other, almost kissing him on the cheek, and whispered, "Today is my day off. I'm going to go home and get my wife so she can pick out the carpet she wants. Don't try to hide any of the good ones. Leave all the rugs just like they are. In the meantime, why don't you help greaseball Louie here find his papers. When I get back, I'll check them out—if he's still here."

He closed one eye in an exaggerated wink, just as he had seen Wallace Beery do at the Nickelodeon Movie Palace. As he turned to go out the door, he added, "You think you can find a carpet that I can buy for about ten dollars?" Peter nodded yes. The big man spun on his heels and walked with a bounce out the front door.

"Now you've done it," Peter said to Angela. "What do we do now? You have got to be a mother to every stray dog or homeless countryman. See what that has got me. When he comes back with that horse-face, stinky Irish wife of his, we will have to sell him a hundred dollar rug for ten dollars. Even after we bribe him with the rug, he may still arrest this jackass Soterios or that little Turkish fart hiding in the back room."

"I can hear you. Stop shouting. Or maybe you think making noise is going to put some stick in your back. That would be a miracle only the Holy Mother Mary could perform." She turned to the confused Louie, who used to be Soterios.

"I am sorry, but you have to leave. Now! When that American Turk comes back, we can satisfy him with the carpet, but you can't be here."

The newly named Louie was still confused—even after Angela explained in detail what had happened. John came into the room and quietly hugged them, first Angela and then Peter. Peter managed to keep his dignity as he shamefacedly apologized for his outburst. He cautioned them to be careful when leaving. It was even possible that the inspector belonged to the Klan and had already turned Louie in. "The Klan is active and violent even in broad daylight," he warned.

John spoke up. "Christ! We can't say three words in American. If there are people in white masks beating up anyone who isn't American, we won't stand a chance. I would rather not get off the ship on this trip, not with those crazy fools in white sheets stopping everybody and beating people. Wait a second...." He hesitated, then resumed, "Things aren't that bad. We've only been gone from the ship for two days. We can get back on it without anyone being the wiser. It will be easy to convince the ship's officers that we are so dumb we let a couple of whores steal our money. We'll tell them that we were trying to find the girls to get our money back.

Reluctantly, Soterios agreed to return to the ship. Peter volunteered to drive them to the docks if they would hide under some old sacks in the back of the wagon. Soterios agreed. They quickly piled in and burrowed under the sacks as Peter opened the double doors leading to the street.

Angela reached under the sacks, took Soterios' head in her hands, and said with a mischievous smile, "Louie, take care of yourself. Come back and see us when you can."

The last thing she heard was John chuckling and saying, "Ha-ho-ho, wait till his mother finds out that for the rest of his life his name is Louie. Looouiee! If you say it quickly, it sounds like a pig squealing. Loooouie-Loooouie!"

At the ship, John told the story to explain their absence, blaming it on the mythical thieving women. As John predicted, it was easy to convince the officers that the two truants had more penis than they had brains.

The second mate looked at the two men standing in front of him. "I never expected to see a Greek who didn't know that whatever happens to your body can be blamed on your crotch." He winked and said to John, "I know that a stiff penis has no conscience, so I am anxious to hear of your adventures with Soterios."

"Well, my friend, I will be glad to tell you, but you must understand that Soterios is no more. That poor fool you see standing in front of you is now called Louie, Louie, Louie!" John laughed loudly as he added, "I wonder what the date is for Saint Louie's Day?"

The new Louie told the chef the truth about what happened to them and why they had to return to the ship.

"I don't know why those bastards in white sheets don't like Greeks. I don't even know why they don't let the blacks alone. Christ! I don't want to steal their stuff or screw their women. All we want is a job so we can bring our families here." Soterios shook his head sadly. "I can understand that jerk of an immigration inspector. He acts just like the petty government officials do in the old country. Bribery or extortion is all they know. They can't stop pushing people around. I thought I had left all that stuff behind in Greece. I never expected to find that same kind of crap going on here in America. I don't know why I expected people to be different in America. I guess crooks are crooks no matter where you are. They may speak a different language but they are all the same. I have a lot to learn about this American paradise."

"Louie, my friend, you must try hard to understand that even though you'll find people like that no matter where you go, the world is full of opportunities. The opportunities are there if you keep your mind clear. If you get bitter and just feel sorry for yourself, your brain will be so busy finding words to explain how unlucky you are that it won't be available for new ideas. Find some time during the day when you will just think about opportunities. Don't let anything but good thoughts and new ideas pass through your brain. I personally use the minutes that I am sitting on the toilet seat as my time for thinking and searching for opportunity."

Soterios couldn't help but smile as he pictured the cook seated on the commode, deep in thought.

"In any event, you and your friend are now safe. The custom inspectors are gone, and you weren't turned in. You can sleep easily until we get to our next ports. New York is first, and then Boston."

The ship was scheduled to stop and unload the immigrants at Ellis Island in New York. Immigrants who chose Boston as their final destination would board the ship after they had been processed at Ellis Island. The approval process took so long that it was impossible for immigrants to get off the ship at Ellis Island and reboard the same ship for the final destination. Most immigrants were met at the dock in New York by family members and proceeded overland to their next destination. A few, for various reasons, chose to finish their journey by ship.

Soterios' ship would pick up immigrants who had cleared immigration and were now ready to join family members and friends in the Boston area. Agents of the ship's owners had contracted for freight, as well as a few passengers who wanted to visit Greece and were waiting to be picked up in Boston. The situation presented Louie and John with another unusual opportunity.

SOTERIOS

CHAPTER 7

BED PARTNERS

L ouie and John, without knowing it, had picked the right time to emigrate. The tidal wave of immigration had begun to swell as more than sixty percent of all Europe's people left their homelands for the United States. The Irish and Germans emigrated in large numbers—three million arrived from 1850 to 1860. Southeastern Europe, Greece, and Italy contributed about six million from approximately 1870 to 1910. The organization and systems to weed out undesirables were being strained to the hilt. However, even if the two had been aware of their good timing, they would not have worried any less.

Louie tossed and spun in his narrow bed each night as he tried to concoct plans so they could get off the ship in Boston until he finally couldn't stay awake any longer.

The trip to New York was uneventful. Louie and John marveled at all the sights but never left the ship. The passengers and immigrants were dropped off, new passengers were loaded on, and the ship left for its final destination

Louie wrote a letter to his brother Costas, who was still in Greece. He had written twice before but had not disclosed the promise that his other brother, Angelo, had forced him to make. Louie regretted that he had promised Angelo that he would be the first one he would help to join him. But, as he recalled, he really did not have much choice. Louie remembered the day on the road to Argos that now seemed so long ago and far away. Louie had felt trapped when Angelo refused to return home until Louie agreed to his demands.

Costas was four years younger than Louie and a product of his father's second marriage. Although they had different mothers, the two boys were close and loved each other deeply. Angelo had always resented his older brothers' close relationship. He felt that because he and Costas had a different mother than Louie, if anyone should be treated as an outsider, it should be Louie.

Louie and Costas were quiet, considerate, and although adventuresome, were not inclined to be reckless and wild. Angelo and Costas however, both loved the rush of adrenaline that comes from taking chances and gambling. They enjoyed playing the knife, paper, and stone game, and were always willing to take a risk on a bet or a dare. Costas, however, did not get extremely upset when he lost as Angelo did. Costas, in fact, seemed happiest when he was involved in some kind of gamble.

In his letter to Costas, Louie explained all that had happened, and this time confessed that he had agreed to assist Angelo before Costas. He gave the letter to the chef to correct and rewrite properly before it was mailed. Louie hoped and prayed that Costas would understand.

As the ship began to maneuver to dock and unload onto the pier at Boston Harbor, John came to Louie with the latest plan. "I hope that this plan is more to your liking than the other three that you turned down. Not only am I running out of ideas, but we are running out of time. Give me a cigarette and I'll tell you."

They were standing at the stern of the ship with the wind blowing straight at them, pushing the ship right into the pier. Louie turned his back to the wind and made a shelter out of his hands to light his cigarette. After the wind blew the match out a third time, he sighed and gave up. John, quietly puffing on his lit cigarette as he watched Soterios, said, "When you can't solve a problem, try another way even if it does not seem logical. Face the wind. Do not shield the match. Let the wind blow the flame into the cigarette, and puff quickly."

Louie did as he was told, and on the second try was rewarded with the acrid taste of burning tobacco.

"You may be pretty, but you're not very smart," John teased. "In any event here is the plan. When the ship docks, we will unload what little freight we have. Then the captain, the mate, and the steward will meet with the owner's agent. At about the same time as the meeting takes place, they will allow the immigrants to go ashore where they will be met by the officials. Any real passengers will be allowed to go directly to customs. The immigrants from Ellis Island will go to a different line. They will be asked, 'What is your name? Where do you come from? Do you have any American money?' An interpreter will be there to help. Once all the questions have been asked, they will go to another room where they will be sprayed with a powder to kill any lice and bugs they may have picked up on the ship. We will join the immigrants when they leave the ship, answer the questions, get sprayed with a little powder, and Hopa! We are Americans."

"John, it seems so simple that I think it will work. It will work as long as none of our crew gives us away. None of the immigrants will. They will be just like the blacks in Virginia. They won't want to be involved. Can we spread a few dollars around so the crew members will not squeal?"

John laughed aloud, slapped Louie on the back, and said, "Finally you are beginning to think like a smart Greek from the shores of Turkey. That is exactly what we will do."

When the great day came, and all the good-byes had been said, John paid the deck crew the agreed-upon price with an extra bonus to the engine-room chief, who was to enforce the agreement. The chief had been arrested for stabbing a merchant sailor in Cyprus, and even though he was acquitted, he had a reputation. Most of the crew were afraid of him.

Louie, hoping to be mistaken for a family member, squeezed between two families from Kalamata and offered to carry the embroidered handbag with which the little, stooped grandmother was struggling. Everything went like clockwork. His heart skipped a beat when John began to cough in the delousing room, but the official was too busy trying to see a girl's breasts as he pressed the nozzle of the sprayer inside her unbuttoned blouse.

The official shouted to the interpreter, "Tell these Spicks to keep their mouth shut and not to breathe until they are through the room. Christ! How dumb can they be?"

They exited the room onto the main street that led to the dock. There were policemen, politicians with flowers in their lapel, and anxious-looking family members searching for the new arrivals. Automobiles, trucks, and horse-drawn freight wagons narrowly missed Jews with long beards and funny clothes. There was noise and vitality. They had arrived. They were in America—this time to stay.

The two men wandered around the city, up through the waterfront, walking and looking around wide-eyed and opened-mouthed. They found themselves near a train station and trudged uphill before reaching Scollay Square, an area that was to become famous among sailors.

Continuing up the hill, they walked between rows of tables sagging under the weight of produce—lettuce, tomatoes, cucumbers, and even fava beans—through which housewives poked and selected. A huge tired-looking horse almost knocked John down as it plodded straight ahead, separating Louie from John as they crossed a street. Louie noticed that he was alone when he detoured to avoid a puddle with bits of parsley floating in it. Alarmed, he looked back the way he had come. He spotted the top of John's head as he passed behind a fat woman who was arguing with a long-mustached vendor. He turned back, avoiding a bedraggled cat with no fur on the tip of its tail, and almost bumped into a stalk of bananas hanging from a rope. John saw him and walked quickly toward him, maneuvering between rows of foodstuff. John winked at him but didn't stop as he passed by. Puzzled, Louie followed him around a corner. John stopped behind a light pole and produced two of the biggest golden pears that Louie had ever seen.

John grinned before saying, "Louie, I saw these pears sitting there with thousands of others piled around them just waiting for me. There were so many pears that no one will miss these. Besides, I was hungry and no one was looking. Here, have one."

"Jesus, John, you're crazy! All we need is to get caught stealing fruit and have some policeman ask us questions. We'll be back on that boat in chains."

"Don't look up, Soter, but one is looking at us now."

Louie turned, still holding the pear in his hand. No more than two feet away, a policeman sat on a black-maned brown horse. The officer's shiny, black-booted leg rubbed against the sky-blue saddle blanket on which B.P.D. in gold lettering was partly obscured. The horse interpreted the scratching leg as a command to move forward. Then, with its eyes fixed on Louie's pear, the animal stretched his neck to sniff at the fruit. Louie smiled and fed the pear sitting on his outstretched palm to the animal.

Louie grinned as brightly as he could at the scowling officer, waved his hand in greeting, turned and walked quietly away. John scurried after him—half-running, smiling, and waving at the official, who just stared at them.

Their next encounter with the law occurred at the entrance to a cemetery that was protected by an iron fence guarding what looked like very old grave sites decorated with little American flags. Two mounted policemen stopped traffic so that a line of children, two abreast, holding hands, and escorted by three Catholic nuns, could cross the street. The schoolchildren's goal was the graves of American Revolution heroes. As he watched the procession cross the street, John inadvertently stopped at the gate to the cemetery, blocking the entrance. The nun leading the children stopped directly in front of John, causing the entire line to stop. As the traffic and the children waited, she asked John to move aside. He didn't understand her words, but knew that she wanted to get past. He backed up, just as another coughing spell overtook him. He turned his back to the nun, faced the cemetery half-wall, rested his head on the wrought-iron fence, and attempted to clear his lungs.

The children, entranced by the horses, giggled and bounced up and down, making one of the horses nervous. The rider kept pulling on the reins to keep the horse under control; the last thing he wanted was to appear unable to contain his horse in front of all the spectators. He lost patience, pulled the horse around, and pounded the ten feet or so that it took to reach John. He bent over the horse's neck, grabbed John by the back of his shirt, and pulled him out of the way. John was suddenly sprawled on his back on the ground. For a split second, Louie angrily confronted the mounted policeman, then helped John to his feet so they could melt into the crowd.

Louie almost bumped into an organ-grinder with a monkey as they made their way across the foot of Beacon Street. Exhausted from walking and the emotional upheaval caused by their adventures, the two men finally collapsed on an empty bench in the Boston Commons.

John wheezed, "I thought we were going to get caught by those American Cossacks. I don't care where you are, but once you're face to face with a policeman on a horse, you've got trouble. But, Louie my boy, this Boston is definitely something special. God, I'm hungry. My stomach is beginning to feel as if the sides were sticking together from being empty for so long."

"John, at least you ate a pear. I didn't get a bite of mine before the horse got it. Come, let's find a place where we can get something to eat. But for the love of Christ, don't steal it. We have some money; let's use it."

They wandered until they reached Tremont Street. An inescapable odor of coffee and cooking food floated out an open door. They couldn't read the sign but knew it had to be a restaurant. Satchels in hand, they cautiously looked into the room. It wasn't much of a place. Four square wooden-topped tables with three chairs to a table were placed end to end in a row down one side of the room. The other half of the room was empty except for a long bench with a high back. It looked like an old Deacon's bench, the kind that can still be found in some old Protestant churches. The end of the bench's left side was held up with an old broken cobblestone, which replaced the carved leg that had previously supported it. Newspapers lay on the seat as if someone had just dropped them while reading.

The woman standing behind the counter next to the coffeepot turned to them when the bell, hooked over the top of the windowed door, announced their arrival. Still chewing gum, she managed to say, "I'll be right with ya, fellas. Take a seat and I'll be back in a minute." She headed toward the rear of the place, twisting to avoid a brown, flat-topped icebox which dripped down the side from the melting ice. She first blew, and then popped, a big bubble of pink gum between her teeth before she disappeared into another room.

The two men stared at her when she finally came back and handed them a stained, hand-drawn menu. Louie blurted the only words he knew in English that signified food—"Ham and Eggs," he said as he held up two fingers. She snorted, and after three attempts to determine whether the eggs should be fried or scrambled, retreated to the back room to place the order. Then she poured coffee and brought them toast and butter, which they promptly devoured. She had to bring more toast before the eggs were ready. Louie kept looking at her when she wasn't facing him. He was fascinated by her ability to chew gum, pop bubbles, and talk at the same time. As she leaned over to wipe off the counter, her breast bounced off the metal-topped sugar bowl just as a big gum bubble popped.

Louie's stomach was almost full, and he was warm and dry. As he continued to admire her, his trousers suddenly began to tighten. She glanced at him, looked away, and then her eyes double backed and stopped at his brown eyes as she saw his expression. She reached up and touched the little bump that all the male members of his family had. It was in the center of his forehead, just above his dark full eyebrows.

Louie reacted to the warm tentative touching of her fingers and rose as if to reach out for her. John quickly intervened. "Not now, for the love of Christ. We don't have time for that now. We can't take any chances. Give her some money and let's go."

"She is good looking and I'm only trying to be friendly," Louie sighed. He reached into his rear pocket for a brown leather wallet with the sides tied together with a piece of string. He pulled a handful of bills out and handed them to her so she could select what she needed. She smiled, and pulled a five-dollar bill from the little stack, turned to go, and looked at him once more. Then, she reached for his hand and swapped the five for a one-dollar bill and gently pushed him toward the door. Louie returned her smile. His white teeth flashed and his skin tone reddened as he blushed. He tried to express his admiration and thanks with his eyes while saying in Greek, "Thank you." His expression made her moan slightly as she whispered, "Here we go again." She twisted her head toward the kitchen, while still holding on to Louie's sleeve and called, "Chris, come out here please."

Chris came out of the kitchen, wiping his hands on a towel thrown over his shoulder. Soap suds splashed his face as the towel whipped by. Over six feet tall, with dark brown hair, he looked down at them through clear green eyes and spoke to them in Greek.

"Well, well, I greet you and welcome you to America. I was looking through the door when you came in and, somehow I knew you two were Greek. I told Molly when I heard you talking that you were countrymen and that's why she called me. My name in the old country was Cristos Choonones, but my landlady says an American-sounding name will help me get a job as a waiter. Here, temporarily of course, I am a dishwasher."

He stopped talking and threw his hands into the air. "Forgive me. I am not usually so rude. I haven't even asked your names. It is this country; everything is moving so fast that I get caught up in it."

John examined him closely. Chris' accent revealed that he came from one of the Aegean Islands. All three started talking at the same time. Their hands seemed to be keeping pace with the words that gushed out of their mouths. The faster they talked, the faster they waved, pointed, and flip-flopped their hands.

"Gentlemen! Please let me suggest something. I have to get back to work, but I should be finished in about two hours. Why don't you two walk around and see the sights? Come back in two hours. I have some ideas that might fit into your plans and would be of mutual benefit."

"That's a good idea. Soterios and I will take a look around and then we will come back."

"Soterios? I thought you said his name was Louie."

"His old name was Soterios. His new name is Louie. You're not the only person who has an American name. I admit I, too, get mixed up sometimes and call him Soterios. In any event, that is another story, which we will tell you later."

The bouncing, bubble-gum-popping waitress with the sugar-smeared breasts was soon forgotten.

Louie and John walked up and down Tremont, Boylston, and Washington Street. They finally reached the fringe areas of what was once the fashionable South End. John kept trying to pay attention and keep track of the twists and turns in the streets.

"Look! Soterios, see that building with the steeple? If we keep that on our right-hand side, then we can find the building with three metal balls hanging over the door."

"What do we do when we get to the three balls?"

"Come on, Soter, pay attention to where we are going. We will never find our way back to the restaurant. When we get to the store with the balls, we will have to go left until we come to the street that the restaurant is on."

"I have been paying attention and you're wrong. I remember that we have to make a right turn in order to get back to the right street. Remember where the cat was sitting on a box next to the pretty girl with the umbrella?"

"Cat? What cat? What pretty girl with an umbrella? We're lost. If we can find our way back, we'll wait outside on the sidewalk until our new friend comes out. You can look at girls walking by from there as well as anyplace."

John led the way. When the two reached the storefront with three balls hanging over the door, John pointed in triumph to the street where they needed to go. They hurried until they got to the restaurant. Once there, they leaned against the storefront and waited. A policeman walking his beat looked as if he were going to question them, but veered off at the last minute to help an elderly lady cross the busy street. Chris finally appeared, wiping his forehead before putting on a small tweed baseball-type hat.

"Well, countrymen, I hope that is the last time that I work twelve hours for ten hours pay for that bastard. Here is a piece of chicken and some bread that I took for you two. Come, we will sit on a bench and let the girls admire us while you eat and I talk."

They selected a bench under a maple tree facing busy Park Street. Speaking rapidly, Chris outlined his plan.

"We Greeks need to stick together. We need to find a way to make a lot of money. It's hard to make enough to live on—never mind thinking about sending some home so our sisters can get married and our brothers can come here. Sometimes it seems as if the whole world came to America for the same reason. This city is full of Irishmen and Italians.

"But we are different from the Italians because they don't have enough sense to help each other. The Italians live in the same neighborhoods, but they are always fighting among themselves. The only time they stick together is in church affairs. The Irish already have most of the good jobs, but they are too busy arguing and drinking to worry about the future.

"Well, first things first. We need to earn money for a place to sleep, food to eat, and clothes to wear. Anything else is luxury, and we cannot afford extravagance. Then, we have to go to school and learn to speak English. If we don't speak good English and become citizens, we will never have enough money to help the family.

"I have met three other Hellenes like yourselves. We have a plan but we need two more good men for my strategy to work. The employment for us is the restaurant business. There is plenty of work available. The only white people who will do that kind of work are the Italians and the Greeks. The best part of working in a restaurant is that we can be paid money and get our meals free as well. That leaves paying for a place to sleep as our only major expense. Some restaurants are open twenty-four hours a day. We have met a man who owns such a restaurant. He will hire all six of us."

Chris stopped talking and kicked out at a pigeon who pecked away at some crumbs next to his foot.

Then he continued, "Now, the plan is that three will work at night and three will work in the daytime. That way we can share the cost of one room by six men. That means that the three who work at night get to sleep in the bed in the daytime and the others use the bed at night."

John interrupted him. "All that sounds good, but I know too much about this world—and especially about fast-talking islanders—to trust you just because your parents were Greek. What is the other arrangement you have made with this generous owner who likes to help Greeks so much?"

"Arrangements? What arrangements? I tell you that we have a opportunity to progress. I will become a waiter, three of you will become cooks (of course, you may have to wash dishes for a while), and the other two will be busboys until the time comes that they can become waiters too. All right, so my good looks may have attracted the owner's wife, but you shouldn't object to that."

"Where are the others from? I don't think we can tolerate another islander."

Louie quickly interjected, "One wise and suspicious Turk and one scheming islander can be controlled if the other four are honest Greeks from the mountains."

Both Chris and John laughed, breaking the tension. Still chuckling, Chris explained further: "You can ask them where they came from when you meet them. They are called Dennis, James, and Fotis. James and Dennis will be the busboys; I will be the waiter; and the other three will become cooks. If we can agree on this much, let's start walking north where the good honest people of this world live. They live in a area called the North End."

The three men walked down Washington Street, alternately dodging horse-drawn wagons and automobiles. Chris explained that only a few Irish families still lived in the North End. For the most part, the Irish were moving up into the better areas of Boston. The tenement houses and narrow streets of the North End were filled with a mixture of peoples. The Italians were more numerous than their Mediterranean neighbors—the Greeks, Syrians, and Armenians. Poverty caused this mismatch of cultures to blend into a hodge-podge mix of people and noisy neighborhoods.

They walked through the produce district, alternately dodging wagons and noisy trucks. The wagons and trucks were unloaded by aproned workmen who carried bags of vegetables on their shoulders. Louie almost had to shout so Chris could hear him above the din.

"Chris, what you have said so far makes a lot of sense. We haven't had a chance to tell you yet, but we are both experienced in kitchen work. I'm a pretty good cook. I have worked on a couple of ships for two years and never had a complaint. We had some tourists on board, and thanks to the chef who was my boss I learned to cook American foods. John knows his way around a kitchen, too. However, in all fairness to you, I want to tell you something important."

Louie hesitated for a minute when John scowled at him. "I am willing to follow your plan for a while, but I want you to know something about me. It seems as if it was a hundred years ago, but when I was in Argos, I met a man who told me something important. This guy wasn't what you would call a good person, but he was rich and had a lot of power. He was also very smart. He could not have gotten rich if he wasn't smart."

Louie had stopped walking so he could talk to Chris face to face. Chris and John had to stop, too, and the three created a backlog as people piled up behind them.

John turned to Chris, "Don't pay too much attention to him. Poor fellow, he can't walk and talk at the same time. Your idea is great. We could have a good thing going here."

Chris was alarmed. He didn't want any problems to get in the way of his becoming a waiter. He listened carefully as Louie continued talking. "This fellow told me the secret of his success. He told me that I would never get rich working for someone else. I am going to be a businessman and own my own business. If I do work for someone else, it won't be for long."

Chris stared at his new friend and choked back some laughter, his eyes sparkling with amusement.

"Louie, my friend, believe me—that is the one thing that we Greeks all want to do. That is why we are so different from the Irish and the Italians. We all want to be in business for ourselves. Don't be surprised or get discouraged, though, if it takes more than a couple of days or weeks—possibly even months—before you can be a businessman in America."

Louie flushed with embarrassment as he realized how silly he must have sounded. John giggled and said, "Sometimes you talk so much that it seems as if you have diarrhea of the mouth." The three broke into loud, almost obscene laughter as they weaved their way through the crowded streets.

The evening breezes from the Atlantic swept the streets as the warmer air followed the sun, which now dipped below the horizon. The six men sat at a table in the small drab cafe that served as a coffeehouse. It was owned by a small wiry man of unknown nationality who had been in America for three years. He claimed he was Macedonian, but John whispered, "Not a chance. He is a lousy Bulgarian."

The *cafenίon* was a unique institution in many of the countries that had once been dominated by the Turks. It served as an unofficial club and a place where a newcomer or a harassed husband could find some solace and conversation. Women weren't allowed to come through the doors. The men would sit and talk for hours over a single cup of thick Turkish or Greek coffee, or a glass of *ouzo* or *raki*. Some mild gambling usually occurred. In the old country, the *cafenίon* was a haven for many males. Some avoided working in the fields by going to the coffeehouse. The work was then done by the women who hurried home from the fields to cook the dinner meal while balancing the latest baby on one hip. In the new world, the *cafenίon* served as a meeting place where the immigrants, who were mostly single men, could congregate and exchange information.

Dennis, the smallest of the group, was round-faced and slightly balding. He was a dapper dresser and a quiet, sincere person. Fotis, who later changed his name to Charlie, was only slightly taller than Dennis. He had black curly hair that flowed over his ears. His skin was darker than that of any of the others, his nose sharp and pointed. A dark birthmark, located at the left-hand corner of his mouth, wiggled and seemed to jump about when he talked. James looked like a pirate dressed in modern clothes. He was tall and handsome with dark eyes that always seemed to be aiming at something. When he smiled, his thin lips moved properly, but anyone who watched felt a pang of anxiety while trying to decipher whether James was smiling or sneering. He walked on the balls of his feet, almost as if he were getting ready to hurl himself forward. John watched him carefully.

The first meeting lasted three hours, which seemed like an eternity; finally everything was resolved. Chris left to make arrangements with the landlady who would receive double the normal rent for the one room with only one bed that all six men would share.

Chris had decided that the waiters—himself, James, and Dennis—should work in the evenings when the tips were greater. John, Louie, and Fotis would work in the daytime. This meant that the bed would be shared by the three men who were not working.

John began to grumble when Chris revealed the sleeping arrangements. "I was right about sneaky islanders. After all, he has managed to get the cleanest bed partners and the best shift for himself."

"John, you're embarrassing me as well as yourself. For Christ's sake, shut up and stop complaining. Forget the thorns and just think about roses." Louie then turned to the other four men. He held Fotis by the shoulders. "I apologize for what my friend here has said. He doesn't mean half of what he says. You haven't had a chance to get used to him yet. It is in his nature to try to find problems where none exist."

"That's all well and good, but if the other three are the clean ones, then that means I am one of the dirty. That little shit is the one who has dribble and snot on his shirt from coughing all the time," Fotis interjected.

"Wait a minute now. I can speak for myself. Louie doesn't have to apologize for me. Forgive me. I am sorry that I said what I did. Sometimes I just say whatever comes into my head."

Fotis seemed to accept the apology then muttered, "What can you expect from a Turk anyhow?"

Louie edged John toward the door as Chris spoke soothingly to Fotis. Before any more words could be said that would prolong the crisis, Chris took Fotis with him to meet the landlady. When they returned to the coffeehouse, Chris ordered another round of coffee and stood facing the seated men as he squinted through the heavy cigarette smoke.

"We are all set. I've spoken to the landlady and she has agreed to double rent, but we can't make any trouble, and no women are allowed. I told her that was not a problem. With six men in one bed, there isn't any room for anybody else." Everyone laughed, breaking the tension.

Chris continued. "We can move in tonight. At least we all will have a place to sleep. Dennis and James are already working tonight in my friend's restaurant. I think I can go to work tonight also. Of course, that means I'll have to keep both jobs until I get my pay from my present job. I don't want to quit until I get paid. Fotis is supposed to start work tomorrow at nine o'clock in the morning. I will talk to the boss tonight. I'm sure he will agree to hire Louie and John tomorrow for the day shift. He'll be happy to fire the two Hungarians to make room for his countrymen. He will pay you two less than he paid the Hungarians, but that can't be helped. We will do what we have to do."

The six men left the coffeehouse and headed toward the tenement house on Revere Street. Their room, which was on the third floor, faced the street. From its oblong shape, they could tell it had obviously once been part of a four-room apartment. An extra room had been created by putting up a wall on one side of what had been the apartment bathroom and re-hanging the door to open inward. This made it possible for the neighbors who occupied the two-bedroom apartment with a kitchen to share a bathroom with the bedroom rented by the six Greeks.

As it turned out, Chris couldn't begin work until the following night, which meant that four men would have to share the room that night. John found himself curled up on the floor with his back to the door. He had to roll to one side every time someone had to go to the bathroom. Each man had one bureau drawer. The few clothes that needed hanging were suspended from a pole wedged into a corner. The single bulb with a bright green warehouse shade generated a triangular light shadow. The last thing Louie heard before he fell asleep that night was John mumbling and cursing, "What happened to the streets of gold?"

The six men, sharing one bed three at a time, lasted for six miserable months. John was first to leave. He made friends with some Cypriot men who had banded into a little community in Salem, north of Boston. James had struck up an acquaintance with a Polish waitress who shared an apartment with her sister and a cousin somewhere around Dover Street. They had a three-bedroom flat and James supposedly was going to rent one room. His presence would provide some deterrent to anyone wanting to take advantage of the unprotected females, and in return the cousins would do his laundry. This left Dennis, Louie, Fotis, and Chris to share the third-floor room.

Chris spent little time in the room, though. He developed a reputation as something of a lady's man. Once he discovered that he possessed a strong baritone voice and was able to sing love songs persuasively, he seldom lacked company. Chris attracted the ladies by singing to them in a convincingly passionate European-accented voice. The three remaining men then shared the room. Now only two slept in the bed at one time. Dennis, who continued to work nights, soon found that he had the bed all to himself.

In later years, one question Louie was frequently asked was "Why did you Greeks always seem to end up in the restaurant business?" Louie would respond by smiling, shaking his head, and saying quietly," It's easier to save money when you eat for free, sleep cheap, and work a lot. We knew that it doesn't matter how much money you make, it's how much you keep that counts. Besides, restaurant work was all the Americans would offer us until we became citizens."

Charles (Costas) Douropoulos

CHAPTER 8
COSTAS

A t first Louie was able to send most of his earnings home. He spent most of his time either working or going to the citizenship classes that the government provided. The citizenship classes were held at the Post Office building on Milk Street. The classes were intended to teach English to all immigrants, as well as prepare them for the tests that they must pass in order to become full-fledged American citizens.

Louie received a packet of letters the day after he took and failed his first examination for citizenship.

The packet of letters included the following letter from Papa Yiannis

> My dearest friend Soterios,
>
> Due to the actions of your brothers, may God forgive them, I have been in constant communication with your parents
>
> Your brothers will tell you why they had to leave so suddenly. Your father and mother are, of course, grieved over the whole situation, but for now they are in reasonable good health. I beg of you to continue sending them money, and to follow the teachings of the Holy Saints.
>
> God's blessings on you. Be generous when you pay for the candles in Church. I hope you can read my handwriting. I wrote part of it while riding on my mule.

Well, the time has come to stop writing and get this letter on the way to you. I promise to write again the first chance that the good Lord gives me. Be certain to continue visiting the House of God and supporting his work. By the way, my wife is expecting a child, but her disposition has not improved.

Your friend,

Yiannis

The next letter in the packet was a letter from Soterios' mother and father.

Dearest Son,

Your mother sends you kisses to cover your eyes and asks the Virgin to bless you. I have asked the good priest to write the words for you to read that I have in my heart. Your brother Angelo deserted us and left for America after we had a bad argument. Why a son of mine would act like he does is not known to me. Your mother and I decided that Costas should go to America to be with you. We will tell you more about why we made that decision some other time. We can survive because we know you will send us money when you get rich.

Before Costas left, he heard from that devil's spawn brother of yours. Angelo was in Corinth and had gone to work with a big man who was a friend of yours. We did not believe Angelo because he said the friend of yours was a smuggler and a bandit. Times have changed the way people think, but we know you would not mix up with smugglers and thieves. We miss you and send our respect and kisses. Your sister is well and sends her love. She hopes to marry someone soon and begs you not to forget her.

Love,

The scribbled signatures were those of his parents.

Louie read both letters many times before he was ready to discuss them with Chris. "Chris, I've received a couple of letters from the old country," he finally told his friend.

"One letter is about my brothers. Both of them have left Greece, but I don't know why. What could have happened that would cause Costas to leave the old folks and my sister unprotected? I'm not too surprised about Angelo because he was always unpredictable, but Costas is—or maybe I should say was—a good son who would never do anything to hurt his parents. Why would he have changed?"

Chris reached to touch Louie's hand as it moved across the table, keeping tempo with his words. "Wait! Before you make a judgement or say things you don't mean, remember that the old gentleman said it is important for you to know the circumstances."

"Ah, Chris," Soterios sighed, "you're right. I need to know what happened. But what in the world could it be?"

He thought of Costas, only five feet five or six inches tall, but broad-shouldered and extremely strong—so different from Angelo. "Costas is pretty quick-tempered, but also quick to forgive any insult when an apology is given. He is a competitor, though, and unmerciful when he answers a challenge. And he hates to lose. Maybe that's what got him in trouble. Or his gambling. Costas loves to gamble heavily, and constantly. He just can't bring himself to turn down a challenge or a bet. Christ, I've known him to bet on the sex of the next lamb that would be born, or on how far a cricket could jump. The size of the wager is not important; he simply loves the surge of adrenaline and the excitement. I'm the only one who never gave up trying to convince him that he should take fewer chances. Everyone else has given up any hope of trying to slow his gambling down. And now I'm not there to stop him."

Soterios again pictured Costas and the younger Angelo, and recalled how the two were always squabbling. "Sometimes his two brothers would end up in a tangle of arms and legs fighting and rolling around on the ground. And no matter how many times Costas beat Angelo, and sometimes even hurt him without meaning to, Angelo kept coming back for more, and refused to back down," he said, shaking his head. "What could have happened to them in the old country?" he wondered aloud.

It would be some time before Soterios would hear the whole story from the middle brother. Their problems, he was to learn years after the events occurred, began in Greece on a perfectly normal day.

Costas wasn't sure whether it was 1909 or 1910. "Christ, for all I know it could be 1911," he muttered to himself. "I miss that older brother of mine. It's strange how we could have two different mothers and still be so much alike. Angelo and I had the same mother, but he is so different from me. What a pain in the ass Angelo can be! I must have told him ten times that his mother and mine, Katerina, married our father when his first wife died after giving birth to Soterios. The little fart doesn't listen. He is still trying to make up to me for the trouble he caused in the fields yesterday. That little stinker thinks I will be flattered if he says we are a lot alike. He is driving me nuts. Look! I am even talking to myself now," he said to a sparrow watching him from the top of a rock wall next to the road. Costas shrugged, just as a rock in the middle of the road tripped him, interrupting his thinking.

The road to Sparta emerged from Tripoli and wound south through a low mountain range sparsely dotted with villages. One village was called Kaparelli. Unlike most mountain settlements, it was bisected by the road, which split the community in half. The school and the largest store in the village were on the western side and the *cafenion* and the church, as well as most of the houses, were on the eastern slope.

The store carried many of the products that the villagers couldn't grow or make themselves. On the other side of the road, patrons of the *cafenion* waited for the occasional traveler to bring news of the outside world.

On the opposite side of the mountain range was a village called Doliana. Doliana was more remote, visited only by travelers who had reason to go there since they would have to leave the road.

Each village was inhabited by approximately five hundred villagers who eked out their livings by forcing the used-up soil to produce one more crop of wheat and vegetables each year. The homes, made of stones gathered from the fields, had been handed down within the families for hundreds of years. Small bands of sheep led by a scraggly goat with a bell tied to its neck, a few donkeys, and scrawny chickens shared the land with the peasants.

The houses were built so that the humans lived on the first floor while all animals were housed in the basements, more accurately described as cellars since they were dug out of the hill, open on one side and secured by a door.

The houses in Kaparelli huddled together on both sides of the road that wound around the mountain. The principal building that sat on a slightly higher elevation of land was the church. The older houses faced inward so that the front doors and windows all faced the center of the village. The sides of the houses that faced away from the village center were solid; no doors interrupted the solid stone walls. In past years the village would have resembled a fortress with the houses facing and protecting one another.

The villagers left the safety of their enclave each day and walked to the fields some distance from the town. The years had been turbulent, with bandits as well as soldiers from the various conquerors roaming the hills. Most villagers realized there was no real safety in the massing of houses, but like sheep when threatened by predators, they huddled together seeking safety in numbers. They hoped someone else would be attacked first.

The coffeehouse and the store where a few essentials could be purchased formed the social center of the village. The heart of the village was the church located on a hill at the south end of the village overlooking the cemetery, where each villager would eventually rest. A heavily traveled path led from the cemetery to the church passing a grove of olive trees that shaded the house where the priest and his family lived.

Periodically the peace of the cemetery was disturbed, usually when more grave sites were needed. The old coffins would be excavated since there just wasn't enough room for only one body in each grave. The excavated bones were carefully washed and stored in cloth sacks before being blessed by the priest prior to being reburied in the family plot. The skull was given special attention. Cleaning and washing the excavated skull was delegated to the oldest woman in the family. Land was too precious not to be used over and over again so the small sacks of bones were stacked on top of the new coffins.

Costas was in Kaparelli to arrange for the delivery of the rough wheat used by his father in the baking of the sweet Easter bread. The flour had to be milled before it was ready to be worked into huge round loaves of braided bread. Each loaf had at the very least, six braided flowers that contained a brilliant red-dyed egg. The egg represented the renewal of life as well as the resurrection of Christ. The selection and purchase of the ingredients to make the bread took on special significance since Easter bread had to be perfect.

Costas concluded his business for the day and decided to return home to Tripoli in the morning. He had considered visiting relatives and the graveyard in Doliana where Soterios' mother was buried but decided not to make the trip. Instead, he made arrangements to stay overnight with the family of the man who operated the coffeehouse in Kaparelli prior to returning to Tripoli.

He loved the smell of the thick sweet coffee that filled the air when it was brought to a boil three times then allowed to simmer in one-handled brass pots. Costas was sitting with a youth whose family lived at the other end of the village. His friend's family consisted of a grandmother on his mother's side, his mother, and an older brother who owned a piece of land covered with grapevines that yielded the red grapes that made the strong and slightly bitter wine that the peasants enjoyed.

The vineyard was old. Because so few of the vines had been replaced with young, vigorous plants, the vineyard was slowly giving up. The oldest son, Stephanos, had made it clear that he intended to exercise his right to claim the property and pointed out that the vineyard could not support more than one family.

Costas sat at a table waiting for the coffee to cool and listening to the youngest son, Dimi, talk.

"Costas, I have a problem," his friend confided. "I met this girl who lives in Doliana a year ago at Easter. I want to marry her and she wants to marry me, too."

Costas blew on his coffee, interrupting the speaker.

"She must be a beauty for you to want to marry her and give up your freedom. In any event, what is the problem? A good-looking clean fellow like you should be a good catch."

Dimi sighed, "Of course, they say they want to marry her off, but because I'm the youngest son, I don't have anything. Her family knows that my older brother will inherit everything. So her brothers will never accept me. They won't offer a sizable dowry since she is so beautiful. I get a lump in my throat every time I think about her. Her aunt, who is a friend of my cousin, told me that Mary is an excellent cook and works really hard keeping the house clean.

She and her three brothers live in the house where her grandmother had been born. Her brothers are lazy bastards and refuse to help her with anything. They spend more time in the *cafenion* than they do tilling the few hectares of land they inherited."

"I know who they are," Costas said as he signaled for more wine. "They don't even take proper care of the sheep they have left."

"That's right. Mary tried to ignore the condition of the sheep, but she couldn't stand to see them neglected for long. Now she has to take care of them as well as do her other chores. Just as she feared, when her brothers realized that Mary would make sure the sheep were watered and led to the areas where they could find green plants to eat, the brothers stopped any pretense of caring for them. Since then, Mary has added the other animals to her workload as well."

"Well, if you know all these details, you must be meeting her in secret. How did you first meet her anyhow?"

Dimi settled into his seat and began, "It was during the breaking of the eggs at Easter that we first looked deeply into each other's eyes. I was the winner of the egg-breaking contest and went to Doliana to challenge their champion. It was the day after Easter, and I confess I was still a little tipsy."

Costas recalled how each family in villages all over Greece dyed and decorated eggs at Easter. After the traditional meal of spit-cooked lamb, family members would crack decorated hard-boiled eggs together. One person in each household emerged as the champion, as long as one end of the egg was unbroken. The champion from each home went to the closest house, and then on to the next house, until only one decorated egg with at least one end unbroken remained in the village. The owner of the unbroken egg was proclaimed the village champion.

Each person would hold their egg so that its tip protruded from their fist, exposing one inch of the colorful, decorated egg. The opponent would hold their egg with the tip pointing downward and gently strike the other egg while saying 'Christ has arisen.' The eggs and roles would be reversed for the next opponent.

Dimi continued explaining how he had met Mary. "My egg was whole on both sides, completely unbroken. I went to every house in Kaparelli and won. I went to the church with the whole village following and even broke the priest's egg. The priest proclaimed me the winner, blessed me, and promised me that I would have good luck for the whole year. I was so happy that I continued to celebrate through the next day. The priest celebrated, too. The next day a bunch of us, including the priest and some people who had relatives in Doliana, went there to challenge their champion.

"Mary told me that when she saw my brown curly hair and heard me laugh like an angel, that's when she fell in love with me."

Costas laughed. "Spare me the lovely little details; just tell me the story."

Dimi blushed and continued talking. "I just want to tell you that she loves me. It's not enough for me to just talk to myself. It's so wonderful that I want everyone to know she loves me."

Costas smiled and raised his glass to Dimi, signaling him to continue. Dimi walked around the table once, then settled into his chair once again.

"The two priests, one from each village, got a little drunk from too many toasts to the risen Christ. They pushed Mary and me toward the center of a circle of people. Mary had the champion egg in her village. Mary blushed as she looked up into my eyes and whispered, "Christ has arisen." I swear to you she was so beautiful that I forgot why I was there. All I could see and think about was this beautiful, slender, angel with moist, glistening, brown eyes looking at me. The priest nudged my elbow and the nudge caused me to drop my egg. I could hear a moan from the onlookers when my egg hit the ground. I was so embarrassed, and I guess so angry, that I scowled. What happened next is hard to believe."

Dimi stopped talking, took another gulp of wine, and began again.

"I was so surprised that I opened my mouth like a fool when she opened her hand and, looking straight into my eyes she smiled, then she let her pretty blue egg decorated with little white doves drop to the ground. Her egg broke, of course. The villagers cheered her. Then the musicians began to play a *Xasápiko*. Mary took my hand and we began the line of dancers with her as the leader.

"The *bazóóki* and the mandolins played. Mary twirled and completed a half turn, looked up at me, and smiled when I asked, 'Why did you drop your egg? You would have been the champion of both villages.'"

"She spun in a graceful twirl, pointing her toes so that her waist turned. She swayed toward me, and whispered above the music, 'It was more important to me that everyone saw that you did not get beaten by me, than it was for me to win.'"

Dimi stared at Costas, sighed loudly, and said, "I know that I was so confused that it must have shown on my face. This angel called Mary smiled, and continued, 'A good and loving woman will never allow strangers see her beat her true love at anything.'"

"Costas, as the Holy Mother knows, at that moment I fell in love. I tripped and stumbled around the circle for the rest of the dance. Her brothers rushed forward after that dance and for the rest of the evening kept getting between Mary and me in the dance chain. They wouldn't let me near her." Dimi stopped talking, hesitated for a second, then shrugged his shoulders.

"I spoke to my own priest. 'Father,' I said, 'you have to help me. I think I am in love. Did you see her drop her egg so she wouldn't win? Now her brothers keep getting in the way. They won't let me near her.' I was so upset I had to stop for air I couldn't breathe."

"'Wait! Now breathe, my son,' the priest said to me, 'or you will drop here in the dirt. Wait a minute, take a breath, and go on.'"

"I did as he said and took a deep breath before continuing. 'I know Mary cares for me. She said so. All I want to do is to get to know more about her. Please speak to her brothers; tell them what a good man I am.'"

"The priest left me and I saw him talking to Mary's priest. Then they both went to talk to her brothers, but it was no use. The brothers were adamant. They would not consider me as a potential brother-in-law. They kept saying it was because I was poor and had few prospects. The priests tried to get the brothers to admit that their objection was due to their reluctance to give up their housekeeper, cook, washerwoman, and herdsman. The priests even offered to help them find wives. Nothing could change their minds. The priests even told them it was a sin to keep their sister in virtual slavery."

The priests continued to plead with the brothers for two weeks then finally gave up in frustration. Mary threatened to stop working. I think they beat her. Anyhow, she never carried out her threat. The law, as well as established custom, is clear. The brothers are within their rights to discipline their sister and not allow her to marry me."

Costas and Dimi emptied their wine glasses, and Costas ordered more wine instead of coffee when he saw how tense Dimi was. Dimi scarcely noticed that, as the evening wore on, they had finished two bottles of wine.

and I managed to exchange a few letters through her cousin and twice we were able to meet and touch each other for a ᵣ.nutes. I have made up my mind that I am going to marry her ₩ay or the other. I can't stand it any longer. If I have to, I'll kill her ᵣthers and anyone else who tries to stop us. I told the priests that I was going to do something soon, and he came up with one alternative. The alternative is dangerous, but he was so concerned that I would become violent and possibly kill or get killed by one of the brothers, that he told me about an old and forgotten custom."

"'Under the right circumstances,' he told me, 'the Church will marry a couple over family objections and will probably excommunicate anyone who attempts to destroy the marriage. The Church will give sanctuary and offer the Holy Sacraments to anyone who is worthy and asks for God's blessings while kneeling in front of the altar. The problem will be getting her to the Church without her brothers interfering. Let me tell you about the plan I have worked out.'"

Dimi told what the plan was and Costas was hooked. The challenge and risk were irresistible. Costas pleaded with his new friend until Dimi relented and allowed Costas to join him in the venture.

"Dimi, for the love of Christ, there isn't anything else to do in this country. You have got to let me get involved. It will be fun for me."

"Costas, you must know that I am touched by your wanting to help. It will be dangerous, though, and I can't pay you anything for taking the risk."

"Payment? Who asked you for payment? I want to do it for the adventure of it. My only request is that we do it very soon. I can't hang around here much longer."

"Costas, I will let you be the godfather to my first child, especially if it is a boy, if you help me with this little task."

After an hour of discussion, the plan was set. Dimi and Costas would go to the local priest and recruit him to communicate with Mary's village priest. Mary's priest would communicate with her so that she would be ready the following evening.

She was to act normal and go to her room as if she were going to bed, but not go to sleep. She should pack her most important belongings and wait by the open window. Dimi and Costas would borrow two horses from Dimi's cousins and ride to Doliana after dark. They would get to Mary's home at about five in the morning. The brothers normally didn't stir from their sleeping rugs until much later.

Costas and the eager groom would simply ride up to the house, throw Mary a rope so she could lower herself to the ground, put her on the horse with Dimi, and ride to the Church before the brothers knew what happened. The priest would marry them, and the brothers, though undoubtedly angry, would be helpless.

Everything went as planned. Mary was safely on the horse with Dimi. Costas let them go ahead while he, as prearranged, acted as a rear guard in the event something went wrong. It went too well. As a matter of fact, Costas thought it was a lot of trouble to go to, and it had been a long, uncomfortable ride for such a boring result. The lack of adventure and the adrenaline rush he enjoyed so much caused him to do something he would regret for the rest of his life.

When he was sure that Dimi and Mary were safely away, he reached for his belt, pulled out an old single-shot pistol that was loaded from the barrel, and used little round iron balls for bullets. He fired it into the air, hollering and whooping, until the brothers, oil lamps in hand, rushed into the dark farmyard.

"My name is Costas Douropoulos. Dimi and I have stolen your sister. Come and catch us!" His horse reared and spun in circles. The terrified old farm animal reared as the wild man on his back screamed and hollered. It bolted again as the brothers, awake now but angry and confused, shouted back. The startled horse, used to plodding peacefully along, rolled his eyes, and with flaring nostrils, bolted in panic. To make matters worse, Costas was not a good rider. As a matter of fact, this was the first horse he had ever mounted, though he had ridden a lot of mules. The horse reared and spun around on his rear legs, as one of the brothers leaped up to grab the reins. Suddenly, the man's head snapped down sharply, as one of the horse's front hooves split his forehead. The man screamed at the moment blood splattered on his undershirt.

The panicked Costas tried to control the spinning horse. One of the brothers yelled, "My God, you've killed him!"

Costas was unable to regain control of the galloping horse until the terrified animal stopped out of sheer exhaustion a couple of miles down the road.

Costas arrived at the Church just as the priest concluded the brief ceremony. They had waited for Costas as long as they dared but, fearing that Mary's brothers would arrive first, went ahead with the ceremony.

"It was an accident," Costas pleaded after telling the story. "Christ, I can't help it if the crazy horse kicked him in the head. Those devil brothers of his won't care whether it was an accident or not. I have to get out of here. To top it all off, I gave them my name, I shouted it out for all the world to hear. Please go to my father in Tripoli and tell him what happened. My mother will be heartbroken, but I can't go home," Costas explained to the priest.

The priest took Costas by the arm and insisted, "My son, you must let me hear your confessions now before you leave. It will be best for everyone, especially me, if I am sworn to secrecy by the confessional."

"Father, I have never ever confessed my sins before, even though I have received the sacraments. This is a good time to begin, though. You must also promise me that you will talk to my brother Angelo. I have caused enough trouble. Promise me just in case anything does happen and Mary's brothers get to me before I can get away, that you will stop my crazy brother Angelo from turning this into an old-fashioned vendetta. As a matter of fact, it may be better not to tell Angelo anything unless you have to."

Mary was crying in huge gasps. Dimi was trying to console Mary, reassure the priest, and talk to Costas at the same time. With a final hug and a characteristic shrug, Costas disappeared into the darkness. He was on his way to America and safety. Once there he would join Soterios, who was now known as Louie.

As the priest attempted to calm Mary, the church door banged open. They looked up to see all three of her three brothers standing in the dawn light, the oldest with a bandage wrapped around his head.

The priest rushed to the door as the brothers, raging and death-mad, entered. "It is too late for you to stop the marriage. If you don't accept it, I will curse you and you will be in danger of excommunication. What is done is done," the priest insisted.

Blood dripping down his eye, the wounded brother spoke out.

"How could you marry my sister to a no-good like that Kaparelli nothing? You may have the authority, but don't for one minute think that the men of our family will stand for it. We will not give them a dowry. No, that's not true. We will give her a dowry; we will give her the head of that Tripoli bum who tried to kill me. Where is he?"

It took another half hour to convince the trio that Costas had gone. Dimi convincingly lied and told them that Costas had gone south to

Sparta where he would take refuge with his mother's kinfolk. The three left, hoping to cut Costas off before he could get to the outskirts of Sparta.

The priest accompanied the newlyweds on the two horses until they too reached the safety of Sparta, where they would live until it was their turn to go to America.

Costas had headed North East toward Athens. Once there, he earned his living working as a stevedore on the tough, dangerous docks of Piraeus. As he worked, he constantly moved his eyes back and forth in search of the avenging brothers. Finally, just as he was getting used to the "hunted" feeling, he had an incredible turn of luck. His gambling losses had always been more than he could really afford until one night, on his birthday, everything changed. No matter what game he played, he won. He played at dice and won all the money a seaman from a Belgium ship had to gamble. He played a version of *mah jongg* with Oriental sailors and won again. He won at cards; he won at guessing how far crickets could jump. When he finally counted his earnings, he had the incredible sum of four thousand American dollars.

Costas booked passage on a ship on the tourist-class deck. Two years after he rode the horse into Doliana, he legally stepped off the ship at Ellis Island. It took him three days and, after a poker game, the rent of his money, to get to Boston where his surprised brother Soterios—renamed Louie—co-owned a restaurant with a partner named Chris.

Angelo "cut" from a group photo

CHAPTER 9

ANGELO

T he priests of the church were held in special esteem because they were the link to God and could protect the laymen from all the evils the Devil constantly marshaled to attack their souls. The Orthodox Church dogma and its Byzantine background were presented to the peasants through icons portraying the saints clothed in heavy and ornate wrappings with golden haloes over unsmiling and grave faces. The smell of incense drifted through heavy air where the worshippers sat or knelt in semidarkness. The altar and the icons were lit by fluttering candles, held upright by gold-encrusted holders. The message clearly sent to worshippers was that the church and its surrogates, the priests and the saints, were destined to special and more luxurious lives because they lived blessed with God's own light; the non-anointed laymen, on the other hand, were fated to live and toil in the darkness. The formula worked for centuries. The only threat to its continued existence was that every so often, a brave soul dared question it.

⅃⅃⅃⅃⅃⅃⅃⅃⅃

Angelo and his father stood glaring at each other, each stubbornly refusing to say anything that would break the impasse. Angelo's image had been destroyed when his father reprimanded him in front of the coffeehouse for spending too much time with two ruffian brothers who the other villagers treated as virtual outcasts.

These brothers lived in another village higher up on the mountain and owned nothing more than a few goats and a little plot of land. They lived alone since Despina, their mother, a little stooped and hunchbacked person, finally died from overwork and loneliness. She was overworked because her two sons neglected the farm, gambled, and drank their lives away. In order to make ends meet, the woman had no alternative but to till the soil and to care for the animals as she had done when she was young. Despina was lonely because the women of the town shunned her ever since she was accused of having the Evil Eye when she refused to sell a magnificent book of the saints.

Widowed when her husband broke his neck falling off his mule, Despina was destined, at the age of only twenty-three, to mourn for the rest of her life. Her husband had been the last of his line so there wasn't anyone to help the widow raise her two sons.

The only thing she had of value was an ancient book of the Holy Saints that had been in her family for generations. Her husband wanted to sell the book many times and had even shown it to the district policeman in order to learn its value. It was protected front and back with two hammered copper covers. The hand-painted pages and images of the Saints were in magnificent color. The lettering was done with heavy black ink, with the capital letters outlined in gold. The style was flowing, with many curls and feathering circles decorating each individual letter.

The book's pages were bound together with a heavy silk-like thread. The covers of the book, when closed, were held together with a silver clasp that resembled a man's hand. The hand's fingers were permanently locked together in the prescribed figuration needed to make the sign of the cross when blessing oneself.

Despina had refused to sell the book, even when the policeman sided with her husband. She stood defiantly with her hands held on her hips and her feet stamping on the floor like a nervous horse.

"That book has been in my family ever since one of my great-uncles brought it back from Constantinople. He had been one of the priests who could have amounted to something. He could have been a Bishop. I can't remember what happened, but I do know that all the women in our family have protected this book. During the black days of the Turk occupation, they risked their lives to hide it."

"We are getting older and we need the money it could bring. Let us take the book to the Bishop and sell it," her husband had pleaded.

"I will tell you for the last time that the book will not be sold so you and your friends can buy more wine. If you two do not stop pestering me, I will curse you both. Leave me in peace."

The two men left the room, beaten and outraged. "She is an evil woman and, I believe, possessed by the Devil. That is why she is keeping the book hidden instead of letting us bring it to the Bishop. If I can acquire such a Holy Book for the Bishop, he will have to reward me or at least recognize how important I am," the policeman muttered. Then he added, "Tell her that if she does not relent, I will ask my cousin who is a priest to proclaim publicly that she is cursed with the Evil Eye."

Despina never relented. The policeman fulfilled his threat, and his cousin, the priest, accused her in public. She was shunned by most of her neighbors and was refused the sacraments of the church. Now she hid the book so her husband could not steal it. No matter how hard he tried, the book could not be found. Her final victory came the day her husband finally died, after lying conscious but paralyzed for three days. He became paralyzed after he drank too much wine, fell off his mule, and hit his head on one of the sharp rocks that seemed to grow out of the ground. He fell into a coma-like state, unable to move or to relieve himself. After he was brought home, Despina had to feed him and wash and wipe the soil from his body. She did so without the comfort of knowing that she was taking care of someone who appreciated and loved her.

Despina bided her time. It was important that she picked the right time. Finally, the moment came when she realized he was about to die and this would be her last chance. She turned the dying man's bed and propped his head so that he faced the door. By standing on a stool, she was able to remove part of the lintel, a board that ran horizontally over the door. There, resting in an upright position and wrapped in a oiled sheepskin was the book. After making sure that he was watching, she unwrapped it and let the light from the candle bounce off the book's side. She slowly undid the clasp, and still without saying a word, opened and closed the book three times. Her expression was triumphant, and without a trace of kindness. She slowly rewrapped the book and returned it to its hiding place. Her husband made a sound of anguish. It seemed to come from deep down inside him. He died moments later. The last thing he saw was his wife staring at him as she held up her fingers, pointed at him in the sign of the broken cross, a favorite symbol of those reputed to be followers of the Devil.

She continued raising her two sons, a lifetime of hard work, with little encouragement and very little gratitude. She never stopped hoping and praying that eventually they would return her love. Little by little, however, even she became discouraged and lost hope. The only one of her childhood friends that remained loyal to her was Sarah. When Despina was alive and struggling, Sarah had tried to shame the brothers into being more helpful to their mother.

"Shame on you, you two big garbage heaps. Shame on you for letting your poor mother do all the work. Look how she has suffered since your father died! It is because of him that the village has shunned her. He wasn't much good when he was alive. He proved that by getting drunk and killing himself by falling off his donkey. I know how lonely it is when a woman is alone. Remember, my husband died a long time ago. The women in the village barely talked to me after that. They were afraid I would steal their husbands out of my loneliness. Bah! Who would want another one? Your mother is working all the time to raise you two, hoping that the good saints will somehow reach down and touch you. Please, can't you try to help her a little bit?"

As the years went by, many of Despina's peers died, including her old enemy the policeman. By repeating and embellishing his story so many times, by the time the policeman died, he convinced almost everyone, including himself, that Despina had the Evil Eye.

Tuberculosis finally conquered her, but not before giving her enough warning so that she was able to make her peace with the Church.

The newly assigned village priest was of the new breed who became a servant of God not out of desperation, since his family was not starving, but because he truly was committed. He had been educated in a seminary outside Athens, married before he was ordained, and did not harbor any ambitions to rise any higher than a parish priest. It was significant that he came from a village in Northern Greece, far removed from his assignment. He was part of an experiment to introduce new ideas and outside influence to the rural areas as the Church began to reform and modernize.

The enlightened priest received Despina without fear of the mythical Evil Eye and listened compassionately to her plea. Her story moved him because the gentle and loving Christ that he worshipped would have understood and forgiven her. They enjoyed the sacraments alone and yet together—he as the embodiment of Christ, and she as the human and long suffering example of humanity.

A few days later Despina sent one of her sons to ask the priest to visit. She had chest pains that wouldn't subside and was concerned. The priest, knowing that she was ill and alone, asked his wife to accompany him. When they arrived, Despina insisted that her two sons leave her with the priest and his wife. She made the priest sit beside her bed. Despina told the befuddled priest's wife how to find the book in its hiding place. When the book was brought to her, Despina lovingly kissed it and gently put it into the young priest's hands. The only compensation she would take for the book was that a single candle be lit for her soul and that her name would be on the list of those prayed for on holy days that the Church reserved for honoring the dead. Despina had made her peace with God on her own terms.

After their mother died, the trouble-making brothers ran wild. Bored and eager for excitement, Angelo joined in many of their escapades as the drab winter months gave way to spring. In the springtime the overworked land seems to gather strength and explode into color. Red poppies and the golden dandelion flowers blended with the pale yellows of wild mustard. Oregano, mint, and thyme bloomed, sending their aroma to mix with the muted fragrance of laurel and lemon that drifted in the air.

The three men between the ages of eighteen and twenty-one, young and vigorous, were terrified that they would become carbon copies of their parents. Unaware that their fear of becoming like their parents caused them to rebel, they opposed their parents by misbehaving. If their parents drank moderately, the young toughs drank heavily. If their parents went to Church, they refused to go. Since their parents loved to dance, these youngsters with the extra energy would not. The life-frightened youths never stopped to wonder why they behaved as they did, and had anyone attempted to advise them, they wouldn't have listened. Out of boredom and, as a form of protest, they constantly mocked adults and taunted young girls, stopping only when they had reached the limits of aggression. They knew that if they overstepped the unwritten boundaries of acceptable conduct, they would face fathers, brothers, uncles, and other male members of the girl's clan.

The sweet but acrid smoke from the hookah would drift about their head as they took turns puffing from the hose. Introduced many years ago by the Turks, the hookah was the preferred way of inhaling fumes from the seeds of white poppy flowers. Bored and frustrated, the three young men tried to find relief by sucking on the water pipe until their senses, dimmed from the fumes, were muddled. Then they would lie on the ground for hours, oblivious of the world around them.

Because weddings, funerals, and holy days provided a diversion from boredom, they were happy to hear that a wedding was scheduled. The girl who was finally getting married was Aspasia. Her mother, Sarah, and Despina had once been close and had remained friends until Despina's death. Sarah had been among the few who refused to believe that Despina had the evil eye. Sarah had bathed and prepared Despina's body for burial and boiled the wheat and raisin mixture fed to the few mourners who attended the funeral. In better times, the two friends had talked about how pleasant it would be if their offspring would marry and produce grandchildren.

The day that Despina died, after being summoned by the priest's wife, Sarah had lost her temper again.

She turned to the two boys standing outside their dead mother's bedroom. "Ptu! I spit on you, you bastards. She was too good for you and your good-for-nothing father. She loved you, the poor soul, and worked herself to death for you. May the good Lord reward her."

Sarah held up her fist then quickly opened her fingers, so that the palms were aimed at their faces. "Na!" she snarled, "Blow at my hand! May the devil get you and the crows roost on your grave."

The only mourners at Despina's funeral were her sons, Sarah and her daughter, and two old grandmothers who were so stooped and racked with arthritis that they could barely make it up the hill. The withered old women went to Despina's funeral as they had every funeral for years. Funerals and church services helped to fill their days.

The priest intoned the prayers with more emotion than usual. The brothers would have left early but there was no one else to lower the body into the grave. They shuffled their feet and rocked back and forth in impatience, as Sarah glared at them. Finally, the last shovel of rock-filled dirt was thrown onto the plain coffin and the ordeal marking the end of Despina's sad life was over.

As Sarah turned to leave, the older brother warned her. "Be careful, you old bitch, I haven't forgotten how you cursed us. We will pay you back for that soon."

The priest was so surprised that he almost dropped the incense burner.

"May the Lord God forgive you. At least wait until you have left your poor mother's grave. I join Sarah in her disgust of you. Get away from here so we do not have to look at you or your brother again." He made a sign of the cross as he said, "May God forgive us."

A few days later Angelo and his friends lay sprawled on a hillside overlooking the village. They passed the hose back and forth from the hookah and finally fell asleep next to a crumbling stone wall. A lizard stopped for a moment and swept its beady eyes back and forth over the sprawled figures. When the crusty creature decided that it was safe to continue its journey, it scampered quickly under a broken piece of granite.

The eldest of the brothers groaned, causing the lizard to poke its head out from under the rock. The drug wore off as the young man tried to recapture the events at his mother's funeral. His younger brother and Angelo began to stir. Angelo got to his feet, shielding his eyes from the sun, and looked down the hill where the city lay. Music drifted faintly up the hill prompting Angelo to remember that a wedding was taking place. A hawk soared in ever-widening circles as it climbed even higher into the blue Mediterranean sky. Angelo squinted into the sun and said, "I wonder what that hawk can see from up there? Does he see anything different today than he sees every day? When you can see vast distances there must always be new things to see."

"I wonder, too," someone chimed in, "but right now I'm wondering about getting something to eat. Let's leave the pipe here and join the wedding to get something to eat and drink."

They tried to rearrange their clothing while making their way down the hill through the small grove of olive trees. Angelo stumbled over a small mound and struggled to recover his balance, elbowing one of his friends who snarled, "You cursed fool! Watch yourself."

"Most mules know enough not to fart into the wind," Angelo replied, "because the stink comes back in their face. You're the one who was cursed, not me. You're the one that Sarah assigned to the Devil, not me."

Angelo pointed to Sarah, who stood on the stairs of the church next to the groom's father who was preparing to address the wedding party. The groom's father was a tall, bald-headed man with a mustache that drooped at least four inches, forming an upside down "U" through which his lips protruded. He had not been born in any of the neighboring villages but came from a village on the slopes of Mt. Manis. He was the kind of man who fell in love and married without bothering to negotiate the size of the dowry.

The mountain men were known for their stubbornness and strength. The challenge of living in the mountains and coping with the severe changes in weather created an uncompromising and confident person. The mountain people were always in the center of every revolt and uprising. It was still the fashion for these men to wear a sash around their stomach under an embroidered vest. The sash was important. It served as a pocket for a long-bladed knife that fit into a formed leather holder The mountain men knew it was important to be able to reach the knife with the left hand while shaking hands with the right.

The wedding party consisted of almost everyone in the immediate area, as well as a contingent made up of mountain people. The couple were married on a beautiful Sunday afternoon. Candied almonds in decorated pouches had been distributed, and everyone was eager to begin the rest of the reception activities. All that stood in the way of the dancing and the food was the groom's father insistence that he make a speech. He stroked his mustache and postured slightly.

"My friends, we are gathered today to witness an event of extreme importance. It is an event that has been repeated many times during the centuries. More than just a marriage, it is a message of commitment. This commitment has been made between a man and women before the eyes of God and their families, to share the rest of their lives together and to raise their children under God's Commandments. In order to ensure that this commitment will survive, we parents and family must also commit ourselves. Now hear me! Hear me well so that you can tell your friends of what I say. My father's name was

Petros; my mother was called Vasiliki. My name is Alexandros, my wife's name is Anna, and we have two sons and one daughter born to us. My oldest son is named Paul, and my daughter's name is Martha. They are both married, which gives me yet another daughter, Diana, and another son, Andreas. I now would like to introduce you to my new daughter, for today she is marrying my son Constantine. I want you to tell all of her father's enemies and their family that she is now one of us. Her enemies are now my family's enemies. We will honor her and protect her, and we will respect her. We, the men of my family and I, promise that any man who offends her will be offending a member of my family."

When he finished his speech, he collected his new daughter, kissed her roundly on the lips, and commanded her to kiss her newly acquired family. He turned to the bride's father, shook his hand, and said only, "I Promise."

The *bazóóki* and mandolins exploded in song as the new bride and her husband led the celebrants in dance.

An hour later, the wedding celebration was in full swing as the three unshaven and rumpled youths strutted into the dance circle. They joined a line of male dancers and attempted to execute the complicated steps of the *Tsámico*, a dance of Greek warriors. With interlocked arms resting on each others' shoulders, they began the shuffling steps of the dance. The visiting mountain people became more and more agitated as the three rogues continued to stumble, while whistling and disrupting the dance.

Anthony, the groom's uncle, spoke to the priest. "Father, you better do something quickly. I don't know how much more of this we will tolerate. If we were back in our own village, those three jackasses would have been dragged off and beaten, if not castrated, by now. We are not going to allow those pigs to be disrespectful of our bride. Her husband is being restrained by his father, but even the old man may not want to hold back much longer."

"It would be blasphemy to disturb this holy day of celebration with violence. Please contain your people a little while longer while I try to reason with those drunken fools and get them out of here. Please, in God's name, I implore you," the priest replied.

When the dance ended, the well-meaning prelate cornered the three as they pushed their way to the table holding the wine cask.

"As a priest, I am asking you to leave this wedding, go home, wash, and shave. Change into clean clothes and sober up. Your actions today are shaming your parents and insulting the bride and groom."

Angelo's companion, through a flow of spittle shouted, "What do you mean shamed our parents? Have you forgotten that my mother was shunned as an evil woman? We are used to being shamed. Get out of my way, you jackass! I want some wine."

The bride's mother, Sarah, pushed through the crowd until she reached Angelo. "Shame on you! These two are lost, and never have been any good, but you, Angelo, come from a good family. Why do you share fleas with these dogs?"

Before Angelo could attempt to answer, his own father, Vasilios, pushed into the circle of angry people.

"I apologize to you and your family. Please forgive my son's behavior. He has always been a little wild, but it is only since he has been involved with these two pigs that..."

Vasilios was interrupted by Anthony, "Enough. Get those three out of here. We must not spoil this wedding by treating them as they deserve, at least not today."

The three toughs finally understood that they had overstepped the line and were in danger. Angelo was frightened and ashamed of himself. His father would not even look at him. His mother was crying in great uncontrollable sobs. He turned and ran through the crowd, looking only at the ground. His eyebrows were drawn together this time, not by anger but by embarrassment.

The quickly sobering but frightened brothers were escorted by the priest and his wife through the crowd, past revenge-promising eyes of the mountain men. The priest got them through the crowd without harm, and they headed to the hills for safety. Angelo headed for home. When he got there, he was so distraught that he paced up and down while talking out loud to himself. He couldn't stay in the house, so instead retrieved a blanket from his room he climbed the hills above the bakery. Thoroughly ashamed, for one of the few times in his life, he prayed and asked for guidance or a miracle.

A miracle never happened. He waited all night for a voice or something to come out of the darkness that would proclaim him as being saved. Nothing happened. He finally accepted the fact that he would have to face his father alone without God's help. The grass was wet, and water dripped from the small green olives that had only recently been born. The morning dew had been extremely heavy and the trail was slippery. Angelo made his way slowly down the hill onto the small path that led through the center of town. He passed the coffeehouse and was carefully making the turn toward home when he was struck from behind on his left shoulder.

"So there you are! Where have you been all night? By Christ, you can barely walk. You are drunk again. I don't know where you came from. You're no son of mine."

The words assaulted Angelo one after the other like bees. Vasilios, stood in the center of the road, relieved that he had found Angelo yet angry that his son had worried him so. The father's emotions were so jumbled that he had shouted in frustration.

"Please, father forgive me, I didn't mean to hurt anyone," Angelo whispered.

"You never mean to hurt, but you always do. We are sick and tired of you shaming us. Why don't you just get out of our lives? We are sick of you. Damn you anyhow."

Angelo paled when he heard his father damning him. He turned on his heel and walked quickly toward the outskirts of town. Vasilios started to call him back and accept his apology, but the street was filling with neighbors watching and evaluating his actions. He couldn't back down now. If he had known that Angelo wouldn't return, he might have accepted ridicule and swallowed his pride—rather than lose his son forever.

Angelo didn't stop walking until he was out of town. He finally sat on the ground with his back against a tree and tried to make a decision. He always found it difficult to make decisions and usually chose to let things work themselves out. Following the path of least resistance was easier for Angelo. He was already on the road going somewhere new, he reasoned, so why not continue? He had made the break, which is what he had wanted to do for a long time. He didn't have any money, but his brother Soterios had written and identified the people he had met on his exodus. Angelo knew the names and who they were.

The difference between the two brothers was that Soterios intended to repay those people for their kindness. Angelo simply wanted to use them. Angelo finally made it to Argos—tired, hungry, and dirty. He went to the address where the smuggler and Soterios had met. The coffeehouse was still there, but no one knew anything about the man Angelo described. When he left the room and climbed down the stairs, a man left his table and followed him. The follower was tall and thin, with a birthmark shaped like a kidney on his right cheek. He wore a plain brown suit with a collarless white shirt buttoned at the top like a priest's collar. He followed Angelo who wandered aimlessly. It was obvious that Angelo didn't have anyplace to go nor did he know where he was going when he turned into one of the narrow streets that climbed steeply up a hill. The whitewashed houses on both sides of the street were so close to the cobblestone road that overhanging porches on the second floor blocked out the hot sun, almost forming a tunnel. Faint from hunger, Angelo negotiated a sharp turn, tripped over a cobblestone, then fell to his knees and groaned as he felt a sharp edge gouge into his kneecap. As he started to get up, a hand reached down and caught him under his armpit and roughly hauled him upright.

The hand belonged to a short, stout fellow who was leading a mule that had a small umbrella tied to its harness to shade the beast's head. Strapped to its back was a stone-sharpening wheel attached to a wooden frame that tilted to the side when the mule negotiated the same sharp turn.

The man and the mule made their living by sharpening knives, or scissors, and in the more rural areas, axes and hoes. He was a gypsy, one of the thousands who wandered west in the fourteenth and fifteenth century, leaving their traditional homelands that bordered Iran and India. The Gypsies traveled through what was then the Ukraine and into Romania, Bulgaria, and usually only the northern parts of Greece, Macedonia, and Thrace. As they wandered from country to country, always unwanted and branded as thieves (which they were) and child stealers (which they were not), they managed to increase their population.

The gypsy was eating figs from a pile he had wrapped in a kerchief as he walked along calling out, "Knives! I sharpen knives!"

A woman shouted from her window. She did not even attempt to cover her hair and shamelessly allowed her arms to be exposed for any man to see.

"Hey Gypsy! Stop by my front door. I have a scissors that needs to be sharpened."

He strutted toward her and smiled, using his brilliant white teeth as if they were a beacon attracting a moth.

"It is hardly worth my while to stop for just one scissors, which only brings me 10 *leptá*. If I could put an edge on other things that are getting dull because they haven't been taken care of properly, then I could stop and give my poor mule a rest."

"Well, my goodness, what makes you think that I am going to need anything that a dark-skinned thief like you has to offer? The only thing I need is to have the scissors sharpened. I like to cut cleanly when I clip my boyfriend's hair and trim his beard."

"I could tell by looking at you how sophisticated you are and that you did not just come from the mountains. Perhaps next time we meet, you will need more from me," he sighed.

As he spoke, he turned the mule sideways and removed a long leather strap from one of the packs attached to the pannier on the mule's back. The strap was looped on both ends. He attached the smaller loop to the wooden handle that protruded from the sharpening wheel. He untied the wheel brake and gave the wheel a test spin. The mule turned its head, looked away, and up and sighed. The man put his right foot into the loop then pumped it up and down rapidly. The wheel started to turn on its metal axle.

Angelo watched the sun-blackened gypsy, who was even shorter than he was. The scissors made a high-pitched grinding noise as the gypsy pressed it onto the spinning stone. He took pride in his work, stopping only when he could shave a small bare spot on his forearm with the sharpened blades. A small circle had formed to watch the process and the gypsy entertained the crowd.

He pulled another sack from the loaded mule and took out two hand puppets. One was of the puppet clown *"Garagíozies;"* the other looked like a mule. He held one puppet in each hand, and by changing his voice and manipulating the puppets, managed to convey the impression that the two were speaking to each other. He sang some songs and told some stories to the delighted crowd.

"There was a famous and handsome Gypsy who was a knife-sharpener. One day he complained to his friend, the mule." With his elbow, he nudged the mule, which raised his head and brayed on cue, "Hee haw!", making the crowd laugh. The gypsy continued, "I am so tired and life is very painful for me."

The mule puppet then replied, "Sure, your backside hurts from riding on me all day. My back hurts from you sitting on it, but my feet hurt more. They have to carry your back and my back too. Maybe these people who are watching can give us some money. Then you can buy some fresh oats and hay for me." Another nudge produced another "hee haw."

By now the crowd had grown. They laughed, jeered, and clapped. They threw coins, which the gypsy caught with great expertise. He missed one, a two drachma coin thrown by the lady with the once-dull scissors. It rolled past Angelo. He picked it up and with a quick burst ran down the street in the direction from which he had come. He ran right into the arms of the man in the brown suit who had been following him.

"Wait now! Wait, I say! Where are you going with the mule's money? You're the bigshot who was asking about my friend, a very important person, and here you are stealing money from a gypsy."

"Let go of me, you bastard. I am hungry and need that money. I know who I want to see. How is that any business of yours?"

"Well, well, well, you may be an ignorant piece of turd from some wretched village, but you do have some spirit. I want to know how a goat-lover like you can know where to find my boss and what you want of him."

Angelo calmed down and concocted a story about how he was wanted by the Royal Constabulary and needed sanctuary. As it turned out, the gypsy was paying protection money to the smuggler and waited for Angelo to return his coin. It was the gypsy who suggested that perhaps Angelo could be of some help.

"We Gypsies are a strange breed. We are tough guys but always feel compassion for others even less lucky than we are." He continued talking as he took Angelo by the arm and turned toward the menacing hoodlum.

"I'll see to it that my fellow thief gets something to eat. He will stay with me and my mule, sharpening knives, while you see whether your boss will agree to talk to him. If your boss wants to talk to him, then you will know where he is. If your boss doesn't want to talk to him, I'll send him on his way."

The hoodlum agreed, giving Angelo a push toward the mule, "Stay with the Gypsy until I get back." He pointed his finger at the smiling knife-sharpener. "As for you, you black-skinned ape, if he is not here when I get back, I'll bite your balls off and hang them on the mule's ears."

Since the gypsy promised food, Angelo quickly agreed. As the brown suit disappeared around a corner, the gypsy turned to Angelo, winked, and said, "Now, as we walk, tell me what your story is and don't lie. Just tell me the truth. If nothing else, it should be entertaining."

"First of all," Angelo said, "I am not usually a thief, but since the thread follows the needle, I don't blame you for calling me one. Strangely enough, I don't mind you calling me a thief, but I am upset that I got caught by a horse's ass like him."

He continued talking, barely stopping to breathe just long enough to gain momentum for the next rush of words. He finally stopped speaking when his guide led him to a little rundown cafe where the gypsy purchased bread, goat's cheese, and watered wine for the promised meal.

"Well, my little Greek friend who used to be a baker, thank you for telling me your story. It is entirely possible that you do have an aptitude for an old and ancient profession, that of being a thief. Let me explain to you a little more about that complex question: When is a person a thief and when is he just a little bit dishonest?

"Let's begin with a definition. A thief is someone who takes without permission something which does not belong to him. Do you agree with that? But, tell me when Christ chased the moneylenders from the temple, kicked over their tables and money boxes, and then distributed the coins left behind by the fleeing lenders, was he not stealing someone else's possessions?

"When the victorious Crusaders took spoils of war from their defeated enemies, weren't they thieves? When the Christians raided the Temples of Athena, Apollo, and other deities, then took the statues and the gold so they could melt them down and form them in the shape of crosses, weren't they stealing someone else's property? When a starving man steals a rich man's sheep in order to feed his starving children, is he a thief? Of course he is! And of course the Christians I spoke of were thieves," the gypsy-philosopher concluded.

A befuddled and somewhat sleepy Angelo replied, "But that is different. They were stealing because they needed to in order to survive, as in the case of the starving children. In the other situations, they were taking things from the bad or misguided ones and giving those things to good people."

"We Gypsies agree with you. That is why we are not ashamed to steal a lamb now and then, or to take a coat or cloak from someone else. We need those things to survive. The farmer always has more lambs. Unfortunately, the rest of the world does not agree with us. We have become outcasts drifting from one country to another because they keep chasing us and persecuting us. They mistakenly call us bad and evil people, liars and child stealers. They beat us and put us in jail. When the men are imprisoned, the authorities force our wives and children to steal even more so they can survive until their husbands and fathers are returned to them. By treating us so poorly and persecuting us, they continue to reinforce our belief that they are the bad people and we are the good ones. We continue to do the same things the Christians did. We take from the bad and misinformed and give it to the good people—ourselves," he concluded with satio faction.

Angelo laughed out loud. He laughed so hard he ran out of breath. He gasped and managed to breath deeply.

"Oh, I would give a million drachmas to see my father's face if he could hear you tell your version of an honest man."

"Well, I just want you to understand that, as there are different kinds of women, there are also different kinds of thieves. There are women who are as pretty as oranges and just as sweet, if you wait long enough for the fruit to ripen. There are women who are like lemons, and no matter how long you wait, they will always be bitter. There are women like gypsy women who resemble artichokes—all thorny and rough on the outside. But ah! When you get inside down to the heart—oh my friend, then you find paradise."

He continued smiling as he spoke.

"There are thieves who steal for the sake of stealing. All they want to do is to get more. They do not need what they steal; they just steal. They have no character. Then, there are thieves who make their living by stealing. They are professionals who only take what they need. They are like farmers who till the soil and take from the earth only what they need. They are also honorable men."

Angelo could not help staring in open-mouthed astonishment and admiration as he heard this totally different philosophy. The Gypsy grinned from ear to ear, then quickly added, as a shadow fell between himself and Angelo, "Of course, Effendi, you too are a man of honor, and are the most successful farmer of all."

Angelo also turned to face the person casting the shadow. The sun was shining behind the figure, casting a blinding light into which Angelo had to stare. The smuggler looked even bigger than what his brother had described.

"If you believe all that mule crap about honorable thieves, perhaps you are the one to whom I could sell the Parthenon," the surprisingly high-pitched voice of the smuggler came out of the glare. "Who are you and what do you want from me?"

Startled, Angelo responded, almost shouting, "I need to find work and a patron who will help me prosper here in the cities because I am not going back to the village. If it turns out that my teacher will be a little dark-skinned gypsy, then I will listen and learn from him."

Angelo paused, seemed to collect himself, and continued, "However, it seems more reasonable that my patron will be a large, powerful man like yourself who needs not only a student but someone who will give him complete loyalty and allegiance. If that person is you, then I will suffer some indignities; but not even you will be allowed to make fun of me."

Angelo's eyebrows drew together as the veins leading to his face pumped furiously and his skin darkened even more. The giant moved even closer until Angelo had to step back or suffer the indignity of having his nose pressed into the man's shirt front.

"What is your name, little sir, and how did a young wolf like you come to find me?" the giant demanded.

Angelo explained how his brother Soterios had been referred to the smuggler and described the meeting between the two. He went on to explain that Soterios had appreciated the advice he had received, but the smuggler had frightened him so much that he had left Argos and made his way to America without the patron's help.

The result of the conversation was that Angelo agreed to work for the smuggler, assuming that he would pass a two-week trial period.

The Gypsy and his donkey disappeared into the twisting streets leaving as part of Angelo's education an unusual philosophy regarding the moral values of thievery.

Angelo spent two years working for the smuggler, and during those two years learned his trade. He helped to smuggle goods from the distribution of narcotics to the transportation of stolen diamonds from West Africa to the diamond centers in Brussels, Belgium. Angelo became second in command to the smuggler. He thought he was important until he realized that his boss was a small insignificant cog in a mysterious organization that was headquartered in Italy.

Unfortunately, Angelo himself developed an addiction to the drugs that were the main source of their income. He developed into a street-smart person who was rarely taken by surprise, but he was shocked when his boss was arrested by the Royal Constabulary. Angelo barely escaped the dragnet that was being spread throughout the Peloponnesian plains. He finally was able to make contact with the decision makers who controlled the illegal activities of the organization in Greece. Little by little, the story of intrigue began to take shape. It seemed as if the fat smuggler had been offered up as a sacrifice.

CHAPTER 10

THE REUNION

The new Pope installed in Rome was stubborn, and a strong and forceful competitor for the Sicilians who controlled the Italian Government. King Emmanuel III was still trying to redeem the nation's pride after the humiliating defeats of the Italian Army in Ethiopia six years earlier. These factors disrupted the normal business activities of the Organization and made the bosses nervous.

At the same time, it became obvious that the Japanese defeat of Imperial Russia in 1905 had disturbed the Organization's supply lines. Turkey, Iran, and Afghanistan were affected. Greece itself was in constant turmoil, which provoked a near-revolt that ended in 1910 at the rewriting of the constitution. This also opened the door for the overthrow of the royal family.

The political scene was such that the Organization needed to buy time to regroup. It decided that each country in which they were doing business would sacrifice leaders of the underworld to the judicial systems of their country.

ㄹㄹㄹㄹㄹㄹㄹㄹ

Angelo was small potatoes, not worth bothering with. He was safe for now. He made his way north almost to the Albanian border and then to the Island of Korfu where he was able to join a ship's crew as a merchant seaman bound for America.

When the steamer docked in New York, Angelo promptly jumped ship. Angelo surfaced in Boston.

Louie and Costas (now called Charlie) were entering the *cafenion* on Tremont Street when Angelo appeared. Angelo had a seaman's jacket on, and his hair was wet and stuck to his scalp as if heavily pomaded. It was early November and a storm blew hard from the Northeast, ripping through the cobblestone streets of Boston and causing every living thing in its path to shiver in the bitter cold. Angelo was tired, cold, and drenched. He had to ask twice before Fotis, who was working the counter that day, for a hot cup of soup heard him. Fotis would have responded the first time if he had heard Angelo, but he was almost deaf. He had been that way ever since he was eight years old after his father had punished him severely for being too curious. Fotis had been trying to see what his father and mother were doing in the cellar stable under their home in Greece.

In the old country the cramped quarters that most of the peasants lived in made it difficult, if not impossible, to have privacy. They slept five and six to a room on sleeping carpets that were spread each night on the floor around the fireplace. The animals, which lived in the basement or cellar under the living quarters of their owners during the cold winter months, had more privacy than the humans. The stable became a favorite place for a man and wife to quickly couple, often conceiving another child. The adults would tell the children to stay away from the cellar stable, which of course caused the children to whisper and wonder about the mysterious activities that caused the muted whimpers and sighs. The eight-year-old Fotis had to know whether his parents were engaged in the same kind of activity as the farm animals often did, and if so, did people do it the same way?

He crept down the makeshift ladder from the trap door next to the fireplace. His mother was bent forward over the railing that separated the sheep from the mule. Unfortunately for Fotis, his father and mother were both facing him. She had her eyes closed as she grimaced both in pain and ecstasy, but his father saw Fotis with wide-open eyes. Without missing a stroke or hesitating at all, his father said in a strained voice, "Get out of here. I will deal with you when I am through."

Soon Fotis was summoned to the cellar. As the terrified boy began descending the stairs, his mother scampered out of the door, too embarrassed to look at her son, never mind help him escape punishment. Fotis could smell his mother on his father's hands as he stood, shaking, before the angry man. His father grabbed his son by both ears, lifted him from the ground, and shook him like a bell, back and forth. "I will teach you to deny me even a moment of what little pleasure I have in this life. You had to listen and try to see us, did you? By God, I will teach you."

He roared and punished the little boy, whose ears had begun to bleed at the uppermost point where they connected to his head. He shrieked in pain, shouting that he could not hear anything.

The priest had come and dripped Holy Water from a piece of cloth that had been blessed by the Bishop into the tortured and twisted ears, but nothing helped. They had sent to the city for the new doctor who had come all the way from Crete to practice medicine on the mainland. Thanks to some new miracle drugs and continued blessings from the priest, some hearing was restored. Fotis never forgave his father, and never understood why his mother had not intervened.

Angelo finished his bowl of thick, lemon flavored chicken and rice soup, leaned back in his chair, and said loudly to Fotis, who had his back turned, "I am looking for Soterios Douropoulos. Where can I find him?"

Fotis did not answer him, not even when Angelo repeated it—this time more loudly than before. When nothing happened, Angelo exploded. He jumped from his chair, throwing the soup bowl and spoon all in the same motion.

"Hey, you stupid turd, I am talking to you! Why don't you answer? Are you deaf? I am looking for Soterios Douropoulos." The bowl hit Fotis over his right eye, opening a gash about two inches long. Outraged men circled Angelo, like wolves surrounding a sick animal. By this time Angelo was totally out of control and dared the men to come closer. He presented such a menacing figure that the would-be attackers hesitated, even though he was outnumbered six to one.

Louie and Charlie had just entered the *cafenion* and were climbing the stairs when they heard Angelo screaming that he was looking for Soterios Douropoulos. When they realized that they were looking at their brother Angelo surrounded by angry men, they charged into the group. It was difficult for Louie, to associate the tough-looking, cold-eyed fugitive with the laughing devil-may-care youth he had last seen waving good-bye to him a few years ago.

"Wait a minute now, my friends. This is my brother. Stop! Whatever the problem is, we will take care of it."

While Charlie saw to Fotis, Louie said to Angelo, "My God in heaven, where did you come from?"

It took two hours for the three brothers to catch up on each others' lives, and even Angelo cried when he learned his father had died the previous spring. Charlie was working in a restaurant called the Elcho Lunch that was owned by two Irishmen. Chris and Louie were negotiating to buy it. Louie had just sold a little four-stool lunch counter to an Armenian for one hundred and fifty dollars. As Louie explained it, he had made an outstanding business deal.

"The restaurant was over by Haymarket Square. It was not in a good neighborhood, but I thought I could increase the sales. Business stayed down, though, no matter what I did. The final straw was when a man came in one afternoon and ordered a bowl of beef stew that cost fifteen cents. He took the beef and carrots out of the stew and wrapped them in a napkin. He said he was going to have the meat and vegetables for dinner that night. He stirred the liquid from the soup, drank it, and left. He was my only customer that day. The worst part is yet to come. He came back in at about seven o'clock and asked me for a cup of hot water, poured some ketchup into it, took the beef and carrots out of his pocket and added them to the water and ketchup mixture. Then he ate it. He had two meals for fifteen cents, and he was my only customer all day. That is when I decided that maybe I had a bad location." He chuckled and continued, "I found someone who knew he was smarter than me and knew he would succeed where I had failed. I immediately thanked God for his gift and sold the business."

Angelo moved in with the two brothers and slept on an old couch borrowed from the Jewish family in the flat above theirs. Angelo refused all offers of employment that Louie was able to wrangle from his friends since every job required manual labor. Also, as Angelo explained, the jobs did not offer future opportunities. The youngest Douropoulos brother spent more and more time in the North End, which was just becoming known as "little Italy."

The Irish were the dominant force in Boston, and would remain in control of the political plums as well as the police department, fire department, and post office. The Italians, by virtue of sheer numbers and a stubborn persistence to support each other through various societies as well as family ties that seemed to extend to extraordinary levels, were the only group able to challenge the Irish federation.

The Italians began to function as a power to be reckoned with, but they never seriously challenged the political or civic-minded Anglo Saxons. The Irishmen wisely decided that the best way to handle the sleeping giant was to let it have its own territory, which for all intent and purpose was self-governed. Non-Italians were encouraged to run for council seats in any district other than those of Little Italy. Policemen knew that if they were assigned to a beat in that area, there was little chance of supplementing their income. Italians paid only other Italians for protection. Any Irish cop assigned to a beat in Little Italy knew he was being punished.

Other nationalities were graciously allowed to settle in the North End for a while. Then little by little, as more Italians moved in, the "foreigners" were encouraged to move uptown. The only exception was the blacks, who were never allowed to move onto the "sacred streets" of Little Italy. The few brave but foolish blacks who attempted to move in found swift and immediate retribution.

Angelo seemed able to make friends with the difficult Italians. He claimed it was because of contacts he had made before he got to America. Louie worried about his brother's activities, but was so wrapped up his own problems that he barely noticed when Angelo would buy new clothes that became more expensive with each purchase. It was in June that Angelo announced that he would be moving to his own apartment, as soon as the new furniture he had ordered arrived. By that time, even Louie and Charlie were forced to recognize that Angelo was mixed up in illegal activities. It was becoming a normal procedure for the *cafenion* to become dead silent when Angelo strutted through the door. His occasional irrational behavior frightened most people. The facts that he now had excellent suits and a gold watch that he constantly looked at, should have indicated that he had a high-paying job. Yet he was unemployed and absolutely fearless. Soon other Greeks were asking him to assist them in various ways, such as obtaining building permits. Angelo always succeeded—for a price, of course. People began calling him "Boston Blackie."

CHAPTER 11
THE MOB

In April of 1914, Louie formed a partnership with another Greek named Teddy and finally owned a successful restaurant located at the top of a small hill which dominated the surrounding streets of Scollay Square. Scollay Square was an area known for its close proximity to the railroad terminal as well as the docks and the produce market. It was destined to be a continuing hub of activity.

The title "Square" was misleading because there was no defined shape to the jumble of restaurants, shops, and theaters that surrounded a small plot of grass that supported the sign that simply read Scollay Square. Years earlier it had been a large square grassy park bordered with a small white picket fence complete with a statue of a man on a horse. All that was left of the park was the small plot of grass and the name Scollay Square.

The restaurant was located next door to one of the most luxurious and expensive bawdy houses in Boston. Its clientele was able to reserve small intimate dinning rooms on the second floor for late night dinners. On the other side of the restaurant was a theater where a variety of stage plays were produced. Teddy was always able to remember which wife belonged to which politician, always seating the correct couple to the appropriate dining area—downstairs for the husband and doting wife, and upstairs for straying husbands and their mistresses. Since there were two separate stairwells protected by doors that emerged to the entrance alcove, it was relatively simple to keep the traffic flowing smoothly.

With Louie in charge of the kitchen, the food was excellent. Despite high prices, the reputation of the restaurant continued to grow at a satisfactory rate. The first indication of any trouble was when a tough-looking Irishman barged into the kitchen one day. Louie was adding the diced, cooked potatoes to the simmering roux to make the clam chowder he was becoming famous for. The stranger said he represented some clients from the Hill who wanted to purchase the restaurant.

Louie braced himself as he lifted the large pot filled to the brim with potatoes and water. He circled the pot with both arms grasping a handle in each hand. His thumbs slipped under the handles and his hands turned upward as he strained to lift and tip the pot at the same time by bracing its bottom against his chest. The steam from the potatoes rose in a cloud, momentarily blinding him as the water hissed in the hot flour and butter roux.

"I can't stop and talk right now as I have to finish this once I start or it will get all lumpy," Louie grunted. "Wait about ten minutes and we can talk, but to tell you the truth, I don't believe we want to sell."

The Irishman looked at Louie straining with the pot, steam billowing around him, and said, "I can't wait too long, and if you want to work this hard when you can make a nice profit by selling the joint, you're as dumb as Patty's Pig." He turned and fanned himself with his hat to move the wet, hot air away. He stopped in the doorway and stated, "I don't want any problems, and neither should you. Next time we talk, just tell me what you want for the place and we can make a quick deal."

Louie finished the chowder base, and with the salad man's help, moved the pot to a wooden table, placed an inverted bowl under it to allow air to circulate around it so it could cool quicker. Stopping to wipe the sweat from his forehead gave him an opportunity to think about the Irishman's comments.

The first luncheon order of the day was placed by a sour-looking waiter. As Louie hurried to fill the order, he reminded himself not to forget to complain to his partner about the sourpuss waiter. He didn't think about the Irishman again until later that evening as sat on a chair on the back dock, sipping a cup of coffee and letting the still-cool ocean air drift over his forehead. He let his feet fall to the floor from the box on which they were propped, when he remembered that the man had said, "I don't want any trouble and neither should you." He called to the busboy refilling bread baskets, "Would you ask Teddy to come and see me when he gets a chance?"

Teddy came in a few minutes later, sipping a glass of red wine.

"That is the difference between you and me, Louie—I drink wine and you drink that old cold coffee. I wish I could civilize you, especially now that we are going to be rich American big shots. The people are still lined up outside."

Louie crossed one leg over the other, put his head down, and chuckled. He swept his head back and forth in time with his foot, which bobbed up and down to the cadence of unheard music.

"Well Mr. Bigshot, before you hurry off to get married now that you have a few dollars, let me tell you of the stinky Irish skunk who was here today."

Louie told Teddy what happened, emphasizing the implied threat. Teddy sucked in a huge breath of air, almost spilling his wine, and groaned. He blanched when he saw the quizzical look his partner aimed at him.

"When I got civilized I also lost some courage. If you remember, the fox back in the old country never rolled onto his back to plead for good treatment like tame dogs do. I am frightened. The only person I know who is never frightened is your brother Angelo. Let's ask him for some advice. He is always getting free meals here with his fancy women and always ordering the most expensive food. He owes us a lot. I'm not complaining but…"

Louie cut him off. "Sure, now that you need him, Angelo is someone you want advice from. Most of the time you barely speak to him, and I know you call him a crook and hoodlum. He is my brother, and if I get pleasure out of entertaining him, that is my business and none of yours. You may find out that he is not the only one who still has some balls."

After work that night, Louie was still angry as he left for the *cafenion*, hailing a cab just outside the door. He finally cooled off as he reached his destination. The cab stopped outside the *cafenion*, where the sounds of the backgammon dice mixed with the murmur of voices could be heard, seemingly muted by the always-present cloud of tobacco smoke. He hesitated before climbing the stairs and wondered again if it was time to think about finding a good sturdy Greek girl and getting married. His sister, who was still in Greece, had married two years ago. And now, with both parents dead, he was free of any other family obligations.

Charlie and Angelo called to him from the bottom step just as he had reached the top of the landing. "Don't go up into that stinkhole tonight. Come with us and we will sit in the Commons, drink beer, and watch girls' asses wiggle."

Louie laughed and descended the stairs much faster than he had gone up. He enjoyed his two brothers so much that it was difficult to think of them as kin. They were in fact his best friends. They found a bench in front of the bird-spattered statue of Paul Revere in the Commons and settled in, watching the crowds drift by.

Charlie was nervous, unable to sit still. Angelo finally asked him, "Charlie, what is wrong with you? You said you needed to talk to us, so come on now, what is it? I thought at first that you had lost a lot of money at the track and wanted a loan, but that's not it, is it?"

"No, it isn't money. I may go crazy, but losing all the money in the world won't do it. It's worse than that."

Louie intervened, "Come on, Costaki, whatever it is, tell us. We can solve anything as long as the Douropoulos bunch sticks together."

"Okay, I will, but I swear to you that I know what I saw." Charlie stood in front of them with his legs spread wide like a prizefighter as he went on.

"You both know that back in the old country I killed a man. I can't help worrying even though I know that the police aren't looking for me. When I came through Ellis Island, no one bothered me. The Greek government did not have an arrest warrant out for me. I have always expected that someday the police would come for me. I got my citizenship papers as fast as I could in hopes that would protect me. God knows I didn't mean to hurt anyone. It was an accident—I swear to God it was."

He stopped talking and turned his eyes to heaven, while making the sign of the cross on his chest, then continued talking. "All I wanted to do was to have some fun. It would have been great. God, I could have been a hero. That poor sap from Kaparelli wanted to marry that girl so much, and her asshole brothers didn't want to lose their slave. Christ, I can't even think of their names now. Anyhow, as you guys know, it was an accident, but I still feel guilty.

"What I mean to say is, I swear to you that I saw one of the broth ers of the man I killed coming out of the *cafenion* the other day. The reason the police aren't looking for me is that the two brothers have found me and they are going to get revenge themselves. I know it. The other day my landlady told me that a guy she thought was Greek came to the apartment looking for me. He had a package that he said he had to give to me personally."

Angelo smiled without moving his lips, "Charlie, please do not worry about that mule turd. I can handle him, whoever he is. He is plowing in my fields. He hasn't got a chance of getting to you."

Charlie replied, "I know that Angelo, but I haven't finished. Besides, I don't want you involved. I went to the coffeehouse, found a fellow villager of his, and in our conversation he told me that my enemy, his name is Panayioti, is in this country. He was in a hurry to find me. He was trying to find me because he had to leave for Chicago. He is gone now, but he mentioned something about returning in three months or so. I'm not afraid of him. Whatever happens, happens. I just can't help feeling terrible about the pain I caused. It all started because I thought it would have been fun to be a hero."

"There is something wrong in this world, and it doesn't matter whether you are in Greece or here—the same thing happens to heroes," Angelo said to his brother.

By now Charlie was slightly dizzy from the beer, but he was still able to ask, "Louie, what is he talking about? What does he know about heroes? The closest he has ever come to a hero is when he saw me take on three sailors at once in a bar."

Angelo stood up, stretched his shoulders, and said, "I will tell you two what I know about heroes. They spend a great deal of their life doing fine and noble and maybe even brave deeds, and sometimes they even get killed. Then one day someone builds a statue of them and then it happens. See, look at the statue in the park—all covered with crap from the birds. That proves that all Greeks are heroes because we are always in the shit."

He looked triumphantly at his two astounded brothers. "By the good God above, you are right," Louie exploded. "Here, for the first time, I am making some real money and that Irish bastard wants to shit on me. Well, he isn't going to wipe his ass on my shirt."

Angelo insisted on knowing what Louie was talking about. He did not appear too concerned at first; however, he became increasingly agitated as the story neared its conclusion. Louie had finished and Angelo was pacing back and forth.

"Do not do a thing either way about this until I have a chance to find out what is going on," he said, and persisted until Louie agreed. Angelo's final words that he dispatched over his departing shoulder were, "Too bad I can't tell Papa how I had to help his two angel sons. He would be so proud of me."

The pleasant evening breezes continued to move the branches of the maple trees, but the night's personality had changed. The brothers reluctantly returned to their separate homes. Each had his own apartment and each had a different lifestyle. Charlie had established a liaison with a pretty Lithuanian waitress. They had moved in together in a second-story flat not far from the Museum of Natural History. Louie lived alone, although he had frequent lady guests. His three-room apartment was nicely though inexpensively furnished. Angelo had a five-room apartment on the top floor of a swank apartment house just off Copley Square. Two of the rooms had private bathrooms. Charlie had been there often, but Louie had been there only once. He felt uncomfortable in the plush-carpeted, gilt-edged mirror atmosphere. He never accepted another of the many invitations Angelo extended. It was not the opulence of the furnishings, nor was it the flashy redhead who was the present live-in that bothered him. What caused him concern was his knowledge that Angelo was involved with thugs and gangsters, although the brothers studiously avoided any mention of Angelo's "business." Louie felt that if he visited, even occasionally, in these environments, his presence would somehow constitute approval.

After promising to protect Charlie, Angelo left town and stayed away for two weeks. The three brothers met again when he returned. They sat at a table in Louie's restaurant in Scollay Square. Angelo claimed that he had been in Toledo, Ohio, and had visited with a friend before the friend moved to Chicago. He was in a rotten mood and refused to discuss the trip. He pouted, drank more than usual, and appeared to be holding himself in check. The evening was about to be ruined and disintegrate into another trip to the coffeehouse.

Louie tried to lighten his brother's mood by showing him the new silverware with the restaurant's name engraved on the handle, "Howard's Sea Grille."

"The silverware is very nice, brother, but who is Howard? And where the hell did that name come from?" Angelo snarled.

"I don't know who Howard was, but we kept the name because of money. The outside sign and the walnut-carved bar sign said 'Howard's Sea Grille' when we bought the business, and we didn't want to spend any money to change the name."

Angelo with his mood getting even more dangerous muttered, "The name is important and you should have ... "

"Hey that reminds me ..." Louie interrupted. "When I got the license, I had to talk to an Irish bastard who was too lazy to spell Douropoulos and he wanted me to shorten it. So he shortened it to Douros. I asked him what his name was and he told me it was Patrick. I told him that in the old country no self-respecting mule would allow themselves to be called Patrick, especially since it rhymes with prick."

Charlie and Angelo both laughed, especially when Louie admitted that he had the license in his pocket before he was brave enough to confront the Irish official.

Charlie reminded Angelo that he had promised to find out who was trying to force Louie to sell the business. Louie went on to explain. "In the past week, three of my main suppliers have suddenly refused to issue me more credit—even though I have always paid on time. Then, those two musicians that Teddy took care of like they were babies—you know, the violin player and the piano player—both quit without notice. All they would say was that they had been offered better jobs. I think someone is beginning to apply pressure on us—just a little bit now, but it will get worse. I know Teddy is getting nervous."

Angelo pushed himself to his feet, "Christ, Louie, I forgot all about it. I'll go right now and get us some answers."

He stormed out the door, hailed a cab, and disappeared as the cab door was slammed shut behind him. He appeared at the restaurant the next day at nine in the morning. Louie knew it was important because Angelo was rarely seen before noon. All Angelo would say to Louie was, "Louie you got no choice. The best I could do for you was to get them—don't ask who they are—to give you a profit of fifteen thousand dollars. They want the joint so bad that they will give you the right, within reason of course, to tell them what you paid for the place, and then add the fifteen grand. Believe me, you got no choice."

Teddy at first wanted Louie to negotiate a better deal, but Louie explained that Angelo insisted that this was the best they could do and any refusal would have deadly consequences. However, if Teddy wanted to try, Louie wouldn't object.

The day after the deal was closed, the restaurant was shuttered, and carpenters appeared to begin an extensive remodel program that included removing a dividing wall between the theater and the restaurant. Suddenly the theater closed also. The legitimate actors were fired then rehired, as they and the staging moved to newly purchased facilities across the street from a fancy hotel in downtown Boston.

Louie walked by the site of his old restaurant every day wondering what was going to happen next. Then one day a new sign—one of the first of its kind in Boston—was hoisted into position. The massive sign had little round bulbs that flashed on and off alternately around the words: "BURLESQUE PALACE." The bawdy house next door did more business than ever. A steady stream of people swirled around the little complex like leaves blowing in the wind. At first some of the best names in vaudeville played there until moving pictures took hold and the old concept of burlesque changed. It degenerated to a "take-it-off" striptease joint. The bawdy houses turned into whore houses. Sailors from all nations visited the prostitutes and tattoo parlors. Scollay Square was lit day and night as the blinking lights from world-famous bars like the Silver Dollar Saloon flashed on and off all night long.

Teddy became a waiter at the Fairmont Hotel and later joined up again with Louie, John, and Chris in an ambitious undertaking called the Pemberton Inn.

Louie loaned most of the profits from the sale of Howard's to friends who were almost always in need, saving only enough to finance his next venture. Charlie was responsible for Louie saving the bulk of the profits at all. He intervened one day just before Louie handed over a substantial loan to someone Charlie identified as a "lazy good-for-nothing." Charlie grabbed the money from Louie's hand.

"Louie, what the hell are you doing? Do you realize that everyone considers you a fool? For Christ sake, show some sense! It is one thing to be helpful, but another to be a damn fool. I'll keep the money and give it back to you when you need it."

As he walked away, Louie shouted at him, "Okay Charlie, you are right, but for God's sake, don't bet my money on the horses."

Louie's old friend John was standing behind Louie, watching the whole scene. He muttered to himself, "It's good that their mother isn't alive to see the outcome of all of her pain. My Christ, what a trio—a sucker for a sob story, a gambler, and a gangster."

SOTERIOS

CHAPTER 12
SURPRISE MEETING

Charlie jammed his old fedora down hard over his thinning hair, hunched his shoulders against the anticipated cold, and stepped out into the frigid but smoke-free air. He was working at a fancy restaurant on Commonwealth Avenue called "Rodger's." His ten-hour shift was to begin in half an hour. If he hurried, he could get there in time, though he wouldn't have an opportunity to deposit Louie's money in a safe place. He patted his chest where the money lay safe and secure in his inside suit pocket.

His suit was wrinkled and even a little greasy from being around restaurant kitchens. Charlie, like most of his peers, went out of his house in the mornings fully dressed. He wore a business suit, shirt, and necktie—always the same necktie if he was going to work. He only changed it on holidays. He wore a soft fedora hat and his good shoes, which he would change for work clothes and shoes after he arrived at the restaurant. His clothing filtered the air that drifted up from the restaurant kitchens while hanging in his locker. The air was filled with the smell of fats used in cooking as well as dust that absorbed odors of meat, French fries, and other foods. A person could identify a cook by the smell of his clothing. Charlie hated that smell, though he didn't dislike his job. He enjoyed the companionship of other men, and the challenge to race the clock by getting food prepared on time and faster than his peers could.

Charlie loved to walk on Commonwealth Avenue where he could admire the huge brownstone houses that served as "Town Homes" for the elite of Boston. The nearby park areas were always decorated with young brightly dressed children and their nannies.

The only thing Charlie loved to watch more than children playing were race horses. He hurried to get out where the air was fresh—away from the smells of the kitchens—so he could admire the long-legged, shiny race horses. He not only liked to look at them, but he bet everything he could, always certain he knew which horse would run the fastest.

When he got to work he changed clothes, making sure that he kept Louie's money in his work trouser pockets. He liked the feel of it. The restaurant was busy that day, and Charlie never thought about the money until he was through working. Charlie finished his shift, cleaned his work area, and was getting ready to change back into his street clothes when the owner's wife came into the kitchen.

"Thank you, Charlie, we had a good night tonight. Thank you for picking up the slack when the fry cook stayed home. I still want to be able to send you a Christmas card or an Easter card when the time comes, but I don't have your address."

Charlie chuckled and said, "Just wish me Merry Christmas! I am always here." He hesitated for a moment before adding, "Now look, I do my job, and I always get here when I'm supposed to. I don't know why it is so important for you to know where I live or with who."

"Charlie, for Pete's sake, there are certain forms that need to be filled out. I can't keep using the restaurant address when they ask for your home address. What are you trying to hide? If I didn't know you as well as I do, I would think the police are after you."

Exasperated, Charlie headed up the stairs to the employees' change room, "Okay, okay, I will tell your husband tomorrow. It's just that …Oh never mind, I'll talk to him."

As Charlie was changing his clothes, he talked to himself. "I guess people do think I am some kind of nut or crook. Of course, in a way I am. I did kill that guy. Well, I should be able to talk to that Panayiotis sometime soon and get this resolved one way or the other. I better call Louie and ask him to go with me to the *cafenion* tonight because that bum should be back from Chicago by now. I hope Angelo isn't there because I want to get rid of problems—not cause more."

Fotis was standing with a cigarette hanging from the left side of his lip, wiping off the counter, when Charlie and Louie entered. Fotis looked meaningfully at Charlie, then pointed with a sideways nod of his head at a table where two men sat with their backs to the bar. Charlie paled and started to turn aside. Louie grabbed his arm firmly and said, "Come on, Costaki, let's get this over with."

There were four chairs at the table. The two empty ones were pulled aside as if someone had recently been sitting there. Charlie walked around the table, stood between the two vacant chairs, and faced the men. Louie stopped and stood directly behind the two men. One of the men, sensing Louie's presence, started to turn to see who was behind him. Louie gently pushed him down while the man looked questioningly up at him. The other man was eating an apple, slicing wedges from it with a wicked-looking folding clasp knife. He was pushing a wedge of apple balanced on the knife into his mouth when Charlie spoke, "Put the knife on the table and let's talk."

The man looked at Charlie, folded the knife, and spit the half-chewed apple on top of the table where it rested against the side of a butt-filled, square glass ashtray.

Charlie took a deep breath and said loudly, "I'm Costas Douropoulos. I've been told that you want to speak to me."

One of the men said as he started to get up, "Oh, that is what this is about." Charlie backed away and spoke, almost shouting,. "Sit down! Don't get up until I tell you to."

The man sat back in his chair said, "You're mistaken. We don't ..." when he was interrupted by another man who was coming out of the restroom, still buttoning his fly. "What's going on here? What's the problem?" he asked.

"Holy Mary, Mother of God," Charlie managed to say when he saw the speaker. The speaker was the oldest of the three brothers. He had a "u"-shaped scar over his right eye, but was very much alive.

Charlie blanched, grabbed the back of the chair for support, and listened dumb-founded as the scarred man spoke.

"Ha, surprised are you? Well, as you can see, you didn't kill me. I'm still alive, thank you. That's more than I can say for my sister, though. She died giving birth to her husband's second son, and that is partly your fault. If you hadn't helped him, he couldn't have married her, and my sister would still be alive. So maybe I should cut your throat anyhow."

"I can't believe you're alive." Charlie reached out carefully and touched him. "Christ, all those years wasted! No wonder no one was looking for me, and nobody ever even mentioned it. I was afraid to ask anyone, and … and … and you're alive after all. That means it is all over. I can't believe it."

Louie interjected himself physically into the conversation by pushing himself between his stunned brother and his opponent. "I am his brother. Our family joins you in sorrow for the death of your sister. I hope we can have a glass of wine together now in memory of her soul. Mutual sorrow and respect for her memory will be a larger memorial than any wild anger or attempt at retribution." Louie reached out to shake the other man's right hand while concentrating on the other's left hand.

The younger brother, Panayiotis, spoke up, "Of course you are right. We went to Tripoli where she was in the hospital dying. They couldn't stop the bleeding. Mary made us promise to find Costas and to shake his hand in friendship. That's why we are here.

"There was a priest there whose name was Papa Yiannis who helped her prepare for her journey to heaven. He asked us to give you this package when we found you as further proof of our good intentions. He reasoned that you would know that we want to be friends if we went to the trouble of delivering this package."

Charlie, still stunned, sank into a chair and waved his hand at Fotis who was watching the scene unfold. Fotis brought a bottle of brandy, five glasses, and a small dish of olives and Greek cheese. Panayiotis poured the drinks and offered a toast to his sister, Mary, and explained that her widowed husband and two babies would soon be coming to America, though they were planning to settle in a place called Hopewell, Virginia. Louie and Panayiotis tried to involve the others in conversation, but Charlie was still agitated and the other brothers were sullen. Louie opened the package, hoping to find something that would break the ice. When that failed, Louie and Charlie shook hands with the brothers, promised to stay in touch, and left for Louie's apartment. The package contained a small icon of the Virgin Mary holding Jesus, which used to sit on the little altar in the Douropoulos home, a small silver pocketknife shaped like a peasant's shoe, and a minia-ture book of the saints enclosed in a silver box that once belonged to Louie's father. The other part of the package was a letter from Papa Yiannis.

Louie telephoned Angelo to ask him to join them. The three broth-ers met in Louie's apartment to read the letter together.

> Beloved Soterios,
>
> I have sent these gifts which were belongings of your par-ents as further proof of the peaceful intentions of the bear-ers. Your father implored you to promise that you will tell the story about your ancestors to your firstborn son.
>
> My existence here in the mother country is the same as before. My wife is still my wife; God's work is rewarding, but it never changes. Continue to live in God's light, and all God's goodness will shower on you. Go to church of-ten, my friend, and continue to light candles so you won't lose the way. Be generous with your gifts to the Church.
>
> Your friend,
>
> Yiannis

Haralambos and Demetra

꒛꒛꒛꒛꒛꒛꒛꒛꒛꒛꒛꒛꒛꒛꒛꒛꒛꒛꒛꒛꒛꒛꒛꒛꒛꒛꒛꒛

PART 2
THEODORA
CHAPTER 13
KAPARELLI

I n 1899 life was difficult in the villages for both men and women. The women, subservient to their men, felt the brunt of the hardship, often bearing and raising their children without their husbands. The men, at least those brave enough to challenge the future, emigrated, promising to send for their families when they were rich. The women worked, prayed to the Saints, and hoped that a miracle would happen that would rescue them and their children. The miracle appeared; it was called America.

When Louie was fourteen years old, a baby was born in the village of Kaparelli on February seventh. Louie didn't know it then, but that event would have a significant impact on his life.

꒛꒛꒛꒛꒛꒛꒛꒛

February 7, 1899

The trilling voice of the meadowlark stopped abruptly when a woman's screams ripped at the hot Mediterranean sky. Demetra, trying to get home before her baby was born, had stopped in mid-stride. She bent over clutching her swollen belly from which the pain emanated in agonizing waves.

As the aching subsided, she struggled farther down the path remembering how the day had begun. Early that morning she had pulled the mule out of its stall under her husband's house to begin another day's work in the fields. Her lifelong friend Eleni was just returning from a trip to the outhouse behind her own nearby cottage.

"Yiasou Eleni, " Demetra called out. "What a beautiful day it is going to be. I am going to prepare the fields for fava beans. The baby is kicking so that he will make my navel untie itself, but if I don't go now I will not have time to get the planting done. Please say a prayer to the Holy Mother to make it a boy with a penis as big as a cucumber so my know-it-all husband can brag all the louder."

"Be careful, Demetra, do not stay too long. It is your first birthing. I will come down later to see if I can help you. Right now I must go. My mother-in-law is complaining that she is hungry," Eleni sighed, rolling her eyes.

Demetra laughed, swung the wooden hoe shaft to her shoulder as she swatted the mule on its rump and swayed down the path that led to the fields. The sun glinted off the waters of the shallow lake that was again filling due to the recent February rains. She was dressed in a long woolen dress that hung down almost to her ankles, and her tough, dirt- and sun-darkened feet curled to grasp any indentation that would give her more support and balance. She had been married only a year, but it seemed a long time since she had left her village of Kamari Tejeas. Her village was just three kilometers away. Its whitewashed houses shone in the sun when she looked over the fields from her new home situated on top of a little hill. She could see the two fairly good sized *horáfia*, the fields she received as part of her *príka*, or dowry. Demetra's new husband had quickly added the required number of rocks to a stone wall to signify that he had taken possession of the land.

Praise the Lord that her husband's mother and father were understanding, Demetra had thought when she moved into their house with her new husband Haralambos. She became pregnant almost immediately, and then to her dismay, Haralambos announced that he was going to join his two brothers in America. He and his brother John had stayed in Greece while the two older brothers, Elias and James, had emigrated to America in 1880. Now, he had announced, it was his turn to go.

Demetra missed her husband, and couldn't help worrying—even though he promised that he would send for her and the new baby just as soon as he could. Although Haralambos drank more than he should, and was not ever going to enjoy working in the hot sun, he was considered a good catch.

As she and the mule wound their way down the hill, Demetra covered her mouth with the edge of the kerchief to block out the dust the mule's hooves kicked into the dry air, and distracted herself by thinking. Demetra never allowed herself the luxury of "resting her brain." She always kept trying to improve her memory. Her mother had told her once that a woman's brain had to be exercised in order to retain its strength. Today she decided to review her husband's ancestral line, her unborn son would someday want to know. She estimated that it would take about twenty minutes to reach the fields, enough time to practice her recitation.

"His father's great-grandfather was the famous Elias Mitropoulos, who had fought side by side with General Kolokotronis. Elias Mitropoulos commanded a company of men responsible for blockading the road between Tripoli and Sparta. They were brave and fought so well that the Turks couldn't reinforce and get supplies to a battalion-sized army. The Turks finally surrendered to a jubilant Kolokotronis," Demetra rehearsed.

Demetra remembered that the hero, Elias, had married a girl named Theodora, but couldn't remember her last name. She knew that Elias and his wife had produced at least two sons; the first they named Georgios in honor of Elias' father. "Georgios married a village girl named Anna Bichikas," Demetra said, patting her large belly as she spoke, "at least I believe it was Bichikas." Georgios had married Anna just before he became ordained as a priest in the Greek Orthodox Church in 1850.

"Georgios Mitropoulos was called Papa Georgios when he established his home in Anna's home village of Kaparelli," Demetra continued. "Papa Georgios did not have a parish of his own. He traveled from village to village administering to the peasants. Because he was a priest, his children assumed the name of Papageorge as a surname."

Demetra swatted a hungry blue fly that was biting her, bringing her thoughts back to the present. She had been a wife for over a year now, she thought proudly. She remembered when she had felt the first stirring of her unborn child, signaling that it was getting impatient to be born. She had crossed herself while still lying on the sleeping rug and whispered a prayer to her patron saint "Please, Agia Demetroula, let my son be born healthy and protect him from the evil eye. If you do this for me, I promise that on your name day I will crawl on my knees from here to the church and light a white candle for you."

But before her husband left for America, a blackbird had flown into their sleeping room, then, while trying to find its way out flew into the mirror. Her husband had been furious with her and insisted that she must have harmed someone who in retaliation had hired a witch to put a curse on her. He was further convinced that the curse was real when the very next day a raven had flown to the top of their slate roof and cawed at him until he drove it away with stones.

Haralambos reminded her that he was leaving to join his brothers in America as he had already planned before she became pregnant.

"Demetra, don't you have any more concern for me than that? Why would you cause me more trouble? You know that I am worried enough about you as it is without having to worry about a curse someone has placed on you."

Demetra thought as hard as she could but could think of no one who would want to hurt her.

Now she sighed, remembering that Haralambos had left for America two months ago, in her seventh month of pregnancy, leaving her in the care of his parents and his brother, John. She talked to herself as she made her way down the path behind the mule. "Haralambos will be so disappointed if the baby is female, and I do wish to please him." Looking up at the sky, she called out, "But please God, let it be healthy!"

That morning, like most mornings she had awakened before the rest of the family and stoked the fire and boiled some water. Then she made a hot tea from dandelion greens flavored with wild mint. After she drank her tea, she left for the fields, talked with her old friend Eleni on the way, and now was standing in the turned earth, still damp from the morning dew.

When she began to feel uncomfortable, she first thought that she simply needed to urinate. She looked around, and seeing that no one was close enough to see, she adjusted the folds of her skirt so they wouldn't get wet. Then she spread her legs under the cover of the skirt so she could stand there and relieve herself. This time she knew she was in trouble when she felt the hot gush of water that preceded a baby's birth. She immediately remembered the old women talking about the "dam breaking from the river of life."

By the time she retrieved the mule, which had wandered away, she was assaulted by the first severe pain. As she propelled herself forward, pulling the beast along, the pain increased. She stopped and gasped then, sucking air into her lungs screamed for Eleni.

Eleni heard her friend's panicked cry as she swept the dust from her cottage floor. As she rushed down the hill, she heard a second agonized scream. By the time she got to Demetra, her friend was down on her hands and knees, pounding the earth with her fists. Eleni rolled her onto her back, quickly examined her and was astonished to see the top of a baby's head beginning to appear. She quickly pulled Demetra to her feet and held her upright from the rear while pleading with her to push the baby out. It had been a matter of minutes from the time Demetra had her first labor pains to the moment that the squalling, bloody baby was caught by Eleni and gently placed on the ground, still attached to its mother by the birth cord. The tiny child lay on the ground with only her exhausted mother's kerchief protecting her from the soil. Demetra lay on her side and kept her eyes closed so the sweat pouring from her brow wouldn't wash dirt into them. She panted from the heat and her exertions asking, "Please, tell me—is it a boy or a girl?"

"Shush now before the Devil finds out about the baby being born and comes to steal its soul. Thank the Holy Mother for the birth and you will see, my love, that she is perfectly healthy," Eleni replied.

Eleni lifted the child so she could place her own kerchief under it, reached into her apron pocket, and pulled the knife from its sheath of bay leaves. The knife had been washed in holy water blessed by the priest, and kept for almost a year in the bay leaves that symbolized the rebirth of Christ. The umbilical cord was cut and tied. Ignoring Demetra's sobs, Eleni bent close to the baby's screwed-up face and spit at its eyes three times. The phlegm ran down the baby's cheeks as Eleni intoned the ancient words.

"Leave the child be, Oh Evil-Eyed One; she is blessed by Christ." Then making the sign of the cross, she turned to the mother, "There, there now, my golden soul, the baby is perfectly healthy. Even though she does not have a handle sticking out of her groin, she is beautiful. Your husband will understand that it was not your fault. You will have time to make a lot of sons for him." Eleni gave Demetra the baby to hold, on the pretext that she had to get some wash water. The after-birth had arrived, and Eleni wanted it buried quickly, before some wandering demons chanced upon it.

Demetra was one of those women who had been created by God to be a mother. She was born to embrace all babies and to hold them in awe. Any baby would do. It didn't have to be a human baby; it just had to be a baby, she would rush to protect and love it. The hens were always indignant when Demetra swooped down on their chicks to hold them and breathe into their staring, unblinking eyes. The ewes were amazed when Demetra shoved them aside to get to their lambs as they lay bleating in the fields. Once she had even attacked two male dogs who were raping a little female, even though she knew that the dog bitch was in estrus. Demetra had felt it was too young for such things.

Any fear of her husband was shunted aside as soon as Eleni placed the furious baby in Demetra's arms. As she stared at this proof of God's existence, Haralambos lost his position as the most important one in her life. Up to that moment she had been dedicated to provide for her husband's comfort. In a matter of minutes his role in her drama had changed. Now he was only one part of the "making of babies."

Eleni returned from the spring with a water pail made of the local clay. It was filled with the clear rich mineral water that flowed from the rocks around a shrine to the Virgin. She washed the little girl, who was furious at being thrust from her warm-water existence into one where icy cold water splashed at her. Demetra laughed at the balled-up fists and flailing feet as she cleaned herself with her friend's newly washed kerchief.

"This is the first time that I haven't missed her father. I don't care if he likes it or not, but his first child is a girl. I wouldn't swap her for a boy now that I have her. Come on, my friend, help me home so I can rest before I finish cooking the pot of lentil soup for dinner."

February of 1899 would mark the beginning of a new life for both Demetra and Haralambos. With her mother-in-law's help, the new mother washed and changed into the second of three dresses that she owned. The baby was cleaned and wrapped in a linen gown that had not changed in appearance from the swaddling clothes of infants during the times of Jesus of Bethlehem. The smell of lentil soup, flavored with bay leaves and vinegar, and the aroma of fresh bread filled the house. Her father-in-law tried to appear pleased at the baby's birth, but no matter how hard he tried, the disappointment that it was not a male child was apparent in his face. Demetra quickly spooned out a bowl of soup and placed a small bowl of good green olive oil next to his bread so he could dunk it in the oil before spooning the rich brown soup onto it.

"Come now, *Patéra*, eat your dinner. I will feed your new granddaughter. Perhaps we can name her Theodora, which, after all, means God's gift." Demetra crossed herself as she said that and looked up at heaven. "As soon as I heal and join Haralambos in America, we will begin again to find your grandson, who is surely waiting to be born amongst God's angels."

THEODORA

꜠꜠꜠꜠꜠꜠꜠꜠꜠꜠꜠꜠꜠꜠꜠꜠꜠꜠꜠꜠꜠꜠꜠꜠꜠꜠꜠꜠꜠

CHAPTER 14
DISILLUSIONMENT

That the emigrants learned how to read and write as well as speak a foreign language, is commendable; but the feat becomes remarkable considering that most of them never had more than four years of schooling in their native land. Many of them learned to read English more proficently than they could read and write in Greek.

꜠꜠꜠꜠꜠꜠꜠꜠꜠_____

Theodora was three years old when she finally met her father in America. Elias and James, her father's brothers, had emigrated to America in 1880. They managed to buy a small ramshackle produce farm in Franklin, Massachusetts. Haralambos, emigrated from Greece and joined his brothers in 1898. Elias and Haralambos worked the farm while James went to work in a grocery store.

Haralambos was waiting at the wharf when his wife and daughter disembarked from the ship at Ellis Island. Demetra bravely boarded the first train she had ever seen and watched spellbound as the landscape flashed past the windows as they headed for the farm.

Haralambos was unloading their trunks from the back of a neighbor's wagon when Elias first met his sister-in-law and his tiny, sickly looking niece. Elias and James had left Greece almost eighteen years earlier, long before their brother began courting his bride. The tiny nation, after years of subjugation, had not been able to provide any kind of an effective school system. Because the two brothers had only reached the third grade, neither knew how to read or write in

Greek as well as they could in English. When Elias had received a letter from Demetra explaining that she had married into the family, he kept it unopened for almost a month. The twelve-year-old nephew of a fellow-Greek read the letter to him. Elias reviewed the letter in his mind as he half-listened to their cries of greeting. He remembered that she had said: "Life is difficult for us here, and we are anxious to come to America. We need help. My husband is too proud to beg for assistance. I am only embarrassed." Elias sent the five-hundred dollars that was still needed so Demetra could book passage.

It was now spring in Massachusetts and during spring Elias' thoughts seemed to center around the rebirth of life and eventually to Easter. He always got homesick and lonely for family and Greece during Easter. The holiday was only a few months away, and this year he was going to spend it with family in his own house.

Demetra held Theodora forward, "Come now and give your uncle a kiss." The toddler, little more than three years old, seemed to hold back as she looked at the rough-faced, sun-darkened man who was wiping his forehead with a dirty blue neck cloth. She looked so helpless with her skinny legs wrapped in a heavy white blanket that drooped in wrinkled folds from her knees that he couldn't help falling in love with his niece. He held her up to his eye level then clasped her in a gentle hug, "Thank God for bringing you." The classical old country phrase brought a gasp of relief and a smile to Demetra's worried face. She rushed forward to hug and kiss this newfound family member herself.

"Praise to the Lord and thanks that we found you." As she hugged him, she softly spoke to him. "I swear to you that someday I will repay you for your kindness and my debt will be carried by my children."

Haralambos was a silent participant until they sat at the table that evening drinking the heavy and rich Greek coffee from Demetra's little porcelain cups. The delicate cups, along with the brass coffee pot, had been unpacked from the single steamer trunk.

"We have used all the money that we had, as well as the gold sovereigns that my wife had saved but never told me about...," were Haralambos' first words.

Demetra interrupted him, "Please husband, do not start that again. I was saving the money from my mother's dowry, as she did before me. That money has always been saved for the most severe emergencies. If my mother had used all her dowry for minor problems, the money would have been spent years and years ago. I did not mean any disrespect to you by not telling you of the money."

Elias interrupted, "Circumstances in this new country demand that we look at things differently. We must learn to adapt and to use any method that will solve problems. By the way, what happened to the land back in the old country? Who is going to look after all of the fields?"

Haralambos replied proudly, "When we decided that Demetra would come here, leaving the old folks with John, I remembered the old saying that a clever man, like myself, does not allow himself to be squeezed into a olive barrel where there is only one way out. I arranged to lease the dowry fields that came with Demetra to Fotis Bichikas' friend. The money he pays me for rent is to be put away so we can buy a return ticket home if I do not like this wonderful country, America."

When Demetra heard her husband's answer, she turned to Elias, "I had to promise this hero, this man of determination, that I would return to Greece if after a reasonable time he refused to stay here. He would not have let us come otherwise."

Elias crossed his thin legs so that they seemed to fold themselves into each other, hung his head as he studied his knees, and muttered, "I hope, little sister, that you do not live to regret that promise."

The families settled into a routine with Elias and Haralambos working together raising produce and hauling it into town where they sold the vegetables door to door.

One evening, almost two years later, after a particularly hot and muggy day, the little family sat on the front porch hoping to catch the cooling breath of a faint breeze that rustled the tops of the trees. Haralambos had fallen asleep sitting on a rocking chair with Theodora tucked into his lap, while Elias and Demetra reminisced. Elias fanned himself with a magazine featuring a front-page photograph of a Byzantine domed church with a white cross outlined by the blue waters surrounding the obviously Greek island. He spoke quietly, not wishing to disturb the sleeping Theodora. "I really love this new country of ours, but I do miss the old country. I miss the afternoon siestas and the easier-paced life. Life over there was more predictable."

"Remember in January, February, and March when there was little we could do on the farm except repair the house and cut firewood? We spent a lot of time in the *cafenion* with the other men. In late

March and early April, we weeded and got the grape vines ready and free of disease. Then we spent April and May plowing and planting the summer crops. By June and July we were through planting vegetables, but some of the hay and wheat crops had to be taken care of. Then, of course, in the summertime when it never rained, we had to haul water. Then it was harvest time in September and October and early November. We spent part of December getting ready for the winter and the Holy Days. We worked hard, but it seems as if life was more pleasant."

Demetra laughed as she responded, "More pleasant for you perhaps, but those two or three months like January, February, and part of December—when all you hard-working men had to do was to work at home for two or three hours a day and then go to the *cafenion*, were not so pleasant for us women. While you got a break from the routine, we still had to make babies, cook, clean, and wipe kids' bottoms and noses, and take care of our husbands as well! When it's time to get the crops in or take care of the animals, then we were expected to help you men do that, too!"

Demetra patted her swollen belly and continued, "Don't forget, we not only help you to make the babies, but we carry them inside of us, and then when it is time to bury them, we have to ..." She couldn't finish talking as she choked on the tears that filled her eyes and heart.

Haralambos awoke and spoke softly, so as not to wake the little girl snuggled into his lap. "There, there my love. God must have wanted the little girl Olga. That is why she died on the day she was born, and now we have filled your belly once more. This next one will be a son—you'll see. And we will have many more children in America."

What Demetra and her husband didn't know was that some of their children were destined to be born in Greece rather than in America.

The family managed to make a living raising and selling produce from the farm. At certain times of the year, they also purchased produce from the wholesale markets and then resold it. At first they sold their product from the back of a horse-drawn wagon. Haralambos enjoyed standing on the back as it slowly made its way through the streets. He would cry or semi-sing in a rich heavily accented voice "Tomaaaatoes. Cuuuuucumbers. Leeeeetuce."

The housewives would pop out of their houses to haggle with Elias about the price while Haralambos would eye them and strut as if he was the sole owner. Elias had to admit that the combination of his business sense and his brother's voice and boldness was good for their business. Soon, more often than not, they began to add to their product line by driving into town and buying produce and fruits at a wholesale market.

When Demetra's next baby was born, it was another girl. She was also named Olga, in honor of the girl baby that had died. Olga was also the name of the Queen of Greece.

Demetra writhed in pain at home for hours before Olga was born. Haralambos paced back and forth in the front yard, listening to the cries that shattered the stillness. Periodically he called to Theodora, telling her to ask the laboring woman how long it would be before his son was born. Finally, the frightened girl only pretended to go into the room where her mother moaned and cried. Theodora kept telling her father that the midwife was confident that it would not be much longer.

When Olga finally emerged, Demetra was the only one who celebrated. Theodora had to tell her father that he had failed again; he had not produced a son. His new baby was another female. Haralambos received the news in silence and walked off into the darkness, beyond the circle of light from the house.

When he returned, he went directly into the room where Demetra, now washed and dressed in a clean gown waited in bed with her new baby at her chest. Haralambos squinted into the half light and said, "It isn't your fault and it isn't my fault either. What is to be, is to be. I was so sure that we had a son. I am disappointed. But, no matter. Hurry and heal yourself so we can try again."

As he turned to walk out of the room, Demetra stopped him saying, "Please wait a minute. Don't you want to look at your daughter? Come! Look at her. See how pretty she is? I think she looks like your side of the family."

"I'll look later. Let's not wake her up now" was all he said before he walked out to the front door where Theodora waited to talk to someone.

Another year passed before Demetra finally produced a male child, setting off a fireworks-like celebration. The birth of a baby was the most important event to a family. The christening of the first male baby born in the United States was earth-shattering.

This baby was born in style. Demetra lay in her own bed, on brand new sheets that had been sprinkled with holy water. One of Elias' friend's sisters, skilled as a midwife, was hired to assist with the birth. Haralambos gladly made the long trip—thirty miles away—to bring her when the time came. Demetra's son was born after a long labor. Initially they thought the baby was turned sideways and stuck inside his mother's writhing body. The midwife admitted to the trauma-tized Haralambos that she might be forced to kill the baby before it could be removed.

Theodora was holding on to her mother's hand, wiping her fore-head with a clean wet cloth when her brother was finally born. She rushed to her father on the front porch and, standing with her hands on her hips and her legs spread wide, defiantly announced, "My mother has given you a son."

Haralambos wondered for a split second why she had said "My mother has given you a son" instead of the traditional "God has given you a son."

He choked back a sob, and in a breaking voice thanked her with all the dignity he could muster. But dignity ran a poor second to his need to celebrate. He uncorked a bottle of *Mavrodaphne* wine he had been saving for the occasion, gravely gave the first drink to his brother, and then, unable to contain himself any longer, threw his head back and shouted, "Hopa! I have a son!" before rushing in to look at the still-squalling baby. The baby boy was soon named Georgios (after Georgios Pappageorgios).

The old church located in the South End where most of the Greeks lived was called St. John's. The immigrants had settled in a ten-block area of tenement buildings, forming their own ghetto-like commu-nity. Prior to the baby's birth, Demetra had insisted on making the long trip to Boston at least once a month where she badgered the priest and lit white candles until the fathers, in exasperation, assured her that the next baby would be male. An icon of the Holy Mother and her baby hung over Demetra's bed illuminated by a vessel con-taining holy oil that was lit as soon as the sun set.

The christening day was supposed to be happy. It all had begun when the priest splashed the terrified baby for the third time and wiped his eyes with the blessed oil. The priest shuddered when the baby's godfather revealed the soon-to-be-baptized baby's name—Georgios Pappageorgios—for the first time. The priest had to intone the name and call upon Christ to accept the child and protect him from evil.

The priest studied the beaming father and wished again that the custom that prevented the mother from coming to the ceremony would change. It was customary for her to remain at home, waiting to hear the name that her child had been given at the baptism by the baby's godfather. One explanation for the custom was that if the child's name was announced before it was protected by Christ through the rite of baptism, it would make it easier for the Devil to find the baby. It was a foolish custom and the young priest was anxious to denounce it. He found it difficult to convince his flock that a name like Georgios Pappageorgios was not suitable in America. He thought he had convinced Demetra two months earlier when he told her, "All of the other ethnic people have adjusted by shortening their last names, so please talk to your husband about giving the baby an American name. It will make the child's life in America so much easier," he explained.

As soon as he read the note that announced the name the infant's godfather had given him, the priest knew that Demetra had been unsuccessful. He sighed as he confronted the father at the end of the ceremony, anticipating a difficult task.

"Congratulations, my son, you have brought your first male offspring into the hands of Christ. I beg you to teach him the ways of the Church as both his body and soul are in your hands."

The priest turned to the baby's godfather, "As you know, our Orthodox faith demands that the godfather truly accept the task of seeing that the child is raised properly in the event that the father does not fulfill his duty."

Both men were anxious to leave, now that their duty was done, so they could begin celebrating. They both made the sign of the cross as they promised the priest that they would indeed fulfill their duty.

"Before you leave this Church, you must sign the baptismal record, but first I want to speak to you. Please give the baby to my assistant. Come, sit in my office so we can talk."

Haralambos muttered, "I don't know what there is to talk about, but let's get it over with."

The new father and the baby's *nounó* (godfather) took seats on a couch facing the priest who sat in a straight-backed wooden chair.

"The name that you give this child today should be recorded exactly the same way at the mayor's office. The two records, the baptismal record and the birth certificate, should show the same name. The boy is going to spend the rest of his life in this country and he should have an American name. Georgios Pappageorgios is a Greek name, not an American name. I suggest that you shorten it. Let me record it as George Pappas.

Haralambos, confused, managed to stutter, "But his name is Georgios, not George. No one will know him. Pappas? What Pappas? You may not know it, but my father's father was a priest. We earned the right to be called Pappageorgios. Why should I change his name? I refuse to change my name just to make it easy for some stinking American. If I have to apologize or give him a phony name in order to register his birth, then I will not register him in your City Hall of Boston. Come! Fill out the baptism record as Georgios Pappageorgios so we can celebrate.

The baby never did get registered as being born, which was to create some serious problems in later years for the boy who grew up to be called George.

Demetra was furious when her posturing husband retold the story in front of all their guests. Elias calmed her as he said, "Come now, let us dance with the guests. Later after everyone has gone you can discuss the baby's name with your husband."

The visitors had scarcely left before Demetra confronted the tipsy Haralambos. The shouting ended when Haralambos finally agreed to give all future babies a real American name.

Haralambos and Elias continued working together despite the fact that they argued violently and constantly. The family lived together on the farm for almost five years before matters came to a head. After a particularly ferocious argument, which ended when Haralambos stalked off the farm, Elias had to face the distraught Demetra and explain what happened. "You are a good woman and your children are as close to me as if I had created them myself, but your husband and I are fighting all the time. I'm afraid the situation is now beyond repair. He has said some things, and so have I, that can not be retracted. Because we are brothers, we are bound together with our mother's milk. This bond is strong enough that after a suitable period we will become close again. In the meantime, he doesn't want to live here anymore. He believes he can get a job in the city somewhere.

I want you to know that you and the children don't have to leave. You can stay if you wish."

Crying, Demetra turned away from her brother-in-law, "I know that you have tried, and that he, in his own way, has tried also. But he is what he is. I married him, and we will stay together as long as he lives. I made a mistake by insisting that we all come to this country. It is all my fault, but we will do the best we can."

The growing family moved into a third-story flat on Spring Street just off Hanover Avenue. Haralambos worked at various jobs, in restaurants, and in grocery stores. But no matter how hard he tried, he could not keep a job. Demetra augmented their income by working in the boardinghouse located right next door. Single immigrant men—anywhere from thirty to thirty-five at any given time—stayed there until they became "Americanized" and then moved on.

Demetra cooked, washed dishes, made beds, and along with taking care of her own brood found time to wash the boarders' clothing. She washed other people's clothes by hand in the evenings after she had put her family to sleep. Even with the additional income, it was difficult to feed her growing family. Her husband spent more time looking for new jobs than he spent actually working. There were days when Demetra went to sleep without anything to eat except breakfast. She lost weight, and her eyes lost the luster and sparkle. Elias continued to visit them when he went to Boston and pleaded with her to curtail her activities, but she shook her head and continued working. She turned more and more to Theodora, who was now nine years old, for assistance.

Haralambos and Demetra went to the free clinics supervised and operated by the medical staff at Boston City Hospital. Doctors there managed to convince Haralambos that if something drastic wasn't done, Demetra would not survive.

James returned to Boston in response to Haralambos' plea for a family meeting. Haralambos insisted that they all go to church first. Going to church was a statement: The problem was serious. After the services, the three brothers sat at the table facing each other.

Haralambos spoke, "I must be truthful and say in all honesty that I have not been a bad man, but I have not been able to provide properly for my family. I suppose I could have done better; but in my own way, I have done the best I could. The fact is that I need help. The doctor has told me that if my wife continues to work this hard, she will die. We must return to Greece where we don't need as much money and where the farm is waiting for us."

James quietly stood up, and walked in a circle before he replied. "You need enough money to buy passage to Greece, and to build a house that is big enough for your family."

Elias spoke up, "I can provide the money for the boat fare home."

"Wait!" James interjected, "Let me offer a plan. We can send just the wife and the children back. They can live with their grandparents. Haralambos should stay here where he can work and make some money. If he gives me his money to manage, I will put it in the bank and invest it. Someday he will have enough money to build a new house in Kaparelli that will be big enough for the family, then Haralambos can rejoin his family. It shouldn't take more than a few years."

Elias protested. "I don't like to see him separated from the family, but you do make some sense, James. Later on we can sell the other house that our family owns. You know, the one next to the home our parents lived in originally. With everybody working together, we can get enough to build a bigger house on the corner of the property."

Demetra, sitting on the rocking chair in a corner, spoke, "May I say something? I am pleased that my husband's family has come to gether to solve his problem. I admit that I should not interfere in a discussion of this sort, when the men are deciding what must be done as opposed to what I, a woman, would prefer. Remember, however, that you are talking about my life and my children's lives. I will need to be convinced that what you three decide is the best for my children. If I'm not convinced, I don't care how sick they say I am, I'm not going."

Haralambos looked at her, shook his head in wonder, and turned back as Elias started to speak.

"I assume, Haralambos, that you will agree to the plan. James and I will provide the money so your family can return to Greece as soon as possible. It also makes sense for James to act as your banker and help you to save money. If Demetra agrees, then I am in favor of it also.

"I would like to discuss one thing though, and that is this: Theodora is too bright to be wasted in Greece. The family will be better off in the village; but as I said, I hate to see her return to Greece because she is very bright, loves school, and is doing very well here in America."

Haralambos protested, "The child is ten years old now, and she is strong as well as bright. Her mother needs her. She must return with her mother. Think how much she can help. She is my daughter. It is my place to decide what happens to her. She must return with the rest."

Elias argued until Haralambos finally compromised by agreeing to let Theodora go to school in Greece for as long as she wanted to.

James turned as if to ask Demetra for her opinion and was startled to see Theodora quietly rocking the chair in which an exhausted Demetra had fallen asleep. James held the lamp higher so he could get a better look at the hard expression on Theodora's face as she stared at her father.

The following day preparations were begun, mostly by Elias, for the family's return to Greece. In October of 1909, the family, without Haralambos, was once more firmly reestablished in the old homestead in the village of Kaparelli.

When they first arrived, Demetra was so tired that she didn't even want to stop at her home village, though they passed within a few kilometers. She had been anxious to return to Kaparelli. Old friends as well as relatives and fellow-villagers had volunteered to take the children into their own homes until Demetra recovered. Theodora stayed with her mother and the baby, Niko. Georgios moved in with the Bichikas family, four-year-old Litsa was taken in by the Orphanos clan, and Olga temporarily moved to the Fotopoulos home.

Demetra adjusted quickly to the slower, more secure lifestyle in the village where she was surrounded by old friends and memories. The clear dry air helped her gradually regain most of her strength and vitality.

It was difficult for the children, who had never known any life other than the excitement of America and life in the tenements, to adjust to the village lifestyle. Theodora described the wonders and the wealth of the new world while her listeners seethed with envy. Her audience of village youngsters included cousins and more distant relatives, who joined the others in secretly whispering that she must be lying and should be punished.

Theodora and Tasia

꒲꒲꒲꒲꒲꒲꒲꒲꒲꒲꒲꒲꒲꒲꒲꒲꒲꒲꒲꒲꒲꒲꒲꒲꒲꒲꒲꒲꒲꒲꒲꒲꒲꒲

CHAPTER 15

RETURN TO KAPARELLI

R ural Greece is separated into tiny parcels of land. Looking down on it from an airplane, it looks as if drunken spiders attempted to divide the earth into an impenetrable web. The lines of the web are crooked walls of rocks, which the people had been piling on top of each other for centuries. It doesn't matter how many rocks were stacked by thousands of men for centuries, there are always more rocks lying about.

꒲꒲꒲꒲꒲꒲꒲꒲

The scorpion crawled over the fingers of Theodora's hand as she lay on her sleeping rug in her grandfather's house. It still took her a few minutes to orient herself when she woke from a deep sleep. She could smell the wet skin of the animals and the not unpleasant smell of straw and wheat stalks. The animals in their stable under the house were moving about, anxious to get out into the fresh air. Her attention, though, now centered on the scorpion as it slowly continued on its own trip across the floor. She screamed, and instinctively thrust her hand upward, throwing the unsuspecting scorpion through the air and onto the middle of the floor.

Her mother had warned her of the little sword that it carried on the tip of its tail. Demetra had frightened her daughter with her words, "The only thing worse than a scorpion's bite is when a snake sinks its fangs into you. The scorpion is a cousin to the spider and the needle on the end of its tail can sew your eyes shut to make you blind. If it bites you in the foot, your whole foot will swell up and fill with pus.

We will have to make holes in the skin to let the pus escape. So, be very careful when you walk in the rocks or downstairs where the animals live."

The terrified Theodora wasn't sure she believed that the scorpion could make her blind, but she knew she didn't want holes poked into her hand.

Demetra, alarmed, called out, "Theodora what's wrong?" But her daughter was too frightened to answer. Demetra called out again, and waited for a response. The silence ended with a loud slam that vibrated on the slate floor. Georgios, Theodora's brother, had squashed the scorpion with a blackened cooking pan. He turned and grinned at her.

Demetra carefully stepped over the flattened corpse, gathered Theodora against her breast and whispered in her ear. "Everything is all right now. You are safe, my lovely." Theodora whimpered and tentatively reached toward the floor with her bare foot.

"Come now, Theodora, get up from there and watch your brothers and sister. The danger has passed," her grandmother called.

Georgios swaggered out the door as if killing a scorpion with the bottom of a cooking pan ranked equally with the slaying of a dragon. He left the oozing corpse for the women to clean up.

Georgios looked so much like Theodora's father that she was reminded of her secret. She was only eleven years old, but she already knew she truly disliked, maybe even hated, her father. Even though it was a sin, she had begun to dislike Haralambos the day she overheard the adults talking. The conversation revealed that he was responsible for the decision that resulted in her leaving school and the wonderful books to which she had been introduced in America.

Theodora was sorry she hadn't learned more in America. She had really struggled to learn the most basic of English words. She was fascinated by the books and tried to learn, quickly deciding that she wanted to be an American teacher. That dream ended abruptly when her mother confirmed that her father had decided the family should return to the destitute and hopeless existence they had escaped a few years earlier.

As soon as they had settled back into their old home, Demetra insisted that Theodora be enrolled in the village school. The teacher, a young man who had been sent to the village by the government only a year before, had not yet become completely frustrated.

Theodora rekindled the spark that had made him want to teach. At first the other children were awed and impressed with the stories that Theodora told over and over again. As she retold her tales of the wonders of America, she began to notice some children making faces and otherwise expressing their resentment of her. They nicknamed her "*Amerikaneetha.*"

The village of Kaparelli was situated on the main road that ran between the cities of Tripoli and Sparta. The road that had been the main link between the Peleponnesos and the cities of the state of Attica for many years, ran through the center of Kaparelli. As the importance of the cities changed, the fate of the villages fluctuated accordingly. Many years later, in the 1950s, Kaparelli, named in honor of a Turk hero, would be renamed Mantheria by the Greek government. Mantheria was the site of an important ancient battle reputed to have occurred somewhere close to Kaparelli's location. Though the cities and villages changed with the times, the road never seemed to change, except that it was constantly being improved or repaired.

Another custom never changed. No matter what government was in power, the responsibility to keep the road in repair was always the same. The people who lived nearest to the road were required to repair it. Despite the fact that the village had the obvious advantage of the main road running directly through it, Kaparelli never prospered. At its peak, only seven hundred people called it home. The community boasted no more than a school with seventy students and one teacher, four *cafenios*, and one large general store. The other towns within a five-mile radius had similar populations, but none were blessed or, as the case might be, cursed by having the road bisect the village.

The road, you see, presented a serious problem because the government insisted that local inhabitants repair the road where it passed through their town. Fortunately, the material to repair the road could be obtained locally where, like mushrooms, rocks seemed to grow out of the earth. The road was built, supported, and covered with rocks that had to be broken into small pieces. The village mayor appeared at the schoolhouse door one day and politely asked the teacher to convene the children.

"Children, we have just received the summons that we need to begin to assist in the repair of the road. School is canceled until the work is finished."

The astonished children, grateful that school would be suspended, cheered when they were certain the adults were out of sight. The next morning, Theodora and her classmates were each issued a two-pound hammer with a round knob on each end. The hammers were used to make gravel-size rocks out of bigger rocks. The older women as well as men were issued bigger hammers and shovels as well as rakes. For the better part of three weeks that year, all school was suspended while the villagers repaired the road.

Theodora wrapped her hands with burlap scraps from bags that had once been filled with lentils and fava beans. The sharp-edged pieces of granite had cut her hands so many times that the burlap was red instead of brown in places. Her hands never had a chance to become toughened with calluses and encrusted with dirt like her classmates. Pampered when she lived in America, she still had soft and sleek hands. They had been washed so often that they were as smooth and silky as a baby's bottom. Her classmates showed her no sympathy; the jealous girls tormented Theodora at every opportunity.

Theodora sobbed and winced every time she brought the hammer down, jarring her fingers and sending slivers of granite flying into the air. Her tormentors stopped picking on her when they saw that she would not stop the incessant smashing of rocks until everyone else did. Her eyes narrowed as she hit the last rock of the day. Then, refusing any offer of assistance, she made her way down past the school to the house where she lived.

The remnants of the original house formed one wall of a courtyard protecting stone ovens and a fire-pit used for cooking. The outhouse was about five feet away. The two doors, which identified the privy as a two-seater, faced the oven. Much of that house had been torn down and pieces of it had been incorporated into the new house in which they now lived. It consisted of three rooms, used mostly for sleeping, situated above the cellar where the animals were housed.

Theodora's baby brother Niko was almost three years old. As always, his green eyes followed her as she moved around the house. Her mother returned from visiting at her cousin Frank Bichikas's house on the other side of the narrow lane that wound down hill to the fields below. Frank came in with Demetra and Theodora's sister Olga, who was now seven years old. Poor Olga was always coughing and spitting up a milky phlegm, and was so thin you could almost see the bones in her chest move. Even though Olga never complained, Theodora knew that the coughing must really hurt her sister. The last time the government-sponsored visiting nurse had listened to Olga's chest, Theodora had overheard a weeping Demetra tell the nurse that Olga was spitting up blood. The nurse had asked a lot of questions, and Demetra had to explain again what the family had agreed should be done. Haralambos would remain behind in America where he had a better chance to find a job, so he could send money to the family relocated in Greece.

Haralambos finally did return to Greece toward the end of 1915, gravely ill and flat broke. He had suffered a mild stroke, and the American doctors feared that a more severe stroke might be imminent. Before he lost consciousness, he managed to shout that he feared he would never see his family again. When he regained his senses, he quickly decided that he wanted to recuperate in Greece. When Haralambos asked James for an accounting of the funds James had been saving for him, James' answer almost precipitated another stroke.

"I am sorry brother," James said, shaking his head sadly, "but the money is gone, or at least I don't have it now. I invested it along with my own funds, and things didn't go as I planned. But what I will do is give you all the cash I have. It is enough for your travel expenses. That is the best I can do right now."

The stroke had affected Haralambos' facial muscles, though the doctor's assured him that his condition would improve as he recovered. Haralambos arrived in Kaparelli with one side of his face twisted into such a snarl that both eyes were almost squeezed shut. Demetra took care of her husband almost as if he were an infant. After six months of constant care and hot facial compresses twice a day, accompanied by hours of her gently massaging of the muscles in his cheeks, the muscles finally relaxed and the ugly snarl-like expression disappeared. He exercised daily by working in the fields, something that he had avoided whenever he could in the past.

The climate seemed to help him regain strength—enough for him to begin making plans for his return to America. His self-confidence, however, suffered a mild setback when a surprisingly well-thought-out plan to make the average peasant's life easier, failed.

Haralambos needed to talk to someone about the failed plan, so he didn't object to buying the wine at the *cafenion,* to ensure that another cousin, Leo Georgeakilis, would hear him out.

"I was coming home after spending one whole day weeding the fava beans we had planted on the field that I got when I married Demetra. The day was very hot and I was tired. I had to ride on that damn donkey for four kilometers before I would get out of the dust. Then, when I remembered that the next day I would have to go out to the fields my mother was given as a *príka,* I realized how ridiculous the whole situation was. My family property, just like everybody else's around here, is scattered all over. To tell you the truth, I don't know how many hectares we own. I haven't totaled them up."

He poured more wine, "Let me tell you, that's not the way things are done in America. Just think about how much easier it would be if all my land were together. Then I wouldn't have to spend half a day just getting to a piece of dirt that may not be any more than half a hectare. Have you ever wondered how much of the total land available in Greece is taken up by rock walls?

"Anyway," Haralambos continued, "I spent a lot of time finding out who owned land next to mine, and, whether I owned land next to theirs. I was so excited about the possibilities that I couldn't wait to propose swapping so we could consolidate the land. It seems to make a lot of sense to me. Why wouldn't anyone jump to the opportunity to own three hectares of land in one place instead of in five different locations? I was even thinking that maybe I should go to Athens and get a big government job putting this plan into effect all over Greece.

"Oh, your glass is empty, let me fill it up for you, Leo," he said as he again poured wine into his cousin's glass. "But, these dumbbells, these peasants who have never left their village—not you, of course, but those stupids—they are too ignorant to understand even a simple idea like this. They accused me of being too much of an *Americano.* They are suspicious of me. Me! Haralambos Pappageorgios. Just because I spent a few years in America, they think I have become too wise for them and I have some kind of a scheme up my boots.

"Bah! The only way most of those stupids got any land at all is by selling and buying their women over the years. Here, have some more wine. The only thing that multiplies in this country any more is the stone walls and the number of hungry children. Bah! I'm going to go back to America where I can be appreciated. Here, cousin, take the last of the wine. I'm going home." Leo emptied the bottle and called out as Haralambos reached the door, "Thank you for the wine, cousin! Remember to come to the *cafenion* tomorrow night. We want you to discuss the international situation with us." Quietly he added, with a smile, "and buy the wine."

The main topic of discussion in the *cafenion* was the need for Greece to assert herself and regain what was generally accepted as her rightful territory. Thrace, Macedonia, and parts of Epirus were under Bulgarian control. The people of bordering Turkey, Austria, and Imperial Russia were beginning to arm themselves as the world seemed to be marching headlong into war.

Those in America, however, seemed unlikely to go to war. As James wrote to Haralambos:

> I wake up every morning thanking God that our brother John left Greece early enough to avoid conscription and is now living in Hopewell, Virginia, where he works in a gunpowder plant. The gunpowder business is very good nowadays and there is lots of work, which pays very well. I admit that the work is hard but also dangerous. That is the risk we have to take. In any event, we are doing what our sainted father wanted us to do. We are sticking together. John is now in a position to help you also, and he joins me in imploring you to come here as soon as you are feeling better, so we can all work together and get rich. The other reason you should hasten to make an ocean crossing is that everybody says that someday the world will go to war. America, of course, will not fight. Here we are too busy making gunpowder and guns.
>
> Please give my regards to your wife and family.
>
> Your older brother,
>
> James

〰〰〰〰〰〰〰〰_____ _____

The day after Haralambos agreed to return to America, Demetra admitted she was pregnant again. She was four months along before she found the courage to tell her husband. They had coupled quickly one night out by the well, with only the animals and the marvelous full moon that visits monthly as witnesses. The whole act had taken place so quickly that it just did not seem fair that such a serious implication would be the result.

Haralambos spun the worry beads with the blue tassels around his fingers, and sighed, "Why trouble trouble when you can't do anything about it?"

Later that evening, as he was wiping the green olive oil from the bottom of the bowl just emptied of greens, he and Demetra argued.

"Demetra, would you please make some sense and tell me why I should take Theodora back to America? She is now almost 17 years old and ready to marry."

"That is exactly why you must take her. The schoolmaster has told us many times how bright she is. Look at her! She is so beautiful that your heart stops when she smiles at you. Haven't you seen how these men around here stumble and almost fall down when she looks at them? I tell you that she has a future in America. She should not stay here and marry some poor dumb peasant. My heart will break because I'll miss her, but you must take her with you. My sister's daughter, Tasia, is going. The two girls can keep each other company until you get to Boston. Take her to Boston and then you go on to Virginia, make enough money, settle your business with Jimmy, and then send for us. I will have your next baby soon and someday we will all be together again."

The baby, Constandina, was born before Haralambos left once more for America. The delivery was difficult for the thirty-eight-year-old Demetra, causing Theodora to worry about her mother. She seemed to take ever so long to recover even from minor sicknesses. Theodora was entrusted to care for the baby while her mother slowly recovered. A week before she left for America, Theodora, carrying the baby in her arms, walked the entire way to her mother's village so that she could say good-bye to her grandmother.

"*Yiayiá*, you've been more than just a grandmother to me," she told the old woman. "You're one of my best friends and I do so hate to leave you. I won't be able to find anyone else who will give me honest answers when I ask secret questions. I'm worried about leaving my mother, too. Since Olga died, Mother hasn't been as strong as she used to be. Then she had such a hard time with Dina, and Dina is so small and helpless that I think she is going to be sick a lot, just like

Olga! Maybe I shouldn't go to America. Maybe I should wait until next year. *Yiayiá,* my thoughts are upside down. Tell me what you think. *Yiayiá,* what should I do?"

Yiayiá, Demetra's mother, sat facing her favorite granddaughter, who was helping her peel the skin from a pile of shallots so they could be marinated in olive oil and garlic. The baby Constandina (Dina) was awake and searching for the old lady's honey-covered finger that she had been sucking on just a moment ago. "What you should do, my 'heart love,' is to go to America. I know your mother better than anyone else in the world. Whose milk did she drink? Who carried her in a nice warm belly for nine months? I know what will make her very unhappy and break her heart. The worst thing you can do is to rob her of the one thing she desires most in all this world—for all of her children to prosper in good health. You can't stay here. You must go so that she can boast to the women about her beautiful and intelligent daughter in America who is married to a rich and handsome man."

Theodora would never forget the smell of the flowers intermingled with the smells of wild oregano and mint blowing over the golden patches of wheat as she walked back home after saying good-bye. No matter how much she wanted to return to America, her village and Greece would always claim her soul.

လၟလၟလၟလၟလၟ

She said a quick prayer as she watched her tearful family getting smaller in the distance. Her mother, brothers George and Niko, sister Litsa holding their new baby sister Constandina—all waved goodbye.

The three travelers—Haralambos, Theodora, and Tasia—left Piraeus on a cold, windy day in 1916.

Theodora

꙰꙰꙰꙰꙰꙰꙰꙰꙰꙰꙰꙰꙰꙰꙰꙰꙰꙰꙰꙰꙰꙰꙰꙰꙰꙰꙰꙰꙰꙰꙰꙰꙰꙰꙰꙰꙰꙰

CHAPTER 16
RETURN TO AMERICA

The world was changing rapidly—populations drifting from one land to another as the immigrants tried to escape the results of war and poverty. The greatest changes took place in the churches, as the congregations demanded that their places of worship become more open and receptive to their needs. The churches accepted social responsibilities for their flock and instituted programs reflecting their role.

꙰꙰꙰꙰꙰꙰꙰꙰꙰

The first World War was underway, innocent people were being killed, and Theodora did not care. Her main concern at the moment was how to get past the long-haired, gypsy-looking seaman in the narrow, pitching corridor. In order to get some air, she had left her companion in the tiny sleeping area they had been assigned. She made her way as far as the second deck and could smell the sea air. The spiraling ladder led to the narrow hall from which she could just glimpse the blue and white painted post to which the lifeboats were attached.

The seaman catapulted into the doorway as the ship lurched. He smiled when he saw her and stood stock still, his back to the wall, and waved her forward. For her to pass him, she would have to squeeze between his lower body parts and the opposite wall. Theodora hesitated and for a moment almost turned back. With a shake of her head that caused her still blondish-brown hair to fly in front of her eyes, she gritted her teeth and forged ahead. At the last minute, she turned toward the sailor so that she faced him as she squeezed by. Her nose came up to his chin; she had to tilt her head upward so she could stare into his eyes.

At first he could not believe that he was going to be so lucky. He had his eyes on her ever since they had left port. True, she was a little skinny for his taste, but she was a pretty thing and her blouses always bulged nicely. Here she was turning to squeeze past him face to face, and her stomach would have to brush against his. He thought all he would get was a little rubbing of his crotch against her buttocks if she turned to the wall to pass him.

Then, the grinning sailor noticed her eyes. They were not frightened. They glared at him as if she were daring him to attack her. As she went by, she turned her head ever so slightly so that she kept looking directly into his eyes. She was past him before he realized it. Instinctively he reached forward to regain his prey before it escaped. When his hand barely grasped her shoulder, she turned quickly and hissed at him like an angry cat. He reacted as if he had placed his hand on a hot oven. She was not just angry; she was furious. Even though all her vision and hearing functions continued to work and send their messages to her brain, she simply lost control. She acted without thinking; nothing registered.

It all passed in a matter of seconds. Theodora was four steps beyond the seaman before she realized that she was safe. By then she was on deck with the cool wind blowing her hair back behind her ears, cooling her neck. She bent over the rail looking into the blackness and wondered again, why in moments of stress did the power to think seem to leave her? She always seemed to win confrontations, but she knew that some day would be different. She remembered the old proverb: "Words said in anger are like the stones that are thrown into the sea. Any fool can throw a stone into the sea, but once done even a dozen wise men can not recover it." But for now, she reminded herself, she had won again. If that was what she had to do to protect herself and get her own way, well, so be it.

Theodora thanked the Holy Mother once again for assisting her in getting out of Greece, especially at this time. It seemed as if the whole world would soon be killing each other. It was 1917 and the armies, from what she'd heard, were maneuvering to see who could kill the most people. Thank God that her brother George was still too young to be drafted into the King's Army. She said another prayer to the stars that popped in and out behind the blackened clouds, turned, and, after looking to see if the way was clear, made her way back to the cabin.

Two days later their ship arrived in New York harbor. They disembarked at Ellis Island and joined the throng facing the frightening process required of all immigrants. Her father had not forgotten all the English words he had learned, but it was Theodora who took control and guided the trio through the maze of official documents. She was at first intimidated by the arrogant and rude behavior of the clerks and petty inspectors. Then an Irish youth dressed in a dirty white smock shoved the hose of the hand-held delousing spray pump down the front of her blouse, scratching her in the process. She got into trouble when she slapped his round face beneath his mop of red hair. A harassed interpreter from Macedonia questioned her until the officials were satisfied that her outburst of violence did not indicate a mental disability.

Her uncle Elias, whom she called *Baba Lia*, met them at the huge doors that led out to the mythical golden streets of New York. He was not as tall as she had remembered him, and his mustache was beginning to get scraggly. He threw the hand-rolled cigarette to the ground and grasped his brother's hand.

"Thank God you have arrived safe and sound, brother! Let me look at you. A little heavier perhaps, but you look good to me." His eyes filled and then overflowed as he held his brother for the first time in years. His fedora was pushed off his head as he hugged and kissed Tasia, too overcome to speak. Everyone started to talk and cry and laugh at the same time, forming a small circle of noise and love.

Theodora picked at her uncle's sleeve and said in a tiny voice, "*Baba Lia*, I am glad to see you also." He looked at the young girl standing before him with her great eyes shining at him and tried to remember the eight-year-old tot she was when he had last seen her.

"Oh, my love, I did not recognize you. You are such a lady now! Kiss me and let me welcome you to the United States once again. Come! Let's go. We need to get to Boston and begin our new life."

They took the train from New York to Boston. Then they got onto one of the new electric trolley cars, which deposited them only a block from their new home on the third floor of a tenement buildings on Harrison Avenue. The very next day the new family went to St. John's Orthodox Church and thanked God for their safe deliverance.

Theodora lit an extra candle and prostrated herself before the icon of her patron saint, Theodora, and whispered, "Please listen to my prayers: allow me to have a fulfilling life, and please protect my mother and brothers and sisters. If you do all this for me, I promise that I will dedicate my life to helping them all come to this country where we can live happily as a family and we will do honor to your memory and name. Help me find a husband who will be kind to me, allow me to have healthy children, and help me become a good woman. I have promised my brother George that I will help him to come here to America, so please, Oh Sainted One, assist me to do that before he gets old enough to have to go to war."

Her cousin was surprised when Theodora turned her body by spinning on her knees and moved forward, almost hopping on her knees to do so. She half-crawled to the life-size icon of the Virgin Mother and repeated her prayer almost word for word. Later, when they were alone in their new home, Tasia asked, "Theodora, why did you move over on your knees to the Holy Mother after you had committed to Saint Theodora?"

The young girl smiled, giggled, and flashed her palms upward as she replied, "Well, I learned that Saint Theodora helped discover the cross that Jesus had been transfixed on, but I am not sure that was enough for her to become a real saint. She was also the wife of the Byzantine Emperor, Justinian. It is possible that she is not all that holy, but it was her husband who convinced the Church to make her a Saint. Just to be sure, I also spoke to the Virgin. I am sure that *she* can help me."

Tasia shook her head and hugged the mischievous girl. "Ah, Theodora, you are even trying to trick and maneuver the saints for your own benefit! Sooner or later even the fox gets confused because it out-thinks itself. But come on, let's try to understand how this stove works so we can cook dinner."

With the help of Greek women who had immigrated earlier from the Peloponnesian Peninsula, the two soon were involved in the transplanted Hellenic culture. There were even a few enterprising families who, having been grocery store owners in their villages, had opened similar stores to sell the traditional foods to their countrymen. The obstacles that had to be overcome before these markets could be opened were monumental, the least of which was arranging for the shipment of ethnic foods from Greece to America. The Greeks knew who the wholesalers were and where the products could be purchased in Greece, but to arrange for import licenses, letters of credit, and the like was beyond them. The centuries-old tradition of turning to the international businessman, the Jewish money broker, was the answer. Once the chain was established, it wasn't long before the transplanted Greek was able to relieve some of the pain of homesickness by filling his plate with edible reminders of the old country.

Baba Lia introduced them to a lady he described as his second cousin and asked both girls to consider her their aunt Jenny. Tasia did not go with them when the two men, Jenny, and Theodora went shopping at one of these transplanted Greek markets. The market was located in Eggleston Square on Washington Street. Like most squares in Boston, Eggleston Square was not square shaped, and unlike most squares did not possess a rotary around which all traffic flowed. It was rather a crossroad where three streets intersected, the major one being Washington Street. The square was soon to be covered with the overhead engineering miracle that would support the tracks on which elevated electric trains would run.

The Greek market owned by brothers Stavros and Paul Anastos was in a corner building on the first floor. Three large windows displayed their wares. The window to the right of the door formed the beginning of the right-hand side of the store's wall. Baskets of dried beans and open baskets of yellow currants beckoned to passersby. A yellowed poster that once had been taped to the window depicted a Greek Evzone standing in front of the Acropolis. A skinny brown cat with yellow eyes lay crossways on the fallen poster, watching the people who walked by.

The other two windows displayed cheap, Greek-looking vases and cans of olive oil among round blocks of cheese covered with white cheesecloth. The front door had been propped open even though it was chilly. The meat counter and the cutting room where the lambs, goats, and occasional pigs were butchered stood at the rear of the store behind a glass counter. The refrigeration was a large walk-in cooler with a wooden window that could be opened in the wintertime to let the cold air in. It had recently been modernized. It could be kept cold with electric motors as well as ice.

Stavros always faced the front door and greeted customers while he cut the various animals into sellable pieces. Barrels of black *Kalamata* olives, green garlic olives, as well as some of the more

191

wrinkled black olives favored by the Italians, lined one side of the aisle. The other aisle was cordoned off by barrels of Greek cheese in its own brine. Some of the barrels were open, displaying a large piece of cheese just barely covered with brine. A knife handle protruded from the white cheese so prospective buyers could sample it. Tins of *baklavá* and *loukóúmia*, the white sugary candies from the shores of Asia Minor, shared a few shelves with jams made from rose petals. To get to the order counter, a person had to sidestep dried apricots and figs as well as wooden boxes of garlic buds.

The order counter was partly obscured by the bunches of mint, oregano, rosemary, and dill that either lay on the top shelf or hung from the overhead racks. The spices were kept on a wooden shelf to the right of the fig boxes and were stored in little brown paper bags. Garlic, cinnamon, cumin, rosemary, dill, cardamom, thyme, oregano, parsley, and many more spices filled the air with pungent aroma. In a corner of the display window in front of the meat rack, where jars of grape leaves, pickled onions, pickled pig's feet, smoked garlic-flavored mackerel lay ready for sale, a sign handwritten in Greek advertised "Mrs. Anastos' Filo Dough." The floor was covered with sawdust, but Theodora noticed that it was clean; there weren't little pieces of debris mixed in with the curls of pine wood.

As she stood in the middle of the aisle looking all ways at the same time, she inhaled all the delicious smells. The flavor of cheeses mixed in with the familiar spices were washed by the sweet oily garlic odors coming from the olive barrels. She inhaled again and suddenly became so homesick that she started to cry. Not large gasping gulps preceded by tears and wails, but little whimpers that were washed by tears trickling in a stream down her cheeks.

"*Hérete!*" The proprietor boomed the Greek word for "Welcome" from the cutting table, "Come! Come in! We are pleased to meet you."

He came around the corner of the display case with his hand outstretched. He had just wiped it with a towel that hung from the cord of his white butcher's apron. Of medium height and just beginning to show signs of flab, the butcher had pale blue eyes permanently crinkled at the corners, evidence that he smiled a lot. He was almost bald, with a fringe of white hair encircling his shiny forehead like an inverted horseshoe.

He introduced himself. "My name is Stavros Anastos. My brother and I own the market. Our home in the old country was in Megala. That is the birthplace of Byzantos, the first architect of the Byzantine style. He was born a meter or two from my father's house." Stavros had surmised long ago that the best way to get new arrivals to relax was to give them an opportunity to talk about their hometown, or *horió*. It worked again, as Haralambos smiled.

"My name is Haralambos Pappageorgio. This is my older brother Elias, his cousin Jenny; and my daughter Theodora. We are from Kaparelli, a sleepy little village just outside of Tripoli. The only exciting thing that ever happened there was when my *katsíka* (female goat) gave birth to three kids."

The store owner laughed without restraint, as he sucked in additional air.

"I'll bet the boys in the village thought it a sad event when this little beauty announced that she would be leaving them for America," the proprietor smiled at Theodora and almost patted her on the head. Instead, he hesitated for a second then held out his hand in a tender handshake. He wondered briefly why he had not patted her head, then decided it was the look in her eyes. He quickly brought his thoughts back to the business of selling food.

Coincidentally, *Baba Lia* was not going to give up this opportunity to enlarge his circle of friends and contacts. He was painfully aware that Theodora needed to make some friends her own age since she, at almost eighteen, was rapidly approaching the marrying age.

"Thank you so much for such a pleasant greeting. It is true that we look like brand new immigrants, but we have been in America for a while. As a matter of fact, I have been here in this wonderful country for many years. I am a citizen already," Elias said proudly. "We have property in Franklin, though I admit it is not much. Like you, we are also business people. My family will be living close by, and I am eager for my little niece to meet some people her own age. My concern is that she will get bored too soon. She went to school in Greece for seven years and was considered the smartest girl who ever went to school in the village."

At this point Jenny interrupted, "Not only the smartest girl but also smarter than any of the boys who had ever gone to school there."

"Well, well. I understand that we have an exceptional person here, and see how pretty she blushes, too. I better take advantage of this situation right now or my sister will hate me for life." Stavros went to the front door and called out.

"Stephanos, come in here for a minute. I want you to meet someone."

A tall curly-haired, brown-eyed young man came around the corner window where the cat was now sleeping. He was wearing a soiled apron and holding a dripping-wet straw broom in his hand. He had been scrubbing the sidewalk for Stavros, who always had the sidewalk washed after a delivery of meat took place.

"Please, my new friends, I want you to meet my nephew. He is my sister's son. They have been here living with me ever since his father died, God rest his soul." He crossed himself, forming the four points of the cross by touching his right shoulder before his left."

"Stephanos, this is the Pappageorgio family and they come from the Peloponnesos in the province of Arcadia. As you know, people from that region are famous for their friendliness and hospitality. Since we are lucky enough now to act as hosts, would you be kind enough to tell little Theodora about the church and the young people's activities while we older folks take care of the business of shopping?"

"Wait a minute," Haralambos interjected, "It would not be proper for a young boy and my daughter to go anywhere in private. I must insist that the two must stay where we can properly observe them."

"Oh, stop being such a tyrant. The two can sit over there by the fava beans and visit with each other. For the love of God, haven't you noticed that all this time she hasn't said one word?" Jenny said indignantly as she gently turned the young girl toward the designated area.

Stephanos hesitated for a moment then spoke to Theodora, "I would much rather talk to you than sweep the floor. If you would like, I will be pleased to visit with you."

Jenny was jolted when the aggressive, outspoken girl almost simpered her reply. "I think it would be very nice if you would take the time to help me get accustomed to this strange place."

Baba Lia smiled and tipped his fedora up over his eyebrows, "Come on, Jenny, she will be fine." Under his breath he muttered, "He is the one who needs help now."

Theodora turned just as she reached the burlap sacks of fava beans that were lined up just below the window and hopped upward. It was the same motion she had used to jump onto the back of Katerina, her donkey, back in the village. Stephanos surprised her when he said, "I have not seen any girl jump up like that since we were home and my sisters were riding the donkey to the fields." They both giggled even though Theodora turned bright red with embarrassment as she quickly tucked her legs under her. She still was wearing long white cotton stockings that reached up under her dress to her knees.

Stephanos said, "Everything here is different. Even the churches are different. Remember how dark and mysterious the churches are in the old country? Well, here the churches are so brightly lit that I feel as if I am involved in the whole thing. I don't feel guilty if I look at a girl in church, I know it's not a sin to be distracted from prayers because in this country the women sit on the same side as the men. Here, a family—children, men, and women—all sit together.

"My uncle is involved with planning the construction of a new church. It will be a cathedral. They are going to build it close to Huntington Avenue. That is a rich neighborhood, you know, and it will be called the Greek Orthodox Cathedral of the Annunciation. Believe me, it will be a wonderful building. When the Irish and the other Catholics see it, they will know we are as good as they are."

Stephanos continued, almost drawing a picture in the air with his hands. "The cathedral roof will be covered with a golden dome. There will be Doric Pillars just like the old temples in Greece on each side of an entry-way, above a wide series of concrete stairs that will lead to a huge carved double door. The main lobby of the church will be huge, with two marble staircases that will end at a balcony overlooking the main church hall. The altar will be centered between life-sized icons of saints that were donated by the biggest contributors to the church."

He hesitated then whispered, "This is a secret, but I know that the center space is assigned to St. George. I saw the drawing of the icon. It shows St. George battling a dragon to the right of the altar where the flickering light from the candle flames will give a special glow to the halo around his head. The locations of the Icons are planned to be highlighted by the filtered light, which will flow in from the leaded glass windows on both sides of the Church. Jesus and his twelve Apostles will look down from the vaulted ceiling as the smoke from the incense and the chanting of the priests slowly rises upward in shimmering waves. On Sundays, the choir will be dressed in white robes, sort of half hidden on the right-hand side of the altar. Just like in Greece, they will faithfully raise their voices in response to the Cantor's demands. There will be a great hand-carved wooden chair especially for the Bishop when he comes to visit."

Theodora was spellbound, awed by young Stephanos' elaborate description.

"Until the building is complete," he continued, "the administrative offices and baptism ceremonies will be held in the basement level. My uncle met with the Bishop and he said, 'It will be more than just a Cathedral for the Greek Orthodox Church in America. It will truly be an expression of faith by the community and a statement that the Church will survive in this new land and will prosper.'"

"Tell me about the special meetings that they have for young people on Sundays after church services," Theodora said.

Stephanos hesitated for a second, as if gathering his thoughts. "Well, some of the more progressive businessmen, the ones who understand how important it is for us young Greeks to get indoctrinated into the new ways, have arranged for us to get together on Sundays. The priest wanted us to gather on a weekday since the Church is so crowded on Sundays. Nowadays, we have a wedding and at least one christening every Sunday. He has to visit the sick and dying as well as hold memorial services to honor the dead. Of course, the businessmen would not agree to weekdays, because they don't want to have to give their nephews and sons the day or evenings off from their work. In any event, we are going to meet again this Sunday afternoon. We are going to review the names of the American Presidents to help us when we apply for citizenship someday.

"There is a lot to learn," he said, giving Theodora a look of warning. "We have a teacher who helps us learn how to speak English. There is a man named Paul Pappas who owns some restaurants. He lectures on American cooking. We tried to have someone teach us how to dance American style, but the priest would not stand for that. Once a month we have a thing they call a 'social' and all of us young people go and meet each other. We dance Greek and have a good time."

Theodora could not help but ask, "Do only the young people go? Do the mothers let the girls dance with boys without being there to watch them?"

"Oh, the old ones come all right. We haven't got rid of them yet.

They sit on chairs around the walls of the hall and visit with each other while they crochet and make believe they are not watching us. They think we don't know, but they are trying to arrange marriages all the time. You know, here in America many people get married because they love each other, and not just because their parents arranged it. Even though they won't admit it, little by little the old ones are losing their power to make us marry by arrangement. It's not like in the old country, where even the girl's brothers sometime still make the arrangements."

Theodora's eye grew wide and shining as she listened.

"I could never do that," Stephanos continued. "I have already told my sisters that I, for one, will not interfere in their lives."

Theodora bounced on her bottom, clapped her hands, and said, "Good for you, Stephanos! I'm happy to hear that you are more reasonable than most men. I never understood why a brother should be considered more capable of picking his sister's husband than she was. I would not want to disobey my father, of course, but I still do not want him to pick out my husband. I will do that for myself!" she announced with confidence.

The two young people talked for another half hour. The adults seemed to have forgotten them. Stavros was kept busy trying to answer all of Jenny's questions, which at first puzzled Elias. Jenny, who always seemed so sensible, kept asking the same questions differently. He finally figured out that she wanted Theodora to have time to get acquainted with the handsome young Stephanos.

A particularly loud laugh from the corner where the two young people sat caused Jenny to turn her head quickly toward the noise. Haralambos was too busy trying to impress Stavros to pay attention to his daughter. Before the day ended, Theodora and Jenny had agreed to go to the baptism of Stephanos' newest nephew on the coming Sunday. Haralambos also reluctantly agreed to let Theodora attend the "Young People's Society" meeting on the same Sunday—as long as Tasia and Jenny went along.

The family left the market, their arms full of paper bags. Theodora carried a tin of *halvá*, the Turkish candy that Stavros had given them as a gift. Stephanos helped them carry the bags as far as the streetcar stop, which he identified for Theodora.

"Here in America everything is marked with signs. When you come here, just look for the sign that says Dudley Street. See, it is the little green sign with the white trim. I know you can not be expected to read the words yet, but ... "

She interrupted him by murmuring something about how smart he was. Baba Lia watched his niece as she continued to captivate the poor boy.

"Where did she learn all those tricks?" he whispered to Jenny, who walked beside him.

The baptism and Young People's Society meeting took place as planned, and Theodora was soon absorbed into the activities of the young immigrants. Theodora was hired as a stitch-puller at the Green Shoe Manufacturing Company, a factory located in a three-story warehouse on Harrison Avenue. Stephanos told her that he thought the market owned by the Anastos family had originally been financed by the Jewish owners of the Green Shoe Manufacturing Company. He believed their last name was Greenberg, but he wasn't sure.

One of the first friends Theodora made while working was a young and cheery, but shy Greek girl named Helen. Even though the two girls didn't know it yet, their lives would be intertwined for many years to come.

Haralambos made plans to move to Virginia to work in the gunpowder plant. His departure had been delayed because he kept insisting that Theodora leave Boston and go with him. He told anyone who would listen: "It is every family member's duty to work and help the father make money, and that means girls as well as boys." But his own daughter stubbornly refused to go, insisting that she could work in Boston just as well as Virginia. Haralambos, concerned about her apparent friendship with Stephanos Tampas, was scornful when he learned that the Tampases had Americanized their name and shortened it from Tampasoukas.

Finally James wrote that it might be impossible to get Haralambos a job in the gunpowder factory unless he got there soon. Haralambos, unable to delay leaving any longer, lectured to Theodora that even in America, she could not get married without his permission. He made Jenny promise that he would be contacted at once if Theodora didn't behave properly.

The next few months passed quickly for Theodora. She was so deeply in love that she ignored Jenny's warnings about the violent temper that Stephanos seemed barely able to keep under control.

It wasn't long before Stephanos asked *Baba Lia* to write to Haralambos for permission to post the traditional banns in Church. Elias refused and tried in vain to explain his reasons to Theodora.

"It is impossible for me to do as you wish," he said, raising his opened palms. "Even if I was convinced that Stephanos is the right person for you to marry, I could not assist you in defying your father. I'm his brother, and as his brother I have to support him. That is the way we have lived. The father makes the rules. Because of his advanced years and wisdom, he is best suited to make the decisions for his children, especially the females, for as long as he lives. You must do as he says."

Theodora angrily replied, "I thought you were my friend. I can't believe that you won't help me, and that you would be so old-fashioned. Do whatever you want, but don't think that I'll forget that you wouldn't support me."

Jenny intervened, finally getting him to agree to write his brother, tell him what Theodora wanted to do, and ask for instructions.

When the return letter arrived, an anxious Elias held his breath, opened it, and read.

> Dear Elias,
>
> No! I insist that you put her on the first train to Virginia.
> I will discuss it with her when she gets here.
>
> Your brother,
>
> Haralambos

Jenny and Theodora

CHAPTER 17

MARRIAGE AND DIVORCE

Tasia and Theodora struggled with their suitcases as they carefully negotiated the narrow soot-slippery stairs from the train to the platform. The conductor offered to help, hoping for a tip, but backed off when Theodora gave him a haughty look.

Haralambos and James, sweating in the humid Virginia heat, walked stiffly toward the two girls. Tasia spoke carefully, almost whispering, to her cousin. "Theo, remember to control yourself. Wait a while before you fight with your father."

Then she spoke loudly to the two men, "*Hérete*, Uncle Jim, Uncle Haralambos! What a pleasure it is to see you."

"*Hérete*, Ladies, we are pleased to see you also. Here! Give me your bag. Let me carry it for you," James said to Tasia.

Haralambos reached for Theodora's bag, but she lurched forward, holding the suitcase as tightly as she could. "Never mind," she told her father, "I don't want your help. I can carry my own bag."

Grimly, he caught the suitcase by the carrying strap, tugging at it while she held on with both hands. The tug-of-war lasted for a few seconds, then Haralambos got it away from her. Holding the suitcase in his left hand, as far away from her as he could, he pushed her forward with his right hand. "That's enough of that," he ordered. "It is time you learned again that it's not your place to refuse me."

James and Tasia talked about how long it would be before Tasia had to return to Boston. Then they discussed the weather and anything else they could think of, all the while trying to involve either of the two angry people in conversation. Neither Theodora nor her father said a word, or looked at each other as James led the way home.

Later that evening, Haralambos sat in the cramped kitchen of the two bedroom flat that he and James shared. He stared at Theodora, who stood with her back to the metal sink.

"It is your duty to help me provide for your brothers and sisters. I can't save enough money without your help. I wouldn't have to explain all of this if I had been lucky enough to have a son instead of a daughter for my firstborn."

"Don't try to make me believe that it's my fault I was born first," Theodora retorted. "You know I would work in Boston and send you whatever money I could. That's not why you insisted that I come to this stinky Virginia and you know it. You didn't want me to marry Stephanos. You want me here to cook and wash for you after I get through working all day. I am not going to be a slave for you the way my mother was. This is America, not Greece. And it's 1918. Times are changing. I have my own life to live," Theodora stopped, only because she had to breathe.

Haralambos leaped from his chair and grabbed her by both shoulders, shaking her hard enough to make her head flop up and down.

"Quiet!" he shouted. "The only reason you have any life to live, never mind your own life, is because I gave it to you. I don't care if we are in Greece or not; you still belong to me and have to do as I say. Forget about marrying Stephanos or anybody else until I say so. You're going to work in your Uncle Jimmy's grocery store starting tomorrow. I will take you there when I go to work in the morning. And when I'm through working for the day, I'll pick you up and we'll go home. What little salary you earn will be paid to me. I will deduct room and board from it and keep the rest for you unless I need it to send to the village. We will both go to church on Sundays, and until you learn proper respect for me and my wishes, we will go straight home afterwards. Don't you think about going anywhere or to any of the church socials unless you ask my permission first."

"You're crazy if you think I am going to ask you for permission every time I turn around. I haven't asked you for anything for a long time. You may be able to control me until I become older, but you won't be able to do it forever. I would rather not do anything than have to ask you for a favor. I will never ask you for another thing as long as I live, never mind my asking you for permission."

"By God," he thundered, "You'll do as I say or I'll get the immigration people and send you back to Greece."

Tasia stayed in Virginia with one of her father's cousins for a month, and before she left agreed to be the conduit so Stephanos and Theodora could write to each other.

Two years passed, and Theodora was almost twenty when she started attending citizenship classes. She learned rapidly and, once she was certain of her newfound rights, reminded her father that he couldn't have her deported.

"In this country people are viewed as being able to provide for themselves once they become eighteen. You can't send me back to Greece; the law won't let you do that anymore. Give me whatever there is left of the money I have earned. I am going back to Boston."

"Bah! Go wherever you want. I'm sick and tired of you walking around with a face as long as my foot. It's no fun having you around anyhow. You haven't said more than ten words to me in a month. How could you be so stubborn? As far as your money—well there isn't any. I used it to buy you food and clothing. So go wherever you want, but don't expect anything from me!"

Two years later Theodora held up her right hand, renouncing her Greek citizenship and swearing allegiance to the United States of America. The little Hungarian boy standing behind Theodora held tightly onto his mother's hand. As he stooped to scratch his ankle, he looked questioningly at Theodora's left hand, which she had hidden behind her back with her fingers crossed.

Theodora was almost twenty-two when she married Stephanos in Boston, in spite of objections from Stephanos's family as well as her own. They were married in the Orthodox church, though the wedding was a relatively quiet scaled-down version with only a few celebrants. Someone mentioned that they were surprised that *Baba Lia* and other family members living in Boston didn't attend. Overhearing the comment, Theodora said, "They didn't come because I didn't invite them."

Theodora read Demetra's letters (penned by her brother Georgios) time and time again. Demetra blessed her daughter's wedding, sent her love, and, in spite of her husband's written instructions, defended and supported Theodora. The newlyweds rented a second-floor, two-bedroom apartment and set up housekeeping. They eagerly joined in any social activities that promised the dancing and song-singing of the old-country. Theodora loved to dance and played the mandolin, while her husband sang love songs in a deep booming bass voice.

Jenny was the first one, other than Stephanos, whom Theodora told about her pregnancy. Stephanos was so certain the child was male, that he started celebrating the birth of his son three months before the baby's birth. When their son was born, Stephanos promised he would love and honor Theodora forever.

The baby, however, seemed to cry incessantly, stopping only when his mouth was full with one of Theodora's nipples. Stephanos began to complain about his lost sleep. Both parents strained to keep their tempers under control as the infant screamed, demanding attention. Stephanos visited the *cafenion* more frequently, returning home later and later each night. At first Theodora, constantly busy with taking care of little Paul, barely noticed her husband's absence until the baby's colic-induced painful spasms subsided. Get-togethers at friends' homes, once the mainstay of their social life, were interrupted as Theodora had to leave the room to feed and change the baby.

By the time Paul was three years old, the relationship once so full of love and promise had deteriorated into a never-ending war, in which each battle often concluded in dead-still silence that would last for days.

Jenny was having her problems too. She had argued with Elias constantly since she admitted to him that she had helped the two lovers communicate by routing letters back and forth. Elias' visits and invitations dwindled.

Jenny, feeling lonely and out of sorts, became a frequent visitor at Theodora's. She would take the streetcar after church services and get off at the stop about a quarter-mile from Theodora's house. One such day Jenny bought some pastries at a German bake shop and appeared unannounced at Theodora's door.

"*Hérete*, Theo! I hope you don't mind my stopping in this way, but I was so sick of the house that I had to go out. Besides, I haven't seen the baby for a while." She stopped apologizing, startled by Theodora's disheveled appearance. "Theo, what's wrong? Are you sick?" Then, noticing the bruises on Theodora's arms and her tear-swollen eyes, she asked, "What's going on here? Is the baby all right?" She hugged Theodora and gently moved her aside to close the door. "Now, sweetheart, tell me what's going on."

"Oh Jenny, I am so ashamed. My husband and I are always fighting. He doesn't love me, and he hollers at Paul all the time. I told him today that I was going to leave him so he put all of my clothes into a trunk and then put Paul's stuff into a big brown shopping bag and went to the *cafenion*. He is getting crazy. Every time I talk to any man he gets suspicious and accuses me of all kinds of crazy things. I don't care what people think! I'm not going to stay married to him any more."

"Calm down, Theo, let's talk about this some more. What happened to your arms? They are turning black and purple—I mean blue. Did he hit you?"

"I am calm. It doesn't matter whether he hit me or not, I'm going to leave him. I'm not going to stay here. Can Paul and I come and stay with you for a while?"

Jenny argued and tried to convince her that she shouldn't take such a drastic move, but when Theodora finally had her convinced that she was going to leave and go somewhere whether she had a place to stay or not, Jenny gave in.

"Of course you can stay with me. We will solve this thing together. Maybe your *Baba Lia*, Elias, will help us. Of course I haven't seen him since you got married, but I know where to find him."

"I don't want any help from him or anybody else except you," Theodora begged. "I will never forgive him for treating you so badly because you tried to help me. Never mind the fact that he turned against me too. I suppose that he and his brothers are going to say, 'I told you so.' I am not going to give them the satisfaction of making believe that they are sympathetic, but all the time just waiting for the chance to tell me that I should have listened to them. I can hear my father now telling everybody, 'What can you expect when a dumb female doesn't take the excellent advice that her father gave?' The hell with them! I can live my life and I can take care of Paul without them."

"Okay, Theo. If that's what you want, that's what we will do. Remember though, that if you give them that message now, they will never forgive you; no matter what happens, they will never offer assistance again."

"Good! That's fine with me. Who needs them anyhow?"

Theodora went back to work at Green Shoe as a stitcher, sewing the soles onto children's shoes as a piecework employee. She preferred being paid based upon the amount of work she did instead of earning a base salary. She was confident that she could earn more that way. As long as they were staying with Jenny, Theodora was able to make enough money to get by. Then Jenny came down with pneumonia, so Theodora had to hire the apartment owner's wife to take care of Paul while she worked. Jenny didn't recover quickly, and eventually needed care herself, so she gave up her apartment and moved in with her cousins.

No matter how hard Theodora worked, no matter how fast her fingers flew between the pumping needle and the leather soles, she couldn't make enough money to support herself and Paul. Breakfast was a luxury she couldn't afford. She tried to manage with one meal a day—lunch—but she fainted one day after a dizzy spell caused by exhaustion and hunger. Nearing exhaustion, she gave up and brought the baby back to Stephanos.

A triumphant Stephanos readily agreed to taking their son. "I will take him back and see to it that he is raised properly on the following conditions: first, my sister will take him and raise him as her own son as long as you agree that you will never attempt to see him again. When he gets older, we will tell him that his mother died when he was born. Secondly, the boy will be better off if only a few people know the truth. For his sake, you must keep this whole unfortunate episode as secret as you can. My sister doesn't live in Boston, so as long as you don't tell people about him, there is little chance that he will be embarrassed by having everyone know his mother was a divorced woman.

"If you agree, and you must for his sake, since you can't raise him, bring him to me on the pretext that he is going to stay for a few days, say your good-byes and never come back."

A week later, a pale, red-eyed Theodora tearfully helped Paul climb down the stairs of the streetcar. They stopped outside the brick-fronted house that would be his new home. Theodora ran her hand around the back of his head, lifting his brown curly hair over his coat collar. She sobbed and cried in whimpering gulps while he looked at her with huge brown eyes and pulled her toward the stairs so he could get the cookies that he had been promised. Stephanos met them at the top of the stairs where a door led to the apartment. He closed the door in Theodora's face as Paul rushed past him into the hall.

Theodora, now alone, clutching the rail, made her way down the stairs, stumbled onto the curbstone, and walked across the street. She passed a little boy about Paul's age who was eating an ice cream cone while holding onto his daddy's hand. Stephanos watched from behind the cream-colored crocheted curtains until Theodora, sobbing into her handkerchief, turned back, looked at the building, and disappeared around the corner.

The next few years were the worst in Theodora's life; she had given up her son, was virtually ostracized from the local Greek community as a divorced woman, and struggled to earn enough money to barely support herself. Her day began in her one-room flat at seven in the morning. Wrapped in a blanket, she would drink her breakfast coffee and nibble on a piece of cheese. Instead of spending the nickel for the streetcar, she walked to work at Green Shoe. The streets were always wet at that hour of the morning, making the horse droppings from the rag-picker and milk wagons slick and runny. Then little brown puddles formed where the runoff collided with the trolley tracks. Theodora dodged the puddles so the cardboard-patched soles of her shoes wouldn't get wet, always trying to keep as close to the curbstone as she could to avoid the derelicts who huddled in doorways.

Once at work she would remove her wet shoes, so her stockings could dry faster, being careful to keep both feet on the floor. Her sewing machine was one of many mounted on a long table and powered by a single flybelt that ran under the table inches from the stitchers' feet. The belt motors located at the end of each table hummed loudly as they powered the needles that pumped up and down, forcing thread through the leather. Soon the motor and the noise from hundreds of flashing needles, which competed with the rasping of the flybelts and the "necessary" conversation of supervisors, made her long for the quiet of the old country.

The day ended ten hours later—interrupted only by a half-hour lunch break, which Theodora hated. When she was busy concentrating on avoiding the needles and aligning the leather properly, she didn't have time to think about how much she missed her baby. The nights were worse. Her one luxury was the radio she had bought at a Salvation Army outlet. It managed to produce recognizable sounds in spite of the crackling and buzzing.

She went to church on Sundays—always alone—and defiantly made her way to the middle of the pews rather than sitting in the back row where she might have hidden from accusing eyes. She always managed to put her dime in the collection basket as it passed by her. After church she would walk in the Commons to feed the pigeons and enjoy the sunshine while she practiced reading English from discarded newspapers she picked up from the park benches. When it rained or the weather was too cold to sit in the park, she either stayed home or walked through the department stores where she would pretend to shop while she practiced reading signs and labels. At home she would sit in front of a cracked mirror and watch her lips move as she repeated difficult words. Gradually her English improved and the heavy Greek accent diminished somewhat. Still, she never understood what happened to the "k" in words like "knee" and "knife."

She visited with Jenny occasionally, and slowly the hurt of not having Paul lessened as she told herself over and over, "You have to be strong and forget about him. What is done is done. Go on with your life. He is better off anyhow." She made some new friends, mostly Americans, at work; and perhaps as a way of emphasizing that she was starting a new life, asked them to call her Ethel.

Theodora received two letters from Greece, one from her mother and one from her brother George. When George's letter arrived, she was surprised to realize that she, now Americanized, thought of him as George rather than Georgios.

> My sister,
>
> I hope that all is well for you, and that you are making lots of money building shoes in America. I know that you must be having bad times because of the disgrace of being a divorced woman. Your brothers and sisters and I know that terrible things must have happened to you to force you into such a situation. You know that we will always stand by you no matter what you did. Father will never forgive you, but I think you should ask him to try rather than to live by yourself.
>
> As for me, things are not good. I tried to come to America and help you but I can't come.

As you know, the Government here is conscripting people my age for the army. The trouble with Bulgaria is getting worse. Since I was born in America, I decided that I should come there and help you and at the same time stay out of the Army.

I went to the American Embassy and told them I was born in Franklin, Massachusetts, and lived in Boston. They checked in America for my records and there isn't any record anywhere. They said if there were any records anywhere, it would have been in Franklin, but the courthouse had a big fire and everything burnt up. It took them two months to find out. When I told Mother, she finally told me why I am not recorded as being born in America. Sometimes our father has a head like a stone. Even though the priest offered to write the American Embassy and tell them that I was born an American citizen, they won't listen.

The only way I can get out of here is to go to smugglers who do such things. They will sneak me into someplace called Cuba first and then to any city in America I want to go. They want a thousand American dollars.

Please, I implore you to remember your promise to me and save money from your wages to help me. I promise to repay you someday, and perhaps I can help you and protect you in America. Please help me.

Your loving brother,

Georgios

Theodora wrote back, agreeing to help and asking for more details. It was to be another year later before George finally received the following letter from his sister in America.

Dear George,

I have arranged the transfer of the thousand dollars that you need for your trip according to the instructions that your smuggler friends gave. They will take you to Cuba and then bring you to my address in Boston.

I expect you to repay me, but it will take a long time. Once you get here you will realize that life isn't a bowl of cherries. I do not make a lot of money, and have really had to save. I did not buy a winter coat last year and went to work in the cold with only my sweater to keep me warm.

I want to tell you again that I have not done anything disgraceful. They, your father and uncles, are the ones who ought to be ashamed. I have never considered asking them, or anybody else for that matter, to forgive me. You are the one who needs help, not me.

Please kiss my mother and brothers and sisters for me, and please hurry. It will be so nice to have someone from my family with me. At least I won't be so lonely.

Your sister,

Theodora

Theodora sent the money to George, who promptly contracted to be smuggled into Cuba, where he crawled into a small boat and landed on the Florida coast. The boat had barely landed when he found himself being jammed into the trunk of a Ford sedan for a long ride to Cincinnati, Ohio. It took him two more years to get to Boston. He never did find out why he was left in Cincinnati.

Theodora (far right) at the Green Shoe Factory

THEODORA

꜅꜅꜅꜅꜅꜅꜅꜅꜅꜅꜅꜅꜅꜅꜅꜅꜅꜅꜅꜅꜅꜅꜅꜅꜅꜅꜅꜅꜅꜅

CHAPTER 18
THE MEETING

Theodora was working at the Green Shoe Manufacturing Co., a three-story brick building on Harrison Avenue that took up most of a city block. Harrison Avenue ran parallel with what was then called Washington Street, over which ran the electric trains that transported the populace to and from work. Poor people, especially the immigrants, called the surrounding streets home. Since very few immigrants owned automobiles, Green Shoes proximity to their homes made it a favorite place of employment for immigrants. Theodora had worked her way up to the fancy stitcher's job. She was known as a pieceworker, one who was paid based on the number of units produced.

A fancy stitcher sewed the pieces of leather that formed the top part of the shoes. The stitching was highly visible and the design it created was what distinguished the style of the shoe. A fancy stitcher who was on piecework was at the top of the shoe stitcher's economic ladder. Theodora renewed her friendship with Helen, a tiny Greek girl who bubbled with enthusiasm, loved everyone, and thanked God every day for whatever blessings He chose to bestow upon her. Theodora was never able to understand how Helen could find the goodness of God's work in the poverty and hard work in their lives.

Theodora's sewing machine was bolted onto a wooden table in the middle of the second of five rows of similar machines. At different times, as many as forty sewing machines hummed and sang as the workers squinted to move pieces of leather around under the pumping needles. Each table was situated under a single light bulb with a metal shade painted white on the underside, which reflected the light straight down. Additional light came from the wall of windows that ran down one side of the room. Helen was not a fancy stitcher but was a stitch puller. Stitch pullers spent most of their time cutting and pulling the stitches from the leather when the stitching was not exactly as it should be. Stitch pullers also trimmed and cut excess threads on the soles as well as the sides and tops of the shoes.

Helen and Theodora made it a habit to have lunch together, sitting at Helen's table when the day was dark and gloomy, and at Theodora's machine when the sun would flow in from the windows. There was always more room at Helen's workplace since she worked half-sitting on a high stool in front of a long bench, but the girls couldn't give up sitting in the sunlight, especially during the long Boston winters.

After work, Helen would invariably wait for Theodora in the street so they could walk to the streetcar stop together. Theodora was always the last to leave because she wanted "to do one more." The more units she completed, the more she got paid. A year earlier, management had been concerned about a union being formed. The bosses, recognizing the leadership role Theodora had with the other women, had offered to make her a supervisor. But since she could make more money as a fancy stitcher on piecework, Theodora declined.

One evening, Helen waited huddled as far back in the doorway as she could to stay out of the slanting cold rain. The metal awning over the doorway, as well as the long sign above it, were painted green. Specks of dirty white frost were beginning to form on the letters "GREEN SHOES" when Theodora came out of the warm building. Theodora and Helen were bundled up with wool kerchiefs over their heads and scarves wrapped around their necks and tucked into the tops of their coats to protect them from the cold. Each wore high-buttoned black shoes that offered little protection from the ice-cold puddles that appeared everywhere on the streets. The biggest puddles, which formed little pools two feet wide at the curbs between the sidewalks and the streets, were unavoidable. It seemed that no matter where the two wanted to step down from the sidewalk in order to cross the street, there was always a puddle.

On this particular day, the girls struggled to avoid the northeast wind that blew iced air from the Atlantic Ocean straight into their faces. They lowered their heads as they navigated across the street, dodging puddles and piles of horse manure from the peddlers' wagons.

They had crossed one street and were about to cross the second when Helen turned to Theodora and shouted through the layers of scarf. "Po, po, po! It is so cold that my brain is numb. I want to talk to you about my Dennis, but my feet are wet, and when I open my mouth the cold air burns my lungs. I tell you that it cannot be healthy to have all this cold entering your lungs. It must be God's intention to..."

Theodora interrupted. "Stop now with what God's intentions may be. Keep your mouth closed and save your breath until we get to the train station. There we can find a place out of the wind for a few minutes so you can tell me about this Denny of yours."

The streetcar tracks ran down each side of the street so that two streetcars going in opposite directions could pass each other. Passengers, lost in their own thoughts and momentarily safe from the outside world, stared blankly at the faces of similar humans whizzing by. Vacant looks on the emotionless faces so much like their own served as an equalizer. For the time, all felt equal in their anonymity.

The massive concrete pillars holding up the roadbed for the elevated railway tracks and boarding platforms were situated between the two sets of tracks. The stairs going up to the elevated trains began at small concrete islands where the streetcars stopped. A passenger who needed to make connections with the electric trains from a streetcar could get off at the streetcar "stop" and climb the stairs without leaving the safety of the concrete islands. Automobiles and horse drawn wagons negotiated through this maze of streetcar tracks, concrete pillars, and passenger-loading islands. Stores, pawn shops, bars, and an occasional restaurant lined both sides of the street. Eager proprietors hoped that those struggling against the elements would stop and spend some of their precious money.

A streetcar left just as Helen and Theodora entered the shelter by the streetcar stop, which meant that they had a ten-minute wait for the next one. The shelter, three-sided with a roof, was not walled in on the street side. A scarred wooden bench covered with wet newspapers tilted on the uneven cement floor against one wall. The floor was strewn with soaked cigarette butts, some leaking brown fluids onto the rain-wet floor.

The two girls hid from the wind, loosened their scarves, and breathed a sigh of relief. A nondescript wet dog peered cautiously into the shelter, turned tail and ran back out as Theodora kicked at him and shouted, "Out, get out of here you damn dirty thing."

Helen protested, "Oh, the poor thing let him come in."

"Are you crazy? Isn't this place bad enough without some dirty dog in here? Come on! I am cold and tired, so what is it you want to tell me about this Denny of yours?"

"Oh Theo, believe me, this man is an angel. I love him. He is so kind and wonderful that I thank God every day that I have him. I am so lucky! He works very hard as a waiter in some fancy place. Waiters make a lot of money, and I just know he will be a good provider. We are going to celebrate his Saint's name day and I want you to meet him. He is my heart, he is my love, and I will die if I do not have him! Please don't say anything bad about how men aren't to be trusted, and how we women have to learn to provide for ourselves. Please just come and meet him. We will have a good time, I will cook some lamb, and we can dance to some new records that he has just bought."

"Ah, Helen, I don't believe that all men are bad. You know how I am. I sometimes just get so frustrated that I hit out at everything around me. I'm sorry that I kicked that poor dog now, but who cares about a dumb dog?" Theodora sighed, then smiled. "Of course I will come! I'll do the cooking so you can spend more time with your Denny. I'll come especially because you said there will be dancing. You know how I love to dance. Is someone else going to be there? Our dances aren't much fun without a long line winding around so the leader can change every so often."

"Of course! Theo, I forgot to tell you that Dennis is going to bring two of his friends. One of the men has a girlfriend so, of course, you and the other man can get to know each other and dance together and have some fun. His name is Louie, and he is a cook. I believe he owns a little restaurant. He comes from Tripoli. Since your home village is so close, I bet you will get along really well. Dennis has known Louie for years, I believe.

"Oh, Theodora, I am so happy with my Denny that I want you to be happy too. Maybe this Louie will make you happy. We don't have to buy the food or the wine because this Louie is going to bring everything and ..."

"All right, all right, Helen. For God's sake, quiet down! I will come and I will meet this Denny of yours and his friend Louie too."

That Sunday Theodora didn't go to church, but instead said her prayers on the streetcar that dropped her off right in front of the tenement house where Helen lived with her aunt. Their apartment was on the third floor of a brick-faced building. Wide stone stairs led to a mahogany-stained door with glass windows on each side. Theodora pushed the bell button to the left of the door. Helen's aunt had been watching through the heavily starched, white-crocheted window curtains for Theodora. She spent a lot of time just sitting in her high-backed chair looking out the window at all the activity below in the street. This time, though, her surveillance had a purpose. Whenever anyone rang the doorbell from downstairs, somebody either had to go down the three flights to identify them before letting them in or take a chance by pressing the button and unlocking the front door electronically. This time, she had seen Theodora climb the exterior stairs just before the bell rang so took only a few steps before she buzzed Theodora in.

When Theodora heard the familiar buzz, she pushed against it and it opened for her. Directly in front of her a flight of stairs led up to the second-floor apartment and then on past the landing. The stairs almost doubled back on themselves as they continued upward to the third-floor apartment. Had Theodora come to visit someone on the first floor, she would have walked down a small hall to the left of the stairwell when she first opened the front door.

As she ascended the stairs, Theodora talked to herself. "Can you believe that I don't know anyone who lives on the first floor of one of these buildings? By God, someday I will own one and will not have to climb so many stairs. You'll see."

Helen opened the apartment door and, scarcely stopping to say hello, headed for the kitchen. The apartment door led into a small hall that ran the length of the three-bedroom flat. Turning left, Theodora entered the living room where Helen's aunt looked out at the street below. A sofa and two tired-looking overstuffed chairs faced the center of the room, their backs to the windows. Helen's aunt turned from the window and beckoned to the visitor.

"Come in, come in! It is so good to see you again. Kiss me, sweetheart and then help that poor excited Helen. She is so nervous I am afraid she will wet herself."

Theodora laughed and did as she was told. Turning back down the hall, she passed the first bedroom on her left, obviously the aunt's room, then went by the arch leading to the kitchen on her right. All the oak woodwork was stained a dark mahogany color. The massive, dark woodwork was topped with scrolled pieces, like castle turrets, wherever possible.

Helen darted from the bathroom directly in front of Theodora, heading for her own bedroom.

Theodora smiled then continued toward the kitchen, the only room in the house that didn't sport the mahogany look. Instead, the upper walls were painted white above a green chair rail that ran around the entire room, except where briefly interrupted by doors leading to the back stairs, porch, and pantry. The wall below the chair rail was tongue-and-grooved wood painted a slightly lighter green. The kitchen table was painted to match the green of the chair rail, but the chairs—four of them—were painted yellow. The door to the wood-fronted icebox was open, and Theodora could see that the twenty-pound block of ice sitting in its container beginning to drip. She closed the icebox door before turning to take off her hat, coat, and scarf.

"Whose bed will the guests put their hats and coats on, yours or your aunt's?" she called out as Helen ran down the hall, this time headed the opposite direction. She laughed when she got no answer and took her wraps to the aunt's room.

The guests—Chris, Dennis, and Louie—arrived with their arms full of food. They had a cooked leg of lamb with some roasted potatoes, a loaf of Italian bread fresh-baked that morning, and two bottles of inexpensive wine. Louie carried the still-warm lamb wrapped in brown paper in the pan he'd cooked it in that morning,. He had negotiated the turnstiles and sliding doors of the streetcar system with the bulky pan and was glad to get rid of it.

It took a few minutes for the nervousness and tension to melt, but Dennis' graciousness and good humor, mixed with the old country ritualistic introductions, took over. Soon everyone settled back and relaxed. Theodora was taken by the handsome and well-spoken Louie, but she couldn't help but notice that his suit was rumpled and his shirt showed soil marks around the neck.

Louie was entranced. Theodora was exactly what he had unknowingly been searching for. He ran his finger around the neck of his almost-white collar and wished he had changed into a fresh shirt before leaving the restaurant. Chris, who was now busy chatting with the old aunt, had nagged him about being more particular about his dress and appearance. Louie wished now that he had listened to his friend.

It was later in the evening, after dinner, when Helen and Theodora compared notes as they washed dishes. The others were being entertained by Chris, who strummed a mandolin and sang songs from the old country.

"Well, Theo, what do you think about Louie? He seems to be a nice enough man. Isn't he good-looking? I like him. He is quiet but he laughs a lot, don't you think?"

Theodora giggled then laughed, "Helen, you asked me three questions and then told me your opinions. You are so funny. First of all, I like your Denny and he is certainly in love with you, too. When you get married and have children, I want to be the godmother. I would love to be your *Koumbára*. As for Louie, I like him well enough, although he doesn't like to dance very much. He is good-looking. He does smell though. No, I don't mean *he* smells but his clothes smell of old grease and tobacco smoke. I wonder how old he is? I wouldn't want an old man who just wants to stay home. I like to go out and visit people and have fun."

Helen looked over at Theodora and then, raising both her hands to the ceiling, spoke as though to the angels. "She likes him well enough. Well enough to be wondering if he will take her out after they are married or will want to just stay home."

Theodora laughed, "Never mind that foolishness! Nothing will happen. He will be like the other dumbbells when he finds out I am divorced. He, too, will disappear like a bad smell in a windstorm."

THEODORA

ᔐᔐᔐᔐᔐᔐᔐᔐ_____ ─────

Louie and Charlie were sitting by themselves in the *cafenion* drinking coffee and playing cards when Louie first spoke of Theodora.

"Charlie, I met a wonderful girl the other day when I was with Chris and Denny."

"I was wondering when you would choose to talk about her. Chris has already told me that you were acting like a tongue-tied monkey when you met her. He said you didn't say two words all the way home. Denny told me how much fun she was and that she is a good cook, laughs a lot, and is very pretty."

"Did Denny tell you anything else about her?" asked Louie.

"You mean do I know that she was divorced? Yeah. That is something that you need to think about—for about two seconds. Then if you want her, take her. Who gives a crap if she was divorced? Or even why! Neither one of us is so perfect that we can demand perfection in others. Just tell me that you want her and then we will kick the crap out of anyone who suggests that she is damaged goods.

"Christ! One of us needs to get married. I am tired of hanging out in these smoky coffeehouses and not having some place to go on holidays. In the name of Christ, if you want her, then marry her, make babies, and have a family! I need a family too. But I like to gamble on horses too much to ask anyone to share my life with me. I'm glad to see the gambler in you showing up once in a while. You've taken your share of risks in the past. Maybe it's time to gamble one more time. You ought to get married and soon too. After all, you're almost forty."

Charlie lit a cigarette and motioned to the waiter to bring fresh coffee, then continued. "Even though our father, God bless his soul, said that the men in our family are able to make babies long after most men give up, you don't have to prove it. Get married now that you're still young enough to enjoy it. Besides, if you have a family, then I will have one too. Now tell me her name and what are we going to do about getting her to marry us?"

"Theodora," Louie said almost reverently.

"Hey, there is a horse in the second race at Suffolk Downs named God's Gift, which is what Theodora means. I'll be right back. I want to put twenty on her to win. Where the hell is that bookie when I need him?"

CHAPTER 19

MARRIAGE AND NEW HOPE

The blue jay shrieked repeatedly as it dove through the falling red and orange autumn leaves at the scampering gray squirrel. The squirrel snatched the peanut and sank even closer to the ground to escape the diving jay, which broke out of its dive but managed to brush the tip of the squirrel's furry question-mark tail. The squirrel chattered in alarm as it dropped the peanut and ran for the closest maple tree. Another jay immediately swooped down and grabbed the peanut, barely stopping before flying to another tree.

Theodora bounced up from the blanket, waving her hands threatening at the offending jays. She squashed Louie's hat as she sank back to the ground.

Louie sat up and complained, "Hey, be careful! Don't get so angry, love. I just had that hat cleaned and blocked. How can you get upset over a peanut?"

"Who cares about the peanut? I don't want to feed those dirty birds. I like the squirrels. Those birds get enough to eat without eating my peanuts."

"You can't always have your own way," Louie muttered as he retrieved his hat. He waved his hand toward the swans floating on the lake and the ducks floating through the air on rigid wings as their outstretched feet reached for a landing spot on the Boston Garden Pond.

"It is a great day," he reminded her. "The sun is warm enough that we can sit here having a picnic and I can buy you enough peanuts to feed every damn pigeon, squirrel, or blue jay in the whole park. I hate to see you get all worked up over foolish things."

"Oh, Louie, that is the way I am. I don't mean to be quick-tempered, but I guess that's just me. I'm less tolerant than you are. I don't ever want to be pushed around so I go to extremes at times. I'm sorry."

"Well, it is only one peanut and one blue jay, and I sure do not want to have an argument with you. And please don't start telling me again that I am not aggressive enough."

"You're right, Louie," she said, squeezing his hand. "Besides, it is time for us to go. It will take us about an hour to get to the party even if the streetcars are running on time. Someday I will have my own car just like the rich people do so I won't have to depend on someone else."

"What will you do with your own car? When was the last time you saw a female driving a car? A car is very complicated, you know; not everyone can drive one. They are expensive, too. But, if you want us to have a car, I will get one for you after we are married and if I can learn to drive one."

"I haven't agreed to marry you yet, but don't start thinking that if I decide to marry you it is because you own a restaurant and will buy us a car."

"Of course I would not think that! But having my own business is not so bad, is it?"

"No, Louie, it isn't that bad at all," she said as she grasped his arm with her free hand while her other hand held the folded blanket."

She looked up at him and said, "Please pick up the basket, my love, and let's go."

"You called me 'my love.' That is the first time you ever did that. I am so tickled that I won't even complain about going to another party as long as you don't make me dance all night long. I still have to go to work tomorrow."

"Oh, come on! You'll have fun. I have to work tomorrow, too. Just because you are almost fifteen years older than I am does not mean that you are too old to keep up with me. Does it?"

"Too old? Of course not! Come on. Let's hurry and catch that streetcar. On the way home we can talk about getting married."

The Greeks looked out of place as they waited for the wedding to transpire in the Baptist Parsonage. It was a beautiful January day, and some of the inhabitants of North Scituate were planning to drive the few miles south to Cape Cod where their summer cottages—still untidy after the 1927 New Year celebration—waited.

Louie was dressed in a brand-new gray suit with thin, black stripes running through the fabric. His blue and white necktie was pulled tightly against his Adam's apple, making the starched collar even more rigid. He had received his first-time-ever free haircut from his old friend Fotis, the barber. Fotis took command of the shoeshine stand and personally smeared a white liquid on Louie's black patent leather shoes and brushed them into a mirror finish. After Louie had bathed and shaved, Chris supervised the adjustment of Louie's coat lapels and pressed his friend's trousers with a hot iron until he was satisfied. Charlie, who wouldn't let Louie sit down, for fear of his ruining "how pretty he looked," finally relented and gave Louie one small glass of *ouzo* just before they got into Chris's car to go to the parsonage.

Theodora looked radiant holding a bouquet of violets against a lacy jacket covering a cream-colored knee-length dress. Helen was not surprised when Theodora refused to wear a veil, saying that it wouldn't be appropriate since she no longer was a virgin.

Theodora and Louie held hands as the Protestant minister standing in front of them droned on and on in his monotone voice. Theodora tried to pay attention, but as she looked at the bare austere walls and compared them to the ornate, jeweled walls of the Orthodox church, covered with icons of Saints staring down on the worshippers, she couldn't help but feel cheated. Louie, standing beside her, happily waited for the minister to finish droning. Louie knew that no matter what the minister had to say, it wouldn't take anywhere near as long as the traditional Orthodox two-hour wedding.

After they repeated the necessary "I do's," the relieved couple went off to sign a registry while the guests waited on the stairs to pelt them with wheat seeds.

Helen looked even smaller than usual as she stood beside the straight-backed six-foot-tall Chris. They were waiting for the rest of the wedding party to gather so Chris could give them instructions on how to get to the restaurant where the celebration was to take place.

"Well, Helen, since you were the bridesmaid and I was the best man, then we are *koumbari*, too. It was a nice wedding. Small, but nice."

"You're right, *koumbaro*, it was very nice. It's too bad that they had to get married by a Protestant minister. But remember that if we were back in the old country, they couldn't have gotten married at all since Theodora is divorced. Now that they are married, they can begin the process of having the Church sanctify the marriage. Then they can receive the Sacraments and baptize their children. I know there are a lot of papers that need to be filled out, but Theodora is smart enough to figure all that out. I never have met anyone who is as pretty as she is—and is so smart too. My Denny and I were talking about that just the other day."

"Where is Denny anyhow? I know he agreed to organize things at Louie's restaurant today, but I thought he would be here by now. I said Louie's restaurant, but I should have said the restaurant that Louie is managing for his friend who is vacationing in Florida."

"I am surprised, too, that Denny is not here yet, but he will show up. I really wanted him to come with me," Helen sighed, "but when Louie asked him for the favor, he couldn't refuse. You would think that with all the people Louie has helped, he wouldn't have any problem finding assistance when he needs it. Denny says that half of the Greeks who own businesses in Boston owe Louie something. Louie has even worked in someone else's kitchen because they were short-handed instead of taking time off to rest. Denny says that the only reason Louie takes any time off at all is so he can get enough strength to go back to work!" She shook her head in disbelief. "Most people work hard to make enough money so they can afford to buy things and take some time off, have a good time, and enjoy themselves—but not Louie. Well, now that he is getting married, maybe he will spend more time taking care of himself and spend some time with his wife."

"You know, Helen, I have known Louie for a long time. I knew him when he was still called Soterios. He is the best man I have ever known. Louie has taught more of our countrymen how to cook and to run a business than I can count. I hope that Theodora will appreciate him and have a lot of patience. After all, he has been single for a long time, and it may take a little time for him to adjust."

At the reception, Charlie watched Louie carefully as all the toasts were made to the beaming couple while the three-piece Greek band—

bazóóki, mandolin, and clarinet—that Chris had hired, played. Louie, still embarrassed at being the center of attention, led the sparkling Theodora in the traditional dance. Others soon took pity on him and joined the hand-holding line, while they hissed in tune with the music. Louie took the first opportunity to drift away from the dance line and headed for the kitchen, stopping dead in his tracks when he saw a grinning Charlie, arms crossed in front of his chest, blocking the swinging door. Louie sighed heavily and headed instead for the table that served as a makeshift bar. There he fortified himself before returning to the happy line of dancers to follow the bright, graceful-stepping Theodora who held on to Chris' handkerchief as they circled the floor.

Eventually, a still-immaculate Chris, acting as master of ceremonies, invited the guests to sit at the long tables with Theodora and Louie at the center seats. The waiters were already bringing out the first course—shrimp cocktails and marinated squid. An imported *retsina* wine was poured, soon followed by roast lamb, rice pilaf, and an eggplant and green bean vegetable that had been simmered in tomatoes and heavily seasoned with mint and garlic. Still-warm loaves of Greek bread and a marinated salad of tomato wedges, cucumbers, onions, and bell peppers seasoned with garlic, oregano, and a heavy green olive oil competed with chunks of *Feta* cheese and *Kalamata* olives for space on the table. Chris toasted the couple and asked them to speak for the first time as man and wife to their guests and family. Louie, now more than slightly rumpled, spoke haltingly. He thanked the guests for coming and gratefully turned the speech making over to his new wife.

Theodora, slightly tipsy and still excited by the dancing and gaiety of the occasion, merely said, "This is the happiest day that I have had for many years. I hoped that a member of my family, my brother George, would be here for my wedding. But he is trying to find his way here from Cincinnati. Please make my husband and me happy by considering yourselves part of our family. Our home will always be open to you. Hurry! Finish eating so we can dance some more."

When Louie heard Theodora's final statement about dancing some more, he groaned—loud enough for Theodora, Chris, and Helen to hear. Theodora looked at him, laughed outright, and winked happily. Chris and Helen exchanged meaningful glances.

Nick

CHAPTER 20

THE NEW FAMILY

Almost one year later, Charlie puffed one cigarette after another as he paced the ten steps between the bench and the corner of the hospital wall that blocked his view of the corridor. He still wore his topcoat, but it was now open, revealing his work-stained white shirt and tie with a too-small knot that pushed into his neck. His fedora was shoved back on his head so the brim pointed toward the plastered ceiling. Louie, his brother, stood with his back jammed into a corner between two benches, one of which held his topcoat and rain-soaked hat.

He snuffed out a cigarette and said, "For Christ sake, Charlie, relax. She will be fine. Doctor Dukakis is with her. He will take care of her. In the old country, babies are born in the fields with only the mules looking on."

"You're a fine one to talk. You ran out of the restaurant so fast when Helen called that I am surprised you changed your clothes! Besides I am not nervous about her having a baby. I'm nervous because I have fifty bucks bet that it is going to be a girl. I better not lose. If it is a boy, I will have to borrow the money from you."

Earlier that day, Helen had been ironing Denny's shirt when Theodora climbed up the stairs to the third floor, one floor above her own apartment in Eggleston Square. Theodora had been packing to move uptown when the pains first started. Helen ran down the hall and called a taxi, then helped her friend down the narrow stairs to wait for transportation to Boston City Hospital. The hospital was relatively new, but had already earned accolades for maternity cases. Supported by the city of Boston, the hospital was willing to accept all classes of patients without great concern whether they could pay or not. Most immigrants and poor folks flocked to the hospital when they had a need. Even though the recently opened Boston Lying In Hospital specialized in maternity cases, the City Hospital continued to attract the affluent as well as immigrants and the indigent. Most services were offered in the clinic mode.

Clinic patients registered at the desk, where they revealed their symptoms to a nurse who filled out a form and directed them to one of the large waiting rooms, an immense open area filled with wooden chairs. The chairs were in rows, sometimes five or six deep. The room was further divided by placards on metal poles that indicated whether the chairs were in section A, B, or C. An attendant would meet the patients at the door and, after reviewing the two-part form each patient had, assigned a number and directed the patient to a particular section. The attendant would place a copy of the form into a box located on the counter where the nurse on duty presided, deciding when it was a patient's turn to be examined by the next available doctor. As the patient was called by number, he or she would shuffle fearfully but anxiously into the examining room.

In some cases the doctors were late-term medical students, usually interns. It wasn't unusual for a doctor to find two people waiting for him in the examining room, one of which acted as an interpreter.

Helen returned from calling Dennis just as the doctor came through the swinging doors. The doctor stopped for a moment, looked at the group, and decided that since Charlie appeared the most agitated, he must be the father.

"Congratulations, Mr. Douros, you are the father of a beautiful baby girl."

He was surprised when Charlie turned to look at Louie, who said loudly, "*I* am the Douros who has a daughter. *He* only has a bet. Tell me, Doctor, is my wife okay? Is she all right?"

"Congratulations then, Mr. Douros, may your daughter and your wife live long and happy lives. Certainly your wife is fine, and as soon as the nurse cleans her, you can go see her and your daughter."

"Thank you, Doctor, for taking care of my wife. I don't care if the baby is a boy or girl as long as my wife and baby are healthy. Besides, there is plenty of time, and with a woman as loving as Theodora, there will be plenty of opportunity to make a son."

The doctor said, "Good for you! Now that's the way to think." Then turning to Helen, he said, "From the way you look, it seems as if your turn will be pretty soon. Is this your husband?" He put his hand on Charlie's shoulder.

Charlie grinned, "No, I am not lucky enough for that, but I am lucky enough to win a bet. Thank you for taking care of our Theodora. Now excuse me, I have to go collect my money and have a drink or two in celebration. *Hopa!* We have a daughter!" he hollered as he charged out the door, calling over his shoulder, "Louie, tell Theodora I will see her later."

The baby girl was named Katherine, honoring Louie's mother, and the trio moved happily into their home in Eggleston Square on West Walnut Park, which had once been the most fashionable street in that part of Boston. It had begun to decline as more and more of the affluent families moved into the outlying areas of Belmont and Milton. Construction of the elevated railway system, which promised to make more areas available to the poor, and the noise of the clanging speeding trains hastened its descent.

Even so, it was still a desirable area in which to live. The South End or Back Bay where most immigrants still lived was only a few miles away, yet few Greeks had made it this far.

The homes were situated on large grassy lots bordered with neat flower beds on both sides of the wide street. Louie and Theodora rented the top floor of what was once a large single-family home. An interior staircase had been added to the north side of the house, which led to their three-bedroom apartment. There was also a porch behind the kitchen surrounding the other stairs, which descended to the backyard. Theodora looked at the large oak tree that stood in the center of the adjoining lot each time she hung clothes out to dry. By looking in the other direction, she could see the top of the building that once housed the owner's horse and carriage, but now served as storage sheds. The garage where her landlords stored their automobile faced the porch where Theodora stood each day, dreaming of the day when she and Louie would have a house of their own, and of course, their own automobile.

Katherine was a beautiful little girl with black curly hair and huge brown eyes. By the time she was a year old, she had learned how to manipulate uncle Charlie as well as her father. True to his word, Charlie adopted Louie's family as his own. His whole world consisted of work, the racetracks in Revere Beach, Louie's home, and the coffeehouse. At least twice a month, Charlie, Chris, and a revolving list of Greek men and women would have Sunday dinner at Louie and Theodora's home, always followed with hours of dancing and singing old country songs.

The streetcar in which Louie was riding jolted to a stop. The man standing in front of Louie lost his balance as he tried to catch one of the leather loops suspended from a brass rod that ran the length of the car. The man missed the loops, which served as overhead handles, but managed to catch the brass rod and knock Louie's hat off in the process. Louie lost a few precious seconds retrieving his hat without spilling the groceries. He finally grabbed his hat then stepped down from the trolley onto the street. There he stumbled over a cobblestone that had been loosened by the vibration of the many streetcars. As Louie left the streetcar stop and hurried across Washington Street, he was still struggling to balance the large bag of groceries as he tried to put his hat back on his head.

He muttered to himself as he waited for a trolley (as streetcars had come to be called) to enter the huge open mouth of the station-house. Inside, the conductor would stop the trolley and, after the last passenger departed, walk to the other end of the car where identical operating handles and devices allowed him to make a return trip without having to turn the car around. Once the outgoing passengers were loaded, the conductor rang his bell, started the car moving forward, and began the process all over again.

Louie was late getting home, where he was to bring the Greek bread and *feta* cheese for Sunday dinner. His only hope was that Chris still would be singing some of the old melodies and that Theodora hadn't interrupted him in order to start serving dinner.

He walked quickly up the stairs of his home, barely stopping to add his coat and hat to the pile on the bed in the extra bedroom, before heading for the kitchen. Theodora looked at him while shaking her head left to right conveying the message, "Boy oh Boy! You just made it in time. Aren't you the lucky one?" Louie just grinned at her, Theodora grinned back and added a big fat wink.

Hours later, after the other guests had left, Helen and Dennis sat at the kitchen table with Louie and Theodora. The women were examining the white, lace-fringed dress that Helen had bought for Katherine's birthday. Louie and Dennis were drinking Greek coffee out of little demitasse cups decorated with tiny pink roses. Louie pushed little pink rose–decorated flat plates out of the way as he reached for a glass ashtray, on the bottom of which was printed Elcho Lunch. Dennis finished his coffee, then turned the coffee cup over on the saucer. A stream of thick brown fluid blurred the roses.

"Come on, Louie, drink your coffee and I will tell you your fortune."

"Sure, I'll do that, but you know I don't believe in your magic." Louie could never understand how the pattern formed by sediment from the coffee grounds as they slid down the cup could indicate the future. "Come on, Denny," he challenged good-naturedly, "what is going to happen to us?"

Theodora looked up, "Oh good! Come on, let's do it. Sometimes it really comes true, you know."

Helen laughed brightly. "Denny is so funny. I don't believe the coffee cups either, but sometimes what he predicts does indeed come true," her head bobbed up and down with her words.

"Well okay, Louie, let's see what your coffee is going to tell us." Dennis turned Louie's cup over and peered intently inside. "Aha! I see on the other side of the cup an outline of something that looks like money. That means that your next venture will be successful. And over here on this side, I can see two more babies. And here is a curved line that looks like a smile when I turn the cup upside down. All that means you are going to be happy, earn a lot of money, and make lots of babies."

The other three laughed and joked about "making babies" until Theodora added, "The babies I can help with, and being happy is guaranteed because Louie promised me that from now on he will concentrate on making us instead of everybody else wealthy."

The doorbell rang, interrupting the conversation. Alarmed, Theodora said, "My God! Who can that be at this hour? It's so late. It must be the immigration officers."

Louie questioned, "Immigration? What do they care about us? I became a citizen when I was in Rhode Island in 1922, and you told me that you became a citizen in Virginia. Theodora, what is going on?" He started to move toward the door in response to the second ring.

"Yes, I became a citizen, but I did something ... well, never mind that now. I'll tell you later," she whispered as she moved behind Louie, peeking over his shoulder as he began to turn the doorknob.

Theodora gasped and stared in disbelief at the tall man carrying a suitcase in one hand and his fedora in the other. The first impression that flashed through her mind was that her father had come. The man who stood before them had the same large protruding ears, prominent nose, and moustache. She stared for another second, then realized it wasn't her father, but was her brother George.

"*Georgi!* Where did you come from? How did you find me?" She leaped forward to hug him, knocking the suitcase out of his hand. It tumbled down the stairs, bouncing off the walls of the narrow hall.

They kissed and hugged, asked questions and gave answers that nobody heard. Louie laughed loudly and tried to shake George's hand, but shook Dennis' instead. Helen laughed and cried at the same time, kissed everybody she could, and thanked the Holy Mother for bringing such happiness to her friends. Dennis puffed on his cigar and extricated his hand from Louie's pumping handshake. He then squeezed past George, patted him on the elbow, and retrieved the wayward suitcase.

Later that night, after Dennis and Helen had left, George had been fed, and Theodora finished washing the dishes, the two men toasted one another, leaned back in their chairs, and blew cigarette smoke at the ceiling.

Louie smiled at Theodora and motioned her to sit on his lap. He then put his arm around her as he said to his brother-in-law, "George, I want you to tell us about your experiences, and what your plans are. But, first tell us what's going on back in the old country."

"Well, Father is back in the village. I hope he stays there this time. We can send him enough money so they can survive and improve the house—maybe even add on a room or two. In any event, he's back there now and mother will take care of him. My sister Litsa and brother Nick are doing fine. Nick should be immigrating very soon now. The last letter I got mentioned his leaving on Christmas Day. My other sister, Constandina, married Spiro Fotopoulos. I know him well, and I don't believe he is the type to immigrate. He will probably stay there and maintain the house and fields. Mother is the same as ever," he smiled and shook his head. "She is the lifeblood of the family and is still healthy enough; but they are getting older. My God, she has had a hard life," he sighed.

"I worry so much about her," Theodora said, squirming deeper into Louie's lap. "She has always worked harder than she should have, and he was never much help." Then she added with bitterness, "He only thought of himself."

"Sh! Quiet now, Theodora. That's enough of that. He is still your father. Don't get started," Louie admonished her then turned to his brother-in-law. "George, what are your plans?

"I worked in a bowling alley in Cincinnati, and I like that kind of life. I would like to save enough money and have my own place some day. In the meantime I hope I can stay with you for a while."

"Staying with us is, of course, what you will do for as long as you like. I can also put you to work and teach you to cook. That also goes for your brother Nick when he gets here. Litsa can stay with us, too. Not everybody can be here at the same time, of course, but we will work that out."

He winked at George, chuckled, then crossed his legs and rocked back in the chair as he said, "I knew marrying her would be a challenge, but I didn't know I was getting the whole family too."

Theodora poked him in the chest and threw her head back, laughing seductively, then said, "I'll show you what a challenge is, and by tomorrow morning you will know once again that I am worth it. Besides that, it is time to start making a son for you."

George went right to work for Louie as a cook until he became a partner in a bowling alley with his cousin. He moved into his own apartment just before brother Nick immigrated. Nick then took his turn staying with Louie and Theodora, also working as a cook. He would still be on hand to greet his sister Litsa when she arrived in America some months later.

〰〰〰〰〰〰〰〰〰

Years later Nick opened his eyes slowly so the light shining in the window wouldn't make his head hurt any more than necessary. His room faced West Walnut Park, and even at this hour he could hear automobiles driving by. If the wind was right, he could hear the rumble and metal clanking on metal from the elevated trains and trolley cars. He turned his head to the right quickly and glanced at the photograph of his father and mother in the silver-plated frame. She looked very severe standing behind her husband with her hand on his shoulder. Nick wondered again whether his parents ever felt any joy in living.

He tipped his head back and looked almost straight up at the brass, incense-burning cup as it swayed slightly in the breeze that wafted through the open window. The cup was attached at three points by a chain hanging from the bottom shelf that held an icon of the Holy Mother and Child. There wasn't any incense burning in the cup, but the palm fronds from last Easter were tucked into the sides of the icon to form a cross. This reminded Nick that the holy days were coming. He began to mentally say a prayer when he was startled by a warm wet stream hitting him in the small of his back. He jumped out of the bed and threw back the covers without waking the two-year-old Basil (Vasilios), the son of his sister and brother-in-law Louie. The child and Nick had been sleeping together since Basil was evicted from his crib following the arrival of his new brother.

As Nick cleaned himself and attempted to blot the urine from the bed sheets, he muttered to his nephew, who was now sitting up and rubbing sleep from his eyes. "Little boy. Life seems easy for you. You don't even have to get out of bed to pee," he whispered, shaking his head.

"I've been living with your mother and father now for over four years. It's about time for me to move out of here and get my own place. It seems like I just got here, but I left Greece on Christmas day, December 25th of 1928, and didn't get here until January. It was really crowded here when Litsa moved in, too, as soon as she got here from Greece. Remember her, little one? Thank goodness we found her a husband within four or five months. She and John are now living in Portsmouth and, as far as I know, she is happy. We'll see them today at your brother's christening."

〰〰〰〰〰〰〰〰〰————————————————

Theodora carried the baby to the car and tucked a blanket under his legs before turning to her brother-in-law John to say, "Don't forget. I don't want him named after my father. You know how I felt about him when he was alive, and my feelings haven't changed now that he is dead. You may be his godfather, but I'm his mother. I don't want to be reminded how my father treated me every time I look at my son."

George drove his brand new 1933 Ford, with Louie and Nick in the front seat. John and Litsa, who held the baby, sat in the back. They were going to the Cathedral where the baby was to be baptized. No one spoke until Louie said, "This is a nice car, George. Theodora has always wanted a car but ... well, maybe someday we will get one."

Nobody spoke again until Litsa said, "Do you think Theo really means that she hated our father so much?"

"I don't think hate is the right word," Louie finally answered.

George quickly responded, " I don't know if she hated him or not, but she's wrong. She doesn't have the right to insult him and all our family that way by refusing to honor him."

"Mother will be heartbroken if the boy is not named Haralambos," Litsa added.

John sighed, "Well, she is your sister and he was your father. Tell me what to do."

Nick spoke up. "I'm glad I don't have to decide, because if I did, I would have to go against my own sister."

Louie sighed, "Oh-oh! I can see it coming. Do you have any idea how mad she will be?"

George said, "She will get over it. Let's have the priest decide."

"Now John," Litsa declared, "it is your right—your duty as godfather—to name the child. I insist that you name him after our father."

Louie pleaded. "John, for God's sake. Don't name him Haralambos. At least name him Harold. You know, when Chris christened Basil, he got mixed up and told the priest to make the baptism record out as Louis William Douropoulos. Theodora had the birth certificate at City Hall made out as Vasilios Douros, and everybody calls him Billy. This naming a baby business is getting out of hand. No wonder she is so sensitive about the whole thing!"

"I've been meaning to ask you, where did the name Billy come from?" Litsa asked.

Louie replied, "Chris says that William or Bill is the translated version of Vasilios."

Just then George interrupted, saying, "Here's the church. Let's get the poor kid named and blessed by Christ. I'm glad, Louie, that you decided to name him Harold."

Louie protested, "Oh no you don't! John is the one who decided. That's his job and responsibility."

⌐⌐⌐⌐⌐⌐⌐⌐⌐⌐_____

By the time George drove up in front of Louie and Theodora's home for the christening celebration, some of the guests had already arrived. Chris opened the door as Litsa climbed the stairs holding the newly christened baby.

"Congratulations, and may your baby live forever and have a full fruitful life," he shouted, shaking Louie's hand as the other guests crowded around them. The baby, frightened by the sudden noise, started to cry. Theodora reached to take him from Litsa's grasp.

"Shhh, shhh, little one, don't cry," she murmured, rocking him back and forth. "John, where are you? Tell me what you named him."

No one said anything. Theodora asked again, "John, what is his name?"

John was on the bottom stair behind George and Nick. Softly, he confessed, "his name is Harold."

"What! What did you say? I told you not to name him after my father. Louie, why did you let him do that?" she shrieked.

"Take it easy, Theodora, we have guests here. Control yourself."

"Control myself?" she screamed, "What do you mean, control myself?" Her contorted face flushed a deep red.

Chris glanced at Louie's expression, which darkened as his eyebrows squeezed together. He recognized this sure sign that his friend was getting angry and attempted to defuse the situation. "*Koumbára*, Theodora! Come now, you have guests. We can talk about this later."

"Don't give me that," his wife hissed between clenched teeth. "You're as bad as they are! You're good-looking and supposed to be smart, but you couldn't even get Billy named properly!"

Louie grabbed Harold out of Theodora's arms, handed the baby to an astonished Helen who was standing beside Chris. He then caught Theodora by the elbow, forcing her backwards into the kitchen in attempt to get some privacy.

"Control yourself, woman," he said sternly. "Now you have gone too far. You have embarrassed me in my own home in front of my friends and have insulted Chris, the godfather of your son. Now shut up and stop your crying."

He took a deep breath then added quietly, "I'll ask Helen to come in here and help you. Listen carefully because I am telling you that you have pushed me too far. Imagine embarrassing me in front of my friends like that."

Theodora was too stunned to say anything. Helen came in, hugged Theodora, handed her a damp towel to wipe her face, and said, "Ah well! Let's see what can I do to help serve the *souvlákia?* Which ones shall I start with?"

The rest of the evening was strained, but Chris was able to salvage most of the gaiety normally associated with a christening. Theodora was dancing when the baby started to cry. She looked at Louie sitting at the table, shrugged, and said in a tone of acceptance, "Harry is crying. I'll be right back."

George

CHAPTER 21

SHORE DINNERS

The wind toppled the teepee-shaped pile of driftwood and pine logs, scattering burning embers and sparks into the blackness. Even though the ocean was invisible in the dark, a person could hear the waves pounding on the round beach rocks. The bonfire had peaked, and its light was so bright that anything outside the surrounding perimeter of faces was lost in darkness.

The circle was created by the last guests of the season who would be checking out of the Pemberton Inn the day after Labor Day. The inn had originally been built as a summer home for one of the owners of the mill that had supplied steel to the Elevated Railway System in Boston. Pemberton was the last village on a little peninsula that jutted into Massachusetts Bay. The town of Nantasket lay at the base of the peninsula. Then the finger of land poked into the bay north of Nantasket for a few miles before its tip curved in a westerly direction, ending with the village of Pemberton.

The beaches at Nantasket, Seaside, Hull, Allerton, and the other small towns were being developed with summer homes and beach property. In Nantasket, there were plans for a large Coney Island-type amusement park, complete with roller-coasters, fortune tellers, and the forerunners of the fast-food industry lining the boardwalk. These establishments sold everything from fried clams in a wiener bun to saltwater taffy, hot dogs, and ice-chilled bottles of Moxie.

Pemberton, though, was a small isolated town, for the most part still the private domain of the wealthy. What had once been the manor home now housed the inn's restaurant, bar, various cardrooms, and five two-room suites. On the main grounds and just to the right of the inn as you faced the white-capped ocean was a swimming pool filled with fresh water.

Ten cottages had been built and scattered around the five-acre property. The architecture was colonial with a railing-enclosed porch that ran around the entire inn, and each cottage had its own porch facing the ocean. Every building was painted white. The weather vane that was perched exactly in the center of the cupola over the widows' walk was painted bright red, though nobody knew why that color had been chosen. Each year, the caretaker scraped the salt off the big red arrow and repainted it the same bright red. The white clapboards that comprised the exterior walls to the front of the inn were painted each year, the building's rear and sides were painted much less frequently. The difference in their appearance was always explained (when anyone cared to ask) as being due to the effect of the saltwater spray on wood. The swimming pool had in recent years been enclosed with a chain-link fence, and only guests of the inn were allowed to use it.

Chris acted as the lifeguard for the pool during the day and functioned as the restaurant's maître d' in the evenings. His friend Dennis supervised the other waiters and waitresses needed to provide guests with the three meals a day of the "American Plan."

Louie, Chris, and Dennis acted as the working partners of the group that leased the inn and operated it each summer from Memorial Day to Labor Day. Louie, who supervised the kitchen, was especially proud of the old-fashioned New England clam and lobster bake offered at the inn each Friday night. The meal was served right on the beach when weather permitted. The guests sat on blankets drinking wine and wiggling their toes in the sand.

Louie loved the smell of the clams and lobsters steaming in the pit. Especially on evenings when God cooperated, allowing all his stars to shine brightly over the ocean and inspiring a seagull to pass in front of a full moon every so often, Louie knew he was exactly where he wanted to be.

The area in which the pit was dug and where the guests sat had been cleared of the beach stones that covered the entire point. A fifty-foot sand circle surrounded the pit, which was about eight feet long and three feet deep, and lined, almost as if cobbled, with beach stones. Each evening, a bonfire would be started, and as the wood burned down into coals, the rocks would be heated. Wet seaweed would then be placed over the rocks and hot coals, causing some of the rocks to crack. Live lobsters would be placed on the steaming seaweed and covered with another light layer of seaweed. Then, a layer of little clams would be added, which in turn would be covered with another layer of seaweed. Then the whole pit would be covered with a wet canvas.

The steam from the heated rocks would seep up and drift through the sides of the canvas cover to tantalize the guests who were being served steaming pots of New England clam chowder. The chowder was served in pots shaped like little black kettles with a pail handle. The pots were made of cast iron and had four legs that stabilized them when they were set on the sand. When the clams had been steamed to perfection, the canvas was taken away. The cooks would remove the clams, carefully standing on boards surrounding the pit so that sand would not be kicked onto the food. They would put the clams into deep trays, pour melted butter over them, and serve the guests.

Each guest also received a little flat tray with a bowl of drawn butter, a two handled nutcracker, and a huge red and white checkered napkin to use once his or her lobster was removed from the steaming coals and seaweed. Waiters poured more wine as the diners merrily attacked the hot, hard-shelled delicacy. Chris would lead a singalong to put the final touch on what Louie called an old-fashioned clam bake.

This was the last clambake of the season, and perhaps forever, since Chris had received notice that the inn would not be available for them to lease the coming year.

Louie shook his head slowly from side to side in an effort to shake off the effect of the last glass of Metaxa brandy.

"You two fellows are probably the best friends that I have aside from my brothers, Charlie and Angelo. Dennis, you're my daughter's godfather; and Chris, you're Bill's godfather. We have been friends for a long time and have been through some hard times and good times together. I guess you fellows know that Theodora and I have not been doing too well lately."

Louie paused, then continued in a cracked voice, "For the most part, whatever problems we have are caused by me. I never did like to go out and party and dance and stuff, and now that we are not getting along, I have less desire than ever to do so.

"We have the kids to think about and we made promises to each other so we will stick together and continue to work things out." He took a deep breath before continuing. "I am going to get involved in that Nantasket Beach area, where I think plenty of development is going to happen. That is going to take a big effort, and I will have to spend a lot of time there. Since it is about thirty miles to Boston and the family, I will have to stay overnight in Nantasket quite a bit. I never did learn how to drive a car so I could not buy one even if I had the money. I'm just telling you these things so that you know what's going on if you hear stories about Theodora and me."

Having acknowledged what they'd been pretending not to notice, Louie broke the silence, "Come! Let's have another drink. The future is waiting for us."

At home, Theodora stretched to reach the soil marks under the kitchen table, bumping her head on the underside of its metal edge. The light cotton dress she wore under the red-striped apron wasn't quite long enough to protect her knees from the lye-based yellow soap that floated in the yellow bucket at her hip. She backed out under the table and half-stood so she could wipe her red, raw-looking knees free of soapy water. She now walked out of the kitchen backwards, carrying the water bucket by its wire handle into the bathroom. There she removed the soap, scrub brush, and rinse rag, and dumped the dirty water down the toilet. She had just finished rinsing out the bucket and squeezing the water out of the rinse rag that used to be Katherine's pajamas when the downstairs doorbell rang. She knew it was the mailman signaling that he had dropped the mail into the brass-covered slot in the front door.

She retrieved three pieces of mail, stopping at the top of the stairs to peek in at the napping children, and carefully walked onto the still-drying kitchen floor to the coffeepot on the stove. After turning on the gas jets to reheat the morning's leftover coffee, she sat in the chair facing the back yard, hiked up her skirt so she could rub her sore knees, and thought.

I really should go ahead and pay the extra four cents for that new kind of soap powder, she told herself. Even Helen is using it instead of stinky yellow stuff. And how I wish I had a mop. Then I wouldn't have to get down on my knees to scrub the damn floor. But, she sighed as she thought, those things cost money too, and "we just don't have money to throw away," as Louie would say. She wondered whether the Depression was really almost over as Louie told her over and over, always reminding her to "just to hold on a little while longer."

The coffee started to boil, interrupting her thoughts and postponing the decision to buy more expensive soap. She poured the now thick, reheated coffee into a china cup and decided, "I'll wake the kids in a minute." As she waited for the hot liquid to cool, she absently opened the top letter.

She lifted the cup to her lips and began to read. Suddenly, stunned by the contents of the letter, she dropped the hot coffee on her just-cleaned kitchen floor, scalding her legs. The letter, from the New England Life Insurance Company, said that Louie was no longer insured because he had cashed in the insurance. They wanted him to return the policy.

She read the letter again, then hurried downstairs to ask her landlord to read the letter. She desperately hoped they would tell her that she had made a mistake. The owners of the house, Mr. and Mrs. Walsh, were third-generation Irish. He was the director and manager of a large cemetery in West Roxbury. Both Mr. Walsh and his wife were friendly. They had taken Theodora under their wing and helped as much as they could—even when Louie had been late with the rent payments. This happened a couple of times when he was in between ventures. Although he easily found work as a chef, sometimes he had to wait for his paycheck. Now was one of those times that he was working for someone else, had not gotten paid yet and as a result, was late in paying their rent.

As soon as Mr. Walsh (Theodora never called him anything else) saw his distraught tenant standing outside the wooden screen door, he assumed she was coming to see him about the rent.

"Come in, come in, Theo! I hope that worried look you have has nothing to do with the rent. I'm not concerned about it being late," he said soothingly. When her frown didn't vanish, he motioned her into the kitchen. "Come in and tell me what is wrong. How can I help?"

"I'm sorry to bother you, but would you read this and tell me what it says?"

He read the letter and confirmed her fears that Louie had indeed cashed in the policy.

That night Louie never got a chance to take off his coat before Theodora demanded to know why he had canceled her children's life insurance. How could he take her children's money? What would happen to them if he died? Why didn't he tell her? Why did he need the money? They had plenty to eat! Mr. Walsh would wait for the rent. What happened to the money? The questions came so fast he barely had to time to think of one answer before the next question came at him.

He had come up the back stairs and was standing in the middle of the kitchen with his hat still on. He sat down on one of the kitchen chairs and just looked at his wife, waiting for her to finish.

"Theodora, please stop. Take a drink of water, and let me explain. The reason I didn't tell you was because I didn't want a scene just like this."

"Never mind the scene—just tell me what you did with my kids' money!"

"Well, I lent the money to my old friend John Adonis. He is sick and, as you know, it is hard to get a job these days. He had a job, washing dishes and ... Well, in any event, his landlord told him to get out of his room because he was two months behind in his rent. I found out he needed the money so I cashed in the policy and that's that."

"What do you mean 'that's that'? *What* is *that*? What about all your bigshot friends who owe you money? Half the Greeks in Boston owe you money! Why don't *they* pay *you*?"

"They will, they will, but I can't ask them now. Times are tough out there. Businesses are going bankrupt all over the place."

"Louie, you have got to stop trying to take care of the world. I love you, and one of the reasons I do is because you have such a good heart. But Louie, we are barely making it ourselves. I am still squeezing every penny I can get my hands on. There are so many people you have made rich, but we are never able to get a business that lasts. People owe you money and your pride won't let you ask them to pay you. What about us? When do you think about us, about me?"

"You? I think about you all the time. Have you ever gone hungry? We always manage to eat, and the house is dry and warm. It is a lot better than what you had when I met you."

"That is true. I won't deny it, but what about the future? What about the kids' future? It's the kids I'm thinking about. Louie, please remember we have three kids to provide for.

Louie put his hat back on his head and said, "Future? When the future comes, then I'll worry about it. Don't trouble trouble until trouble troubles you. I'm going. I'll sleep some place else tonight. I want a little peace and quiet where I don't have to worry about the future." Just as he started down the stairs, he turned and said, "I'll be back in a couple of days. In the meantime, call Charlie if you need anything."

Baba Lia

George, Theodora, Nick, Litsa

CHAPTER 22
CONFLICT

The next morning, Louie had to wait for a couple of minutes while a burly Negro and the short legged Greek manhandled a 30-gallon drum of grease into the back of a gray truck with a missing front fender. "*Yiássou,* Stratos. How's business? Hello Peter, how is your family?"

Stratos wiped his forehead with a red kerchief that he took from his rear pocket, lifted his arm so he could put the overall strap back on his shoulder, and hesitated before answering.

"*Yiássou,* Louie. Whadda ya say?"

"Save your money," Louie responded, winking at Peter who was standing on the tailgate looking down at him.

Stratos took Louie by the arm and pulled him aside. "You 100% on da dollah when you tell me that I can start little business pickin' up old grease from da restaurants. Another Jew who is started a cleanup place for the grease besides da other one."

Louie laughed and replied, "If you're trying to say I was right that you could make a living picking up old grease, and now there is more than one person you can sell it to, then I understand." Turning to the grinning Negro, he said, "What do you think, Pete?"

Pete replied, "You got it, Mr Louie. I was born here and I don't always understand what he is trying to say, except when he says he can't give me a raise. He sure does know how to say that!"

Stratos got into the truck, unhitching his overall shoulder strap again before saying, "Louie, I shoulda can pay you back da hundred dollars pretty soon now, but would be big help if youdda ask some of da restaurants down dere in Nantasket to give me da old grease. Those places sella lotsa French fries and fried clams. I can down go every month and pick 'em all up."

"Stratos, just because some of our countrymen are giving you the old grease for free doesn't mean everyone is going to do that. You are going to have to pay for it, just like everybody else. Remember there are other people out there who are in the same business. The world doesn't owe you a living; it's up to you to figure it out. But, I'll talk to a couple of people I know. In the meantime, give Pete here a raise; he has kids, too," Louie motioned toward the younger man, who grinned broadly. "Pay me later. So long, Pete. Save your money. See you later."

He walked around the truck carefully so he wouldn't brush up against the grease-smeared tailgate and opened the screened back door of the restaurant, kicking the half-wild alley-cat out of the way. A flight of stairs that led to the second-floor serving kitchen that was used for private parties and banquets faced the screen door. Louie turned left and walked down two stairs to the main serving kitchen that was beginning to get steamy hot from the simmering contents of large pots on the gas-fired stoves. Louie waved to the powerful-looking, bald Albanian who was scrubbing burn stains from the bottom of a ten-gallon pot, then he greeted the stout, flat-faced man preparing the salad table. "Yiássou, Leo. What is new?" Louie turned to his right so he could see behind the steam table, and asked, "Where is Charlie?"

Charlie's voice answered, "Come on downstairs, Louie!"

Louie walked behind the steam table and descended the stairs that led to the food preparation area. There, walk-in coolers and meat-cutting tables stood next to the two storerooms, one for food stuff and one for liquor. Charlie was struggling with a hind quarter of beef, preparing to separate the top and bottom rounds from it. The room used for storing liquor was enclosed with a chicken-wire fence supported by a wooden frame that reached almost to the ceiling. Louie could see a man inside the caged-in area counting bottles of whiskey and scotch. "Yiássou Charlie. Isn't that Chris in there?" he said pointing to the cage.

"Hello, Louie. Yes that's Chris," his brother acknowledged. "Didn't you know that he is buying half of this place? He is going to be a partner."

"He is? A partner huh! This is a big place. Where did he get the money to buy into this size of an operation?"

Charlie grunted as he severed the last piece of fat holding the top round in place. "He did what you are always saying we ought to do. He saved his money."

"Well, good for him. I'm happy that somebody is successful. What about you Charlie? Are you going to be a partner too?"

"Louie, I don't have enough money left to buy a hotdog stand—never mind a big place like this. You know the horses have all my money. I'll work for Chris. He will pay me well. I'll be okay. But what about you? Why are you here? You look troubled."

"Oh, I don't know, I just wanted to say hello. Have you heard from Angelo since he got deported?"

"Angelo, my ass. You didn't come to talk about Angelo. We can talk about him later. Something else is bothering you, I can tell. I've got an easy menu to prepare for today, so let's sit down and have some coffee. I'm ready for a break anyhow."

They went back upstairs to the first floor kitchen and dining room. Louie went out the swinging doors that led to the tables while Charlie poured two cups of coffee and gave an assistant cook some instructions. The dinning room was empty except for the large, elderly ex-waitress who stood in her stocking feet, filling salt and pepper shakers. Charlie called out to her. "Bess, Louie and I are going to discuss some family business, so set up the upstairs dinning room first today."

They both lit cigarettes. Louie added a teaspoon of sugar to his coffee cup and stirred it slowly as Charlie waited for him to talk.

Finally he began. "Charlie, I'm going to be spending a lot of time in Nantasket setting up the new restaurant and getting established. If everything goes well, I will run the place from Memorial Day to Labor Day, shut down for the winter, and then I can work in Florida ..."

Charlie interrupted, "Nantasket is not what you want to talk about. Tell me what is going on with you and Theodora. We're not stupid, you know. You weren't there the last time the gang was at your house on a holiday, and Theodora wasn't her old self either. Now you're talking about going to live at Nantasket and working in Florida in the winter."

Louie lit another cigarette then absentmindedly stirred his empty coffee cup, banging the spoon on the sides. Charlie refilled Louie's cup and waited again.

Finally Louie said, "We still love each other—at least I know I love her. I was just too old and set in my ways when I married her. You know, I am fifteen years older. No, that's not it. It's a lot of little things. I just am not able to be successful enough for her. Now, please understand—I'm not criticizing her. If I had picked the average Greek girl from the old country who would have been satisfied with nothing more than a loving husband, kids, and enough to eat, then I wouldn't have a problem. But, I married an exceptional woman—one who is beautiful and smart enough to know how to be successful. Theodora is competitive and wants to be a winner. She wants to be a respected member of any community, and she should be. She loves the kids and is a wonderful mother. Christ, she sacrifices herself every day on the altar of motherhood! So naturally, she demands the best and won't yield an inch when what she perceives that her children's welfare is threatened."

Charlie interrupted Louie again, "But, you love the kids, too, and you want the best for them also. I don't understand what you're saying."

Louie shook his head and said with emotion, "I don't understand why we argue all the time either, except that at this point neither of us is going to give in. We are both too proud and stubborn. It's possible that given time, things will work out, but at the moment I have taken my position and she has taken hers. I will continue to live at home, and for the most part, things will appear to be normal—at least on the surface. We are not getting a divorce or even separating. I will just be away from home more than usual, and when I am not there, I would appreciate it if you would look in on them."

Charlie stood to face his brother. "You mean all of this is about pride? Louie, you're situation isn't any different from most marriages. Don't get too dramatic about your problems. Why, you're making this sound like some dumb movie with all this talk about taking a position! I have never known you to be so stubborn, especially about something this important.

Charlie looked closely at his brother and said softly, "She must mean an awful lot to you. You must love her so much that you are willing to risk losing her rather than give in. Are you afraid that if you concede that she will think less of you?"

"I don't know Charlie," Louie sighed, "but at the very least, she knows that I am man enough to love her."

_____

At first, Louie's restaurant in Nantasket did very well. Business was brisk and profitable, though Louie never seemed to be able to accumulate extra income. He branched out, entering into partnerships with friends and family members; but once again, he couldn't seem to increase his net worth. Eventually, business dropped off, and Louie ran out of energy. He struggled to make just enough money just to pay the bills.

As the years went by, Louie and Theodora adjusted to a different lifestyle, Louie gradually drifted between home in the spring, Nantasket Beach in the summer, and Florida in the winter months. Theodora went back to work at Green Shoe. True to his word, there were few holidays that Charlie didn't spend with Theodora and the kids.

Theodora and Charlie sat at the kitchen table listening to the "Easy Aces" on the radio after Thanksgiving dinner.

Theodora filled Charlie's shot glass with brandy and said reprovingly, "Now Charlie, that's enough. You're drinking more than you should. The kids and I worry about you going all the way back to Boston on the streetcars after you've been celebrating with us."

"Ah, Theo! Don't worry about me. Besides, I don't take the streetcar anyhow. I walk up to the cab stand and hail a taxi."

"A taxi? My God, Charlie, that's expensive!"

"What else am I going to do with my money? If I don't spend it on you and the kids when I come to see you, I'll lose it on the horses."

"Charlie, I can't tell you how much we appreciate everything you have done for us over the years. So many times I have wondered what we would have done if you weren't around to help out."

"Theo, come now, don't make a big deal out of it. I enjoy it. Whatever I do is because I don't have a family of my own. You guys are my family. Louie is my brother, and his family is my family. You and I both know that if the shoes were reversed, Louie would be doing the same thing for me. *We are all that we have,"* he said solemnly, then added, "By the way, Theo, does Louie know that you bought a car?"

She giggled. "No, he doesn't. Won't he be surprised? You know, I've been working at Green Shoes for the past seven or eight years, and I've been doing very well. Since the unions got in, the pay got pretty good, so I saved money each week and finally got a car. It isn't much of a car—just a 1945 Nash Rambler, but it works pretty good."

"Good for you, Theo. You're a go-getter. I'd like to see Louie's face when you write to tell him about the car. I don't think he can stand another surprise like he had two years ago," he chuckled. "Louie was so funny when he told me about it at the *cafenion*, laughing at himself so hard that he could barely talk. Theo, he was so proud of you, he wanted to tell everybody, but he was too embarrassed. The way he tells it, is that he came home from Florida and went to the house you were living in when he left. He carried his suitcases all the way up to the third floor and found a different family living there. He borrowed their phone and called your brother George. George pulled his leg a little bit and said you'd bought a house, then he told him where it was. Louie told me all he could say to George was 'where did she find the money to buy a house?' Then he went to the house and stood outside for ten minutes admiring it. He sure is proud of you."

"Thank you, Charlie. That's good to know," Theodora said with a smile. "We talked about it for a long time that night. I explained how I'd been saving nickels and dimes for so many years that I lost count. The kids and I ate lots of bread with our meals, and I made sure the kids drank lots of milk and water so their bellies would be full. We turned off the lights a lot and kept the heat turned down low, but we saved a little money each week. That's where the money came from. I think Louie and I enjoyed talking to each other that night."

She turned away so Charlie wouldn't see her wipe tears away, then continued. "Louie really laughed when I told him how I earned ten dollars from the plumber who was trying to sell showers."

Charlie sat up, poured himself another drink and said, "This is my last drink, Theo. Tell me about the showers."

"Well, this Greek guy I know is a plumber and he wants to sell and install showers. He can't convince us cheap Greeks that you use less water by taking a shower than you do taking a bath. So this is what we did. " Theodora giggled, sipped Charlie's brandy, and continued. "I invited seven of my lady friends, all Greeks, served them coffee and *kourambiethes*, and when the plumber came in. I introduced him. He is younger than we ladies are, but not too young. He's tall and has curly hair. He comes from Macedonia.

"Well anyhow, we all went into the bathroom, you should have seen us as we crowded in there. He put the plug in the tub and turned the water on. Then, he made believe he was soaping himself as if he was taking a shower. Some of those old hens got a little squirmy when this handsome guy rubbed himself pretending he was washing. Anyhow, he pantomimed the whole thing then turned the water off, showing the ladies that there were only a few inches of water in the tub— much less than if someone had taken a bath. Two of the ladies signed up right there, and the others wanted to talk to their husbands first. The plumber was so happy with everything that he gave me ten dollars in addition to the free shower installation we had agreed on."

Charlie laughed, "Theodora, you are something special. No wonder Louie is so proud of you. Now, where are those kids? I promised Harry we would play poker for pennies before I left."

"Thank you, Charlie. I'll get the kids. But, I want to tell you that, in my own way, I'm proud of Louie too. You know, with all of his faults, he is all man. When he makes up his mind, nobody pushes him around. Not even me."

Theodora, Katherine, Louie (formerly Soterios)

CHAPTER 23
COMPROMISE

Louie and his eldest son, Basil, who had been named after his grandfather Vasilios, sat together in the living room the evening before the son went into the army. Louie rose up from the sofa, walked to the fireplace, and carefully poked at the fire, moving the logs just an inch at a time to keep the sparks contained. He wore an old gray cardigan sweater with the first and third buttons missing, which created little pockets as the fastened buttons strained to hold the sweater front closed. The long sleeves from his white shirt showed beneath the sleeves of the cardigan.

Louie shivered slightly and commented, "Gosh, I'm cold all the time nowadays. I guess it's true that your blood gets thinner in Florida, and it takes a long time to thicken up when you come back here where it's always cold."

Bill looked at his father and said, "I don't know, Pa, whether that's true or not. It doesn't seem to make sense, but you sure do seem to mind the cold nowadays." Meanwhile, he thought to himself, 'the old guy is getting old. That's why he is cold all the time. Florida is probably the best place for him. Cripes, he is at least sixty-two.'

Louie started to reply, but stopped to cough deeply. Still coughing, he walked into the hall toward the front door, opened the door, and went out on the porch hacking. Bill watched as his father spat out large gobs of phlegm into the rhododendron bushes. The old man slowly returned to the hallway then headed for the kitchen to get a glass of water.

Theodora passed him in the hall, on her way upstairs to the bedrooms. "Louie, you've got to stop smoking so much. One of these days you're going to choke on all that stuff in your lungs." She leaned forward to look around the edge of the door into the parlor where Bill was now stirring the fire. "Billy, don't make a mess in there. I'm going upstairs to sew for a while, then I'm going to bed. You talk to your father for a while, and I'll see you in the morning. Good night."

When Louie came back into the room, Bill said, "This discussion that we've been having must rate up there in importance with Katherine's wedding and engagement party. Ma doesn't usually let us come in here. She only takes the sheets off the sofa and chairs when she is going to dust and vacuum in here."

Louie laughed and said, "I guess she uses the parlor on Christmas, Easter, or when company comes. Years ago we lived in another house where she was able to lock the doors to the parlor. One time she couldn't find the key just when the priest was coming to ask her to be president of the women's auxiliary. She really wanted the job but was playing hard to get—you know your mother. Anyhow, she finally found the key just as the priest was ringing the doorbell, and barely had time to pull the sheets off the sofa and stuff and stash them in the closet."

Bill chuckled and said, "You know, Pa, it would be a lot easier for me to leave for the army tomorrow if I knew you and Ma were going to be okay. I don't worry about Katherine or Harry. Katherine is married, and Harry is going to be fine. But, you two are getting older—especially you Pa. I'm getting concerned about all your coughing, and you still work harder than you should. If you and Ma were more like those families you see in the movies, all lovey-dovey and stuff, I wouldn't worry as much."

Louie looked at Bill, then circled the room, pretending to study the photograph of Katherine and her husband's wedding. He paused for a second to look at a portrait of Bill, taken when he was three years old, next to photographs of Harry and other family members. He pinched the dying leaves off a plant in a vase shaped like an old Grecian *amphora*. He dropped the dead leaves in an ashtray that was shaped like the Parthenon. So many memories of Greece, Bill thought as he watched.

Finally, Louie stopped in front of a rubber plant tucked into the corner just to the right of the French doors that opened into the hallway. Centered in the mantle above the door was a framed plaque covered with black velvet. Embroidered on the velvet, in what appeared to be gold thread, was a sentence written in Greek. Louie clasped his hands behind his back and looked up at the plaque.

"Bill, do you know what that says?"

"Sure, Pa, it says, *Ké Aftó Thá Perásee*"

"Your grandmother embroidered that. What does it mean in English, Bill?"

"Ma told me a long time ago that it means 'That, that too shall pass.'"

"That's right son. And that is a good motto to remember whenever life takes a whack at you or when times are really hard. Remember, 'that, that too shall pass.' The hard times will eventually go away and you will have an opportunity to make the next 'times' better. You do the best that you can.

"Put another log on the fire, Bill, and come over here and sit next to me. You're my son and I haven't spent enough time with you. I don't believe I have ever told you how much love and pride I have in you." He lit another cigarette before adding, "I've been in this country for forty years and I still don't use words properly, but you know what I'm trying to say."

When Bill sat on the sofa next to his father, the old man held his son by the hand and continued. He spoke quietly, in an almost formal manner.

"I have satisfied the commitment that I made to my father many years ago. I have told you the family history—what happened in the old days, as well as events that took place more recently. You must not be the judge of your ancestors. It is your place to try to understand them. It is also your responsibility to tell your children about the past. You must share your knowledge of the past in order to prepare them for the future.

"Your mother and I had a lot of dreams. Some of them came to be and some of them didn't. Still, we accomplished a lot in our time. Never had a lot of money, but we always had enough to eat. I believe that I have a lot of friends, but it's true what many say—that I am a lousy businessman. However, I know you will find that I have the respect of my friends as a good person. What is interesting is that the same people who ridiculed me for being a soft touch were the first ones who came to me when they needed help." He shook his head and sighed, "Your mother and I are not the ideal couple, but I don't know where any of those are. Your mother and I drifted apart, though we have always lived together for the sake of you kids. You always knew that you had a mother and a father."

Louie got up from the sofa, walked to the mahogany-stained radio that was covered with a crocheted cloth. He looked at the photograph of himself and Theodora, with two-year-old Katherine sitting on his lap. "Look how beautiful we were," he murmured to himself, before turning once again to Bill.

"When you get married, you will find that you will have many decisions to make that have more than one solution or option. Think of these options as being black for "no," white for "yes," and the compromise color being gray. When it is difficult to settle the problem with either the black or the white, use the gray solution. A married couple will often have arguments when one will say black and the other will say white. It is rare, but sometimes they will find that there is no gray. Then one of the two must have the sole right to pick either black or white, or the argument will go on forever. In our case, we had never agreed on who should make the final choice of black or white. I suggest that you settle that question before you get married." Louie glanced again at the photograph and said softly, "Unfortunately, Theodora and I never did."

After a brief silence, Louie pointed at Bill and said, "You must never blame your mother for anything. Right or wrong, no matter what she does, she is your mother and deserves your everlasting loyalty. Place her first on the list of people you are obligated to.

"Many years ago before we got married, we made commitments to others as well as ourselves. With those commitments, we decided what kind of life we would live and what kind of person we would be, and we dedicated part of our lives to that commitment. Once we married and had children, the other parts of our lives were committed to each other and our children. There was never any conflict between your mother and me regarding the commitment to our children. Sometimes, though, there was conflict between what she had promised herself as a way of life and the self-promises or commitments that I had made to my own self. It was difficult—sometimes impossible—for us to do the things that would make life easier and happy for ourselves unless we deviated from our commitments. I don't know if being that dedicated to a personal belief is a mark of a good strong person or just a stubborn person, one who is too weak to be willing change. I just know that is what we are.

"The most important test of a man's character is that he must always like himself. In order to like himself, he must honor his commitments. He must feel that the things he does are consistent with his own philosophy. When the final day of reckoning comes, he needs to be able to say, 'I have made some mistakes, but in my own way I have tried to atone for them.' I have lived my life in such a way that I accept my accomplishments and failures.

"I have lived my life and told my story. My children will be able to say, 'I know who I can be because I know where I came from.'

"I want you to think about all your cousins who now live in this country where they have an opportunity to achieve any goals they set for themselves. They now live in a land where the success they achieve is directly proportionate to how hard they work and what sacrifices they are willing to make. That is the greatest gift their parents have given them."

Louie slowly rose and stood in front of Bill, close enough so their toes almost touched. Bill was forced to look up at his father. Louie frowned, wanting to emphasize his next sentence. Then relenting, he reached out, put his hand on his son's shoulder and concluded.

"It has taken generations of people whose strongest motivation was to improve their family's life to get you here. Ever since the Hard One struggled out of the hopelessness, poverty, and pain—to the sacrifices that your mother and I made—everyone's main goal was the prosperity of family.

"Don't let us down, Bill. Remember us! Honor your commitments."

וקו

EPILOGUE

L ouie died in Boston, surrounded by his family, in 1953.
Theodora took her citizenship vows, for the second time, in 1944.
She didn't cross her fingers the second time. Bored with Boston, she
moved to California to be near Basil and Harold. After a few years,
she missed her daughter and grandchildren so she moved back to
Boston. Independent, she lived alone and drove her own automobile
until she was eighty-six. She died of a stroke in 1988, furious that she
could not make her body do as she wished.

Charlie died in Boston, deeply mourned by his adopted family.

Angelo was deported after being arrested in Toledo. He left Greece
suddenly and reappeared in Belgium, where he married a Belgian
girl named Maria. Interrogated and imprisoned by the Gestapo during World War II, he contracted tuberculosis while in prison. He met
Louie's two sons when they came to Belgium with the Army of Occupation. He died in 1960 in Antwerp.

Haralambos returned to Greece for the last time in 1926. He finally expanded the homestead in Kaparelli, after Demetra asked
Theodora and her brothers for assistance.

Demetra died in Boston. Her last major task was to escort two of
Constandina's daughters to America. The two girls, sponsored by Nick,
lived with Nick and his wife Sarah until the girls married.

GLOSSARY

These Greek words are used in the text:

Armatóli .... Albanian collabarators or police
baklavá .... filo-dough covered walnut pastry
bazóóki .... type of musical instrument.
cafeníon .... coffeehouse
Garagíozies .... a certain puppet clown, a fool
halvá .... a sweet pastry
hérete .... greetings, I hail you
horáfia .... fields, places where things grow
horió .... village, home town
katsíka .... a little female goat
Ké aftó thá perásee ... And that too shall pass
kléphtai .... outlaws, guerillas, rebels
Koumbára .... best man's wife, your child's godmother
Koumbáros .... best man, your child's godfather
kourambíethes .... a powdered sugar Greek pastry
Kouréas .... barber
leptá .... money, pennies
loukóúmia .... Turkish pastries (Turkish delight)
Patéra .... father
phakés .... lentil soup
pláka .... market place
príka .... dowry
souvlákia .... meat on a skewer
Tsámico .... type of Greek dance
Xasápiko .... type of Greek dance
yiássou .... congratulations, to your health
Yiayiá .... grandmother

ORDER BLANK

To order additional copies of this book, please provide the following information:

Name: _____

Address:_____

City: _____

State: _____ ZipCode:_____

Please enclose $14.95 plus $3.20 postage for each copy and send your request to:

Five And Dot, Inc
7026 Colina Lane
Rancho Murieta, CA 95683

California residents, please add $1.27 sales tax to the purchase price.

For more than 5 copies, please contact the publisher for multiple copy rates.